From
Child Abuse
to
Foster Care

From
Child Abuse
to
Foster Care

Child Welfare Services
Pathways and Placements

Richard P. Barth, Mark Courtney,
Jill Duerr Berrick, and Vicky Albert

Transaction Publishers
New Brunswick (U.S.A.) and London (U.K.)

First Transaction paperback printing 2011
Copyright © 1994 by Transaction Publishers, New Brunswick, NJ

This book is printed on acid-free paper that meets the American National Standard for Permanence of Paper for Printed Library Materials.

Library of Congress Catalog Number: 2010024344
ISBN: 978-0-202-36397-4
Printed in the United States of America

Library of Congress Cataloging-in-Publication Data

From child abuse to foster care : child welfare services pathways and
    placements / Richard P. Barth ... [et al.].
        p. cm.
Originally published: New York : Aldine de Gruyter, c1994, in
series: Modern applications of social work.
Includes bibliographical references and index.
ISBN 978-0-202-36397-4 (alk. paper)
    1. Child welfare--United States. 2. Foster home care--United
States. 3. Adoption--United States. I. Barth, Richard P., 1952-

HV741.F84 2010
362.730973--dc22

                                                            2010024344

Contents

Preface

Permanency planning was once considered a revolutionary change in child welfare practices. The intent of permanency planning was to create a child welfare system with clearly defined pathways and timeframes for children and families. The inverse of foster care limbo and drift was to be certainty and permanency. Metaphorically, children were expected to follow the road into long-term foster care only if they first went by the roadhouse of reasonable efforts to prevent placement and, failing those, received roadside reunification efforts and, failing that, could not find room in the adoption parking lot. This orderly journey was to begin and conclude within a 2-year period if at all possible.

The permanency planning revolution appears to be stalled. Leaders in the field have recently written an article in social welfare's most prestigious journal entitled, "Permanency Planning: Another Remedy in Jeopardy" (Fein & Maluccio, 1992). Three of the Children's Bureau funded National Centers of Child Welfare Excellence are calling for a new paradigm for child welfare based on "family continuity" rather than permanency planning. The most substantial reform of the landmark 1980 federal child welfare legislation is imminent.

Ironically, we are just beginning to learn about the pathways of permanency planning. Whatever the future might bring with regard to new paradigms of child welfare, the change will be gradual, and the fullest understanding of the operations of the current child welfare system will be essential to a well-managed postrevolutionary and, it is hoped, not reactionary era.

This book has three parts. In Section I, Chapter 1 introduces the main issues of the book and provides a framework regarding concerns about child welfare services and the strategies employed to address them. Chapter 2 provides a unique analysis of the ecology of child abuse and neglect and of foster care caseloads and offers program- and policy-relevant analyses about the impact of program funding on front-end services to assess child abuse reports. Chapter 3 considers the characteristics of child abuse reports and their relationship to ongoing services. Although the child abuse reporting system is the gateway to the child welfare system, the vast majority of children reported for child abuse do not receive additional child abuse reports or additional services. This chapter helps to unravel several mysteries of this critical but little studied aspect of child abuse and child welfare practice. The little that is known about the pathway from a single child abuse report to entrance into the child welfare system is greatly increased by information provided here on multiple reports and multiple types of reports (e.g., physical abuse and sexual abuse).

Section II addresses the factors that explain the child welfare service careers of children. The changes in the dynamics of the foster care system described in Chapter 1 raise a number of issues for policymakers and child advocates addressed in this section. How well are the goals of permanency planning being met for children entering foster care? Are children going home in a timely manner? Are some children more likely to go home than others and, if so, why? Of those who do not return home, who gets adopted? Which children and youths are most likely to spend some or all of their time in institutional care? What are the prospects for the increasing numbers of infants entering foster care? Are they going home to their families at the same rate as children who entered foster care in the past? What are the implications of the rapid growth of "kinship care" on these phenomena? The chapters in this section attempt to bring new information to bear on some of these questions. They employ analytic methods that are of increasing use to child welfare researchers interested in outcomes of a categorical nature (e.g., will a child be adopted or not) or in factors associated with transition rates of children between one state and another (e.g., the rate of children being returned home to their families). This examination of the pathways of children through care begins with a provocative review of the limitations of previous efforts in this regard. We focus on studies of the length of time children spend in foster care. These are interesting both because they provide a context for our examination of the family-reunification process and because they illustrate the strengths and weaknesses of various approaches to understanding the course of children through foster care regardless of the outcome being studied.

Chapters 4 through 7 focus on the examination of factors associated with certain *pathways* of children through the foster care system from initial placement of children to the outcomes of their stays in care. This analysis differs from the other work reported in this book in two significant ways. First, unlike the caseload dynamics analyses of the aggregate foster care population (i.e., Chapter 2), these studies focus on the outcomes of foster care for *individual children*. It is intuitively clear that an understanding of how child, family, and foster care system variables affect a child's course through the system can have a significant impact on policy and practice for children and their families. Second, in contrast to the many prior studies that employ a cross-sectional or point-in-time look at children in care, the pathways studies are *longitudinal* in perspective. For a number of reasons that we will discuss, many questions of interest to child welfare policymakers and practitioners can be answered only through the use of analytic methods that measure change in a child's status over time.

Each of the chapters in Section II relies on administrative data pertaining to the lives of children in foster care. This type of information has enjoyed limited use in child welfare research to date because of problems in collection and analysis. Yet, analyzing administrative data offers compelling advantages for child welfare and other social service research that are not obtainable through other research methods. The most significant of these are the availability of very large populations for study and the ability to follow change over time in the status of these populations. Because of the advantages of administrative data, we are now able, at relatively little expense, to examine large numbers of children's child welfare pathways in detail and over extended periods.

Despite these strengths, no research strategy is all-powerful. Such data offer us little information, for example, about the children who proceed through child welfare services or the environments in which they reside. Section III focuses on common child placements along the child welfare path. With data from more than 1,000 questionnaires and interviews we draw a picture of the out-of-home care environments of kinship foster care, foster care, specialized foster care, and group home care. By employing the same measures of child behavior we are able to describe the characteristics of children in each of these settings.

We also assess and then contrast the practices, satisfactions, and aspirations of the providers.

A longitudinal overview of the paths taken by children in California through the foster care system will help to form a comprehensive view of this process and should answer a number of questions about the children and families who have contact with the child welfare services system, about the child welfare services system itself, and about recommendations for child welfare services in the future. The final chapter integrates the volume's findings with other trends in child welfare services to offer a vision for the next decade.

ACKNOWLEDGEMENTS

The book is a product of the Berkeley Child Welfare Research Center, which was established with a 5-year grant from the U.S. Department of Health and Human Services, Children's Bureau, and the Office of Planning and Evaluation in October 1990. The Center is hosted by the Family Welfare Research Group of the School of Social Welfare at the University of California at Berkeley. The fundamental mission of the center is to serve as a knowledge-building and -disseminating resource for improved child welfare services. We gratefully acknowledge the help of Cecelia Sudia and Penny Maza in establishing and developing the Berkeley Child Welfare Research Center. Portions of this research have also been supported by interagency agreements with the California Department of Social Services (CDSS) to provide research support to the State's Child Welfare Services Strategic Planning Commission, to study child abuse and foster care pathways, and to provide technical assistance to the Child Welfare Services Budget Allocation Oversight Committee.

We acknowledge many service providers and administrators who have endeavored to teach us how to present information in ways helpful to practitioners and policymakers. Any failure to do so in this volume is not their fault—we acknowledge the possibility that their good training is wearing off. Bob Goerge, of Chapin Hall Center for Children at the University of Chicago, and Fred Wulczyn, of Columbia University and the New York Department of Social Services, provided vision and technical assistance to our efforts to harness the power of California's administrative data. Although our work profited considerably from all of their efforts, we acknowledge full responsibility for the conclusions in this book.

Portions of this work have been published. Our thanks to *Children and Youth Services Review* for allowing us to republish substantially revised, yet still derivative, versions of Chapters 9 and 11, The National Association of Social Workers for permission to publish sections of Chapters 7 and 8 and *Child and Youth Care Forum* for portions of Chapter 10, and *Social Service Review* for portions of Chapter 5. Neil Gilbert, coprincipal Investigator of the Child Welfare Research Center has also provided a range of useful research strategies and needed perspective. Sylvia Pizzini offered many ideas and much welcomed enthusiasm. Marianne Berry is coinvestigator of the California Long Range Adoption Study discussed in Chapter 7. Many graduate students, including Sally Allphin, Devon Brooks, Sally Brown, Lacie Gray, Melissa Jousm-Reid and Barbara Needell have assisted with various parts of the research reported here. Sharon Ikami, Susan Katzenellenbogen, and Renee Robinson have provided much word-processing support. Harry Specht, Jim Steele, Judy

Ambrose, Stephanie Smith, and Carol Welsh have all taken on additional administrative work created by our efforts to patch together the staff and support we needed for such a large undertaking. We appreciate Jim Whittaker's confidence in our work. Finally, we thank our spouses for sharing our commitment to children's services—often, more than we shared our time with them during the preparation of this book.

I

Examining Child Abuse and Child Welfare Caseloads and Careers

1

Understanding Pathways to Permanency

Child welfare services have long intended to support children's safety and well-being in their families and, short of that, to pursue brief, therapeutic, and cost-effective out-of-home care for the children. The Adoption Assistance and Child Welfare Act (AACWA) of 1980 (P.L. 96–272) embodies those intentions and focuses services on safely maintaining abused and neglected children in their birth families whenever possible in preference to out-of-home placement. The Act (1) encourages the use of home-based placement prevention services; (2) mandates reporting mechanisms intended to monitor the course of children in foster care and force agencies to plan more effectively for the future of foster children; (3) limits the extent of placement in nonpermanent substitute care placements; and (4) describes specific protection for parents of children in substitute care (such as allowing parental participation in treatment planning, and placement of children in close proximity to their parents' home). *Permanency planning*, the underlying philosophy behind the AACWA, assumes prompt and decisive action to maintain children in their own homes or place them, as quickly as possible, in permanent homes with other families. Simply stated, permanency planning means safely reducing entrances into foster care and expediting exits from foster care via reunification and adoption.

Although the goals of permanency planning are laudable, they have not all been met. Just how many or few have been met is reason for much debate. Most telling, perhaps, efforts to keep abused and neglected children in the homes of their birth parents have not resulted in long-term stability, let alone a decrease in the foster care population. Between 1982 and 1991, the estimated number of children in foster care (as estimated by the foster care census at year's end in the United States has increased by

64% from 262,000 to 429,000 (see Figure 1.1). This growth has exceeded the growth in the population of American children, which has been relatively flat during those years. The total number of children served in out-of-home care per year has increased from 434,000 to 636,000 in 1991 (a 46% increase). Figure 1.1 suggests that the growth in out-of-home care has resulted from steadily greater growth in entrances to care than exits from care. With both entrance and exit rates increasing, foster care is touching the lives of more families each year.

The observant reader will note that the figure does not go back to a time that precedes permanency planning. Indeed, 1982 was about the time that implementation was just beginning in many states. The reasons for this are worth more than a footnote and, indeed, have significance for the analytic interpretation of permanency planning. It has routinely been reported (e.g., Costin, Bell, & Downs, 1990; Pelton, 1989) that the nation's population of children in foster care exceeded 500,000 children prior to permanency planning and that permanency planning was initially responsible for "dramatic effects" (Fein, 1991) on the number of children in foster care placements. Available evidence strongly suggests, however, that there was no dramatic decrease in social services–supervised children in foster care. The often-cited figure of 503,000 was an estimate computed from the Shyne and Schroeder (1978) study of 315 public welfare agencies across the United States and bears little resemblance in method or definition to the estimates for 1979 or 1980 or to current estimates. Since then, there may have been modest per capita decreases in foster care due to more active efforts to prevent placements and the growth in special needs adoption. Additional reexaminations or clarifications of the impact of changes in child abuse definitions on child abuse reports, child abuse investigations, family maintenance, and foster care remain necessary. There is little to suggest, however, that permanency planning resulted in a substantially lower foster care population in the early years and that the successful program later stalled. The significance of this clarification is that we do not need to search for reasons for a permanency planning breakdown or tailspin. The implementation of permanency planning has shown a steady and predictable increase in the foster care population, with the exception of the late 1980s when the crack cocaine epidemic resulted in sharp increases.

We can find some reassurance about the accomplishments of the AAC-WA by using indicators other than the number of children in care. Average and median lengths of stay in foster care have declined since 1977. Data from the Voluntary Cooperative Information System (VCIS) informs us that between 1977 and 1987 there was a 46% decrease in the median length of stay in care for children still residing in substitute care (see Table 1.1). (Lengths of stay began to increase again in 1988, partially reflecting

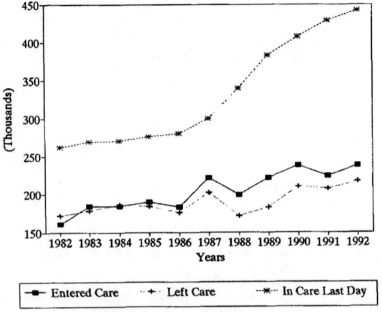

Figure 1.1. U.S. child substitute care population.
Source: Voluntary Cooperative Information System (VCIS).

the slowing in exit rates.) In 1987, one-half of the children stayed in foster care longer than 2.4 years; by 1989 (the last year for which such data are available) one-half of the children would stay in foster care 1.4 years or less. Statewide data on children who left substitute care each year also show a considerable shortening in stays from a median of 8.9 months in 1985 to 6.6 months in 1989. These national data are constructed from a sample of up to 31 states participating in the VCIS. (As discussed later, such statewide data are useful for description but offer little to explain why lengths of stay changed.)

Changing Child Welfare Services Clientele and Dynamics

Although foster care has been growing, the characteristics of children entering the child welfare system (CWS) have been changing. For example, an increasing number of children enter the system with serious medical, emotional, and behavioral problems. A random sample of children receiving placement prevention services in 1985 in California reveal that approximately 40% of the families had known health problems and 55% had drug or alcohol abuse problems (SDSS, 1986). Another study

Table 1.1.   Length of Stay of Children Still in Foster Care

Year	First Quartile (months)	Median (years)	Third Quartile (years)	Ninth Decile (years)
77[1]	11.2	2.4	5.8	8.8
80[2]	—	2.1	4.6	7.7
82[3]	6.9	1.7	4.3	7.4
83	6.8	1.6	3.5	6.5
84	6.2	1.5	3.3	6.0
85	6.7	1.5	3.2	5.9
86	6.1	1.5	3.4	6.1
87	6.1	1.3	2.9	5.0
88	7.2	1.4	2.9	5.0
89	7.0	1.4	2.8	5.1

Notes:

[1] The figures for 1977 were calculated by VCIS from the national foster care data gathered by Westat.

[2] The figures for 1980 were computed by VCIS from the national foster care data collected by the Office for Civil Rights (OCR)/HHS.

[3] The figures for 1982 through 1989 were derived from the VCIS data.

Source: VCIS Research Notes (February, 1993). American Public Welfare Association. Washington, DC.

conducted with identical methodology in 1989 of children referred for child welfare services indicates that just 4 years later, 51% of families had known health problems and 88% had substance abuse problems (CDSS, 1989). The 1985 data show that 29% of children referred to child welfare had previously received some child welfare services and their cases were closed; by 1989, that percentage had increased to 40%. These data are confirmed by studies from other parts of the nation indicating high mental health needs for children in out-of-home care (e.g., Dubowitz, Feigelman, & Zuravin, 1993; McIntyre & Keesler, 1986).

Although the magnitude of the phenomenon is still unclear, many more infants have been entering the foster care system due to drug exposure than in the past. In 1989, 27 California counties that responded to a survey concerning drug-exposed infants reported a total of 3,150 infants who were declared dependents of the court as a result of a positive toxicology screen (SOR, 1990). In a General Accounting Office (1989) study of 10 hospitals, an estimated 1,200 of the 4,000 drug-exposed infants (30%) born in 1989 were placed in foster care at birth. In New York City, between 1984 and 1989, the number of infants entering foster care at birth quintupled. By 1989, 4.5% of all births in New York City were followed shortly by a foster care placement (Wulczyn, in press). Though only a modest proportion of drug-exposed children enter the CWS because of a chaotic and dangerous home environment, officials in New York state estimate that 75% of foster care children come from alleged drug-abusing (including alcohol abuse) families (CWLA, 1990). Nationally, as many as 80% of drug-exposed children declared "dependent" in 1989 may have received out-of-home placements (Feig, 1990).

The CWS is responding to these dramatic shifts in causes for entering foster care and the ages of children. Although the shifting ethnic mix of the nation's child population would lead one to expect some proportional growth in the population of non-Caucasian children receiving child welfare services, receipt of these services is not proportional to the ethnic mix of America's children. For example, children from Asian-American and Hispanic families in California are less likely to be in foster care than their overall numbers would indicate, whereas Caucasian children live in foster care at a rate that is proportional to their share of the child population. On the other hand, African-American children are about four times as likely to be in foster care as their overall numbers would indicate and now exceed 40% of all children in foster care in California. This does not tell us, of course that African-American children are given services that exceed or fall short of need or that services are underprotective or over-intrusive. This volume provides substantial new evidence—and reinterpretation of some old evidence—that clarifies differences and similarities in child welfare paths for African-American children and other children.

The nation's child population has also been getting younger, contributing (along with perinatal substance exposure) to a change in the age distribution of foster children. The VCIS child welfare data base indicates that the median age of children who left the nation's substitute care system became slightly lower between fiscal years (FY) 85 and FY 88— 12.7 years old in FY 85 and 11.1 years old in FY 88 (Tatara, in press). The same trend toward younger recipients was found among children who entered care (10.2 years old in FY 85 to 8.2 years old in FY 88).

The percentage of California foster children under 5 years of age grew from 32% in 1980 to 38% in 1985 and declined slightly in 1993 we expect that these age trends are consistent with those in other large states (Goerge & Wulczyn, 1992). The growth in this group accounts for over one-half of the growth in the overall child welfare population during this period. This trend (along with the crack epidemic that has directed many infants needing protection into foster care) has changed the age distribution of children receiving welfare services.

We will examine the implications of the changing age distribution on child welfare pathways at several points in this volume. The characteristics of adoptive families are also changing. In California, foster parents accounted for 40% of all adoptions involving child welfare services children in 1980 compared to 92% in 1991. Adoptive parents are also increasingly likely to be relatives, single, or related to the adopted child.

The changes in the dynamics of the foster care system and the ongoing concern over the continuing presence of large numbers of children in foster care have raised a number of issues for policymakers and child advocates. How well are the goals of permanency planning being met for children entering foster care? Are children going home in a timely manner? Are some children more likely to go home or be adopted than others and, if so, why? What are the prospects for the increasing numbers of infants entering foster care? Are they going home to their families or getting adopted at the same rate as children who entered foster care in the past? What are the implications for permanency planning of the rapid growth of "kinship care"? Are foster children placed with relativ s more or less likely to go home to their natural parents than children who are placed with nonrelatives?

Some idea about local caseload trends can be gleaned from point-in-time, cross-sectional "snapshots" of child abuse and foster care counts. Local caseload counts can be aggregated into county or regional data and then grouped into state data and then summed into national estimates. This approach offers only crude images of our progress in implementing P.L. 96–272. This level and type of information needs to be supplemented by data on individual clients to explain the course of services for individual children better. Available aggregated data are far less instructive, for example, about the likelihood of a speedy return home for an African-American child compared to a Latino child or for a 6-year old child compared to a 6-month old child (or a 6-month old African American child compared to a 6-year old African-American child). Nor do these data tell us about the likelihood that a child abuse report will result in services for a child who is sexually abused as contrasted to a child who is neglected and whether the child who does not receive ongoing services will be likely to be reported again in the near future. Then, we also want to know the probability that a child who has been in foster care for over 2 years (the permanency planning standard) will be adopted and what factors affect that likelihood. In essence we know something about child abuse reports and something about the foster care census and something about the likelihood of adoption, but until now, our reliance on snapshot statistics has limited our ability to learn about the pathways between these events.

In this volume we endeavor to piece together a description of the likely experiences for individual children, and groups of children in the American CWS. In addition, we provide a description and preliminary explanation of trends in child welfare services caseloads. The authors intend to tell a story that teaches about child welfare service careers, or pathways, and that teaches ways to think about child welfare information. Every child welfare practitioner and student knows that child welfare service providers collect a substantial amount of data about their clients and their decisions. The purposes for these data are often as much of a mystery to their collectors as are the clarity of the regulations that require its collection. Marcia Lowery of the American Civil Liberties Union (ACLU) tells a story of going to a state child welfare agency that the ACLU was suing and asking for a series of important data runs about children's pathways through care (personal communication, March 25, 1993). The agency dragged its heels providing this information. Ms. Lowery reports that she was increasingly convinced that the agency was hiding information from their audit. Finally, after confronting agency directors, the directors explained that they collected the data but that they were not reliable enough to use. (Our experience tells us that the agency may not have known how to coax much useful information from the data even if it were collected with greater precision.) Researchers are just beginning to realize the usefulness of these data, and this book is partially a description of how such data can be used to shed light on child welfare practice and policies.

TOWARD DYNAMIC DATA

In this volume we make use of descriptive statistics and varied and innovative statistical analysis both to contribute to a better understanding of the issues we raised above and to ask new questions about how the foster care system functions. The use of administrative data to examine child abuse and foster care dynamics is relatively new. Similarly, the analytic techniques employed in this study have a very limited track record in social work research, let alone child welfare research. Child welfare is a fast changing hard-to-pin-down area of human services. The methods we employ provide the best opportunity for a dynamic look at the pathways through permanency planning.

We endeavor to present the best and most recent data available on the flow of children in and out of the child abuse and child welfare system. This could not be done with a single source of data. There is at the time of this work no state or municipality that we know of that has a totally integrated data system that follows every child or family from the point of their first child abuse referral to the time of their last exit from child welfare services. The time is not far off when such systems will be available, and officials in many states and municipalities have a vision of such systems twinkling in their eyes. A subsequent challenge that they will face is related to the proper analysis of these data. Ideas about that process are a substantial contribution of this volume.

We have based our description of child welfare service dynamics on a variety of complementary sources ranging from telephone interviews to caseload flow data based on county-level child abuse reports to administrative foster care data from the country's most populous state.

Social workers have been known to complain that their practice is "clerical" rather than "clinical." Indeed, careful recordkeeping is a vital component of the CWS, which is so integrally involved with evidentiary court standards and with authorizing payment for a variety of client services (Barth & Sullivan, 1985). Much data, and arguably too much data, are haphazardly collected and stored in agency files waiting for a case record reviewer to abstract them. Since the late 1970s, researchers have been developing computerized data bases in a few major states. Illinois has continuous computerized data on children in foster care going back to 1976. David Fanshel and John Grundy developed a computerized data base for children in foster care in New York City (Fanshel & Grundy, 1975) and published the first substantial report from administrative data in 1982 (Fanshel, 1982). This report called for better collection of some key data items—in this case, parental visiting of children in foster care. This was just the beginning of an era that has seen expanded data bases and more sophisticated analytic tools.

The next steps in the administrative data era involved state reports on the "conditions of children" in service systems. These included the pioneering *State of the Child* (Testa & Wulczyn, 1980) and *Children and the State* (Hugi, 1983) published about the children in Illinois. These and a copycat report actually named *Conditions of Children in California* (Wald & Kirst, 1988) were reports on the *status* of children, not their condition. The distinction is critical to understanding that such reports, which are primarily based on administrative data from a variety of service sectors (e.g., education, health, and child welfare), are based on children's status within a service-delivery system. As such, they indicate the proportion of children born following prenatal care (a good status), the high school drop-out rate (a bad status), and the foster care rate (a higher foster care rate is considered a bad status for a state but foster care is certainly a better status for a child than being left in a dangerous home).

From each of these statuses, some inferences are made about the "conditions" of children. These inferences are based on theoretical relationships between the status and the child's likely welfare. In this use of administrative data, with a few exceptions (such as child deaths), the well-being of individual children is not considered. Now, under generous support from the Annie E. Casey Foundation, every state has the possibility to get support to develop a *Kids Count* program that tracks status indicators of children across time to see whether there is improvement in the status of children. Casey also sponsors a national report entitled *Kids Count Data Book: State Profiles of Child Well-Being* that tracks change in such indicators as state infant mortality, teenage unemployment rate, and juvenile incarceration rates (e.g., The Center for the Study of Social Policy, 1993). These indicators are chosen because they are available from yearly reports (based on administrative data) and, we assume, because the indicators more clearly indicate well-being than status. (Some of these indicators are still open to debate, however; such items as women in the labor force whose youngest child is between 6 and 17 are not easily categorized in terms of desirability.

These "state of the child" reports have become more sophisticated and useful as they develop consistent data elements to be used across time and place. Still, they lack even the most minimal explanatory power, because the data elements are not linked to one another and not linked to individual children. Simply put, after reading these documents, it is very difficult to tell what we should do—only that we should do it better.

Caseload Flow

The approach used for analyzing caseload flow applies sophisticated data-analysis techniques borrowed from econometrics and biostatistics. This approach, referred to as *time-series analysis*, allows investigators to use aggregate county- or state-level demographic indicators (e.g., number of children), economic indicators (e.g., unemployment rates), and public policy changes (e.g., changes in child abuse reporting laws) to explain emergency response or foster care caseload changes (e.g., Albert, 1988; Plotnick & Lidman, 1987). Time-series analysis allows the investigator to test simultaneously the relationship between various indicators and an outcome indicator of interest. Thus, it is far more powerful than simple counts of seemingly independent demographic and child status variables.

The questions addressed in time-series studies based on aggregate data resemble those asked in studies that use individual-level data gathered for each child or household in the sample. For example, individual-level analysis may address such questions as; What characteristics closely associated with the likelihood of a particular child remaining in foster care for a long time? In time-series analysis, this question can be thought of in terms of the extent to which the number of children with a particular characteristic (age or race) affect the size of the foster care caseload. Although individual characteristics can be controlled for in both types of studies, because of the nature of the aggregate data used in time-series analysis, it is generally not feasible to control for as wide an array of individual characteristics as can be controlled for on an individual level. In general, aggregate data restrict the selection of questions more sharply than do individual-level data.

Time-series analysis offers many advantages that are not found with other types of analyses. By employing aggregate data in time-series analysis, considerable information can be gained about global demographic changes or economic developments. In addition, it is possible to determine the consequences for the caseload under alternative assumptions about external developments. For example, it is possible to forecast changes in birth rates while holding all else constant. Future caseload sizes and their associated costs also can be determined when using time-series analysis. Because time-series analysis relies on secondary data sources, the costs associated with such analyses are minimum. A well-crafted time-series analysis can mitigate the problem of missing data by using various estimation techniques, such as linear interpolation. In Chapter 2 we demonstrate the capacity of time-series analysis to explain changes in child abuse reports. Still, the benefits of aggregate-level administrative data are far greater for policy analysts and program developers than they are for practitioners.

Individual-Level Analysis of Administrative Data

Data collected in the course of children welfare services administration become most useful to practitioners—and arguably policymakers—when analyzed at the individual level. Individual-level administrative data contribute to our capacity to identify meaningful relationships between a child's status and outcome. For example, the status of placement in "group home care" is difficult to interpret, because it may be beneficial insofar as it results in additional services that yield a more rapid transition to a more familylike setting. Such case characteristics as age shed some light, however, on the meaning of this status. Group care is clearly a less desirable status for a 16-month-old than for a sixteen-year-old, because, from a developmental perspective, the 16-month-old should be developing family bonds, whereas the 16-year-old should be pursuing independence from them. Still, if a group care placement makes it possible for the young child to be promptly moved to a permanent placement, then the meaning of this status remains ambiguous. Finally, if an event history analysis concludes that 30% of 16-month-olds do not leave group care until they are 20 months and are no more likely to be returned to their birth parent or adopted within 2 years of entering care than similar children placed in less institutional settings, then, the deleterious child welfare characteristics of the status of group care for young children are confirmed. (See Chapters 6 and 10 for more consideration of group care.)

The great advantage of administrative data for studying pathways through child welfare services is that they are routinely collected over a long period. The Illinois foster care data system has records on children's entrances, exits, and placement moves since 1976. As a result of the ingenious work of the Chapin Hall group at the University of Chicago, these computer records have been reorganized to describe the entire placement histories of children in a succinct and accessible way. Child welfare researchers and policymakers can use this information to understand transitions between placements and how the probability of those transitions has changed with evolving social problems and policies.

A major question about administrative data is their accuracy. Although administrative data produce noise, we believe that a clear signal can generally still be heard. To some extent, we trade some errors for others. For example, in surveys of child welfare providers, a 50% response rate is considered good. Our ability to estimate the biases of the remaining sample is limited. Yet, administrative data routinely identify between 90 and 100% of the cases. In survey or case record review research, a sample of 500 cases is considered extraordinary. More often, samples are in the 100- to 300-respondent range and have such limited statistical power that only the most basic comparisons can be made. The capacity to test for statistical interactions between client and service characteristics is lost. This is a major disadvantage from the practitioner's standpoint, because they have so many questions about which approach used with which client results in what outcome. They are skeptical of less. Studies that rely on administrative data routinely call on thousands of cases that allow for the testing of complex interactions. As the readers will learn later in this volume such samples and the powerful statistical methods that they allow permit researchers to determine the likelihood that, for example, a Caucasian (or African-American) child who is 12 (or 3 or 9) years old from a single-parent (or two-parent) family and living in a kinship foster home (or group home) will be reunified from foster care within 2 years of entering.

Strengths and Weaknesses of Administrative Data

Despite our appreciation for administrative data, it is not the answer to every research question. We know that social workers do not generally or consistently record data with great accuracy (O'Brien, McClellan, & Alf, 1992). Some of our colleagues have asked us whether we can really trust these data or whether the data are too tainted by missing and mistaken information to be useful. We reply that some data are more trustworthy than others. We believe that social workers complete data accurately when the data are tied to court reports, when they are needed to reimburse foster or adoptive parents for their monthly expenses, and when they know that the data will be used. Social workers are also more likely to report data accurately when these data are to be audited electronically (e.g., if the record indicates that á case is closed but there is still a payment going to the foster parent and the data system spits out the case following a logic check). Still, data errors are made—and made routinely.

To date, case record reviews have been a more common child welfare research strategy than administrative data. Analyses based on case record reviews can be useful too, unless you totally agree with Malcom Bush (1984) that "case records that record the lives of children in child welfare systems are written, *inter alia*, to deny the failure of interventions, to justify the refusal to serve "bad clients" and to justify the decision to extend hegemony over "good clients" (p. 1). Accepting that case records are a selective record of case activities, one must point to yet another major shortcoming. The labor intensity of research using case records makes such studies hard to conduct on a sufficient scale to produce powerful results and almost impossible to replicate. As a result, we continue to see case record reviews with idiosyncratic populations and small samples (e.g., Slaght's [1993: $n=129$] study of risk of entering foster care or Grinnell & Jung's [1981: $n=129$] study of relative foster care). These studies may incorrectly conclude from these low power samples that, because length of stay or placement type is not differentiated by case characteristics, the CWS lacks rationality. The authors, the reviewers, and, probably, most readers fail to understand that the effect of the phenomena on length of stay or placement type would have to be *enormous* to be detectable with such small samples. In our preference for administrative data to answer questions about pathways through child welfare services, we agree with the great social science statistician Jacob Cohen (1990), who wrote in his seminal article entitled "Things I have learned (so far)": "One thing I learned over a long period of time is the validity of the principle that *less is more*, except of course for sample size. I have encountered too many studies with prodigious numbers of dependent variables, or with what seemed to me far too many independent variables, or (heaven help us) both.   I have so heavily emphasized the desirability of working with few variables and large sample sizes that some of my students have spread the rumor that my idea of the perfect study is one with 10,000 cases and no variables. They go too far" (pp. 1304–1305). Powerful research can be done with limited variables and many cases. Of course, the more carefully these data are collected, the more dependable the results.

Surveys of Service Providers

Whereas administrative data are pointing the way to a greater understanding of pathways through the CWS, they are not as good at identifying the quality of services that contribute to those pathways. Goerge's (in
press) report from administrative data in Illinois is one of the few that
analyze the contribution of caseload size and changes in social worker to
reunification. (Somewhat against expectations, he found that caseload
size had little impact on reunification but that changes in social workers
resulted in expedited reunification.) Knowledge of services can best be
obtained from interviews, case record reviews, and questionnaires; there
is, at this time, simply no substitute. The third major section of our book
looks at the characteristics of out-of-home care based on interviews and
surveys of out-of-home care providers, including kinship foster parents,
conventional foster parents, specialized foster care providers, and group
care providers. Furthermore, the studies gather information about the
behavior, health, and educational characteristics of those children. These
data were collected based on sampling frames created from administrative data with the intent of answering questions that our administrative
data could not. We believe that they provide a unique opportunity for
bringing vividness and meaning to what is otherwise simply a "placement" status.

Fiscal Data

A common tool for policy analysis is expenditures. The more the
expenditures, the better (or worse) the policy depending on the value
attached to the effort. Fiscal data are derived from administrative payment data and also provide a valuable piece of evidence about child
welfare services. Federal expenditures for child welfare services have
increased from $547 million in 1981 to and estimated $2.4 billion in 1991
(U.S. Committee on Finance, 1990). The vast majority of these increased
costs ($1.9 billion) are for placement of children and related administra-
tive costs payed for under Title IV-E of the Social Security Act. Increases
in adoption assistance administration and payments were proportionately larger but, at $150 million, amount to only 8% of foster care costs in
1991. Federal expenditures for in-home child welfare services to pay for
social work efforts to preserve families as funded under Title IV-B were,
comparatively, flat. The ratio of foster care expenditures to child welfare
services expenditures grew from 2 to 1 in 1981 to 8 to 1 in 1992 (U.S.
Government Accounting Office, 1993). We expect that local government
and private contributions may have exceeded this figure by many times.
Of course, federal spending is a relatively small portion of the pie. States

and local municipalities contribute about 60% of all child welfare services costs (American Public Welfare Association, 1990). Federal, state, and local costs associated with the child welfare services in California, for example, exceeded $1.3 billion in California by 1991. This reflects increases in expenditures between FYs 1984–85 and 1990–91 of 277% for foster care, 231% for child welfare services, and 25% for adoptions (not adjusted for inflation). In contrast, California's child population grew by just over 12% over that period.

OUR APPROACH TO THE STUDY OF PATHWAYS AND PLACEMENTS

National data are not yet available to describe the lives of children served because of abuse and neglect. Although we are moving toward data systems that can capture the national picture, the most detailed analyses available are from individual states (e.g., Goerge & Wulczyn 1992). In this volume we draw on these reports as we endeavor to present a dynamic look at the child welfare system. In particular, we call on a variety of sources to present a clearer picture of the child welfare services system in California. To lay the groundwork for understanding each of the chapters that follow, we first present a brief overview of the California child welfare services system. Although other states may have somewhat different procedures, we expect that they are more similar than dissimilar. All are at least structured to meet federal child abuse and child welfare guidelines. California responds to approximately one-sixth of the nation's child abuse reports and has nearly one-fifth of its foster children. Because of its size, it is normative.

In California, referrals for child welfare services are initiated via a child abuse report. The child abuse reporting law mandates that professionals who have contact with children and parents report all situations where they have a "reasonable suspicion" of child abuse. Some of the mandated reporters include teachers, day care workers, social workers, and medical professionals. Children are often reported under categories of maltreatment such as physical abuse, sexual abuse, general neglect, abandonment, or emotional maltreatment. (This "front end" of the system will be discussed in somewhat more detail in the next two chapters.)

Once a child abuse report is received by the county child welfare agency, decisions are required immediately regarding whether or not the child can safely remain at home. (The process through the CWS is described in graphic form in Figure 1.2.) In the child welfare services system this initial stage is called Emergency Response (ER). If, in the

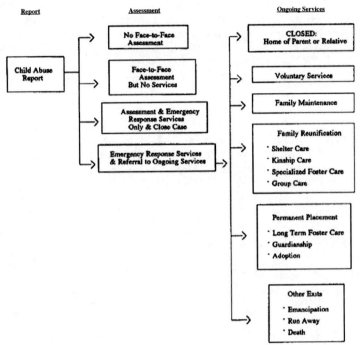

Figure 1.2. Child welfare services in California: pathways through care.
Note: For simplicity not all loops were drawn; for example, children may be
referred for child abuse during ongoing services.

professional opinion of the child welfare agency, the child's safety would
be compromised without judicial oversight and child welfare involvement, a petition is filed with the juvenile court to provide ongoing judicial
supervision under a dependency action.

Child Welfare Services are administered by the state's 58 county social
services agencies and involve thousands of government and private
service providers. Services include prevention and education programs
and supportive social services. Services are also provided under juvenile
court order to maintain children in their own homes (called Family
Maintenance, or FM) or to reunify them with their parents if removal was
necessary initially (called Family Reunification, or FR). Permanency Planning (PP) services (adoption, guardianship, long-term foster care) are
available for those children who cannot safely be returned home. According to the plan, children can move from program to program and home
again for 2 years, after which they must be reunified or moved to the
permanent placement program. In practice, some children are reunified

years after entering care. Children usually leave the child welfare service system when they are reunified with their families (Goerge, 1990). Others leave the system through adoption, guardianship, running away, transferring to another county, or emancipation. These are the "terminations" described in Chapters 5 and 7.

The decision to intervene in the lives of families is extremely difficult. At stake is the safety of children. Also at stake is the unnecessary intrusion into family life. Balancing these critical points is an extremely challenging task. Some theorists on the topic would suggest that decisions are made too often at the expense of family privacy (Besharov, 1990; Pelton, 1989). Others express concern that children are too often left in dangerous situations (Finkelhor, 1990). We do know that decision making in child welfare is becoming increasingly difficult. Part of this difficulty may be explained by the massive shifts that have taken place in the 1980s in the sheer number of children coming to the attention of the child welfare services system, the nature of the families needing services, and the intensity of children's problems.

THE FUTURE OF PERMANENCY PLANNING

Despite some changes in lengths of stay of children in foster care, the apparent limits of permanency planning have been decried by very dedicated and concerned scholars and practitioners. Some lament that too many children are entering foster care too easily and remaining there too long (Pelton, 1989), some are concerned that long-term foster care is undervalued as an important resource for children (Fein, 1991); and others worry about the incapacity of the current permanency planning framework, which calls for one permanent family at a time, to address issues arising from kinship foster care (D. Lakin, personal communication, March 21, 1993). Almost everyone decries the discharge of youths from foster care with too little preparation and no permanent and safe family to assist them in their reach for adulthood (Barth, 1990; Maluccio, 1991). Permanency planning is increasingly considered too mechanistic and time bound and constraining of choices that might best fit the child's needs (Maluccio, 1991).

Perhaps the most vexing issue involved in the rethinking of permanency planning is kinship foster care. As discussed in greater detail in Chapter 9, children living in foster family homes are now, as likely as not, to be living with relatives. This was not anticipated by the foremothers and forefathers of permanency planning and raises difficult questions about legal requirements to pursue termination of parental rights if children cannot go home and when and whether to place adoption above long-term foster care as a permanency planning goal.

As a result, the National Resource Centers on Foster Care, Special Needs Adoptions, and Family Based Services are calling for a new paradigm for permanency planning: *family continuity*. The principles of family continuity include strengthening the core family; the integration of family preservation concepts with permanency planning (so that intensive services become available when foster care or adoptive placements are endangered); the emphasis on family continuity begins at the first placement; and emphasizing the child's extended family and the connectedness of the child to each family.

Although this volume will not definitively be able to assess the success of permanency planning nor predict the value of a transition to a family continuity concept, the issues addressed herein are salient to the understanding of both. With a variety of data sources, we look at the stability of placements, the differences between kinship and nonkinship placements, the transition to adoption, and the familylike characteristics of out-of-home care arrangements. These provide evidence regarding the current operations of child welfare services, the need for a paradigm shift,and the utility of that shift.

Pathways and Practice

Child welfare service providers determine the pathway that children take through the CWS with every small and large decision they make. Administrative data sets with more than one million records like those that we discuss in this volume can help to explain what happened to children, but every one of those records is based on a social worker's and judicial response to a family and child in crisis. Pathways depend on practice. Basically, practice determines decisions that set the child's route through either the CWS or home. Certainly, available resources, laws, and family and child concerns also determine the outcomes of child welfare interventions. Yet, social workers' decisions to place a child in foster care with a grandmother four apartments down the floor, rather than to provide intensive family preservation services to the child's mother in her own apartment, contributes to the ultimate form, duration, and result of services.

Inversely, knowledge of pathways contributes to practice. If that were not so, then writing and reading this book would be in vain. The practitioner who understands that research on child welfare pathways indicates that children who enter kinship foster care often remain there for a long time and that children who receive family preservation services often have relatively short-service durations understands the significance of these decisions. Knowledge about the probability of recidivism following kinship care and family preservation provides additional practice-shaping information. The decision to place a young child in group home care is usually done after much review, but it is done more readily if there is substantial reason to believe that a resource-rich and structured program will result in a more speedy reunification or prompt adoption. Alternately, the failure to find such affects raises additional questions about the utility of group care.

The examination of pathways suggests that a child receiving child welfare services never rests and, instead, circulates like blood through a closed system. This image negates a more proper image that depicts the child welfare path of children as comprised of a mixture of stability and change. Children often stay at home or with kin or in an out-of-home care settings for a considerable time. Although a few children have many child welfare placements, many of them have rather few before their cases are closed. The characteristics of each of those placements is particularly significant. Decisions about the value of pathways determine what those settings bring to a child in the moment and over time. So, for example, a residential care program may offer a child exposed to chaotic living circumstances to a structured, safe, and secure setting that enables the child to regain his/her sense that the company of others is orderly and valuable. Yet, group care is not best to teach subsequent lessons about family relationships and each person's management of the love and loathing of family life's intimacy. Living with elderly relatives may nurture a child's well-being during the formative preschool years but may fail the child when he or she needs structure and support during late adolescent years. Professionals must understand what a child can expect to receive in the way of care at each stopping point in the CWS.

Each residence that a child is in can be judged from the child's perspective according to the likelihood that the setting will be safe from reabuse; stable and lasting; developmentally advantageous; and satisfying to the child. Because a review of available research on the success of family preservation and family maintenance and reunification, adoption, guardianship, and long-term foster care at achieving these goals is available elsewhere (Barth & Berry, in press), our discussion has a more modest purpose. Here, we will simply report that the outcome literature's evidence is clearly to indicate that each of these services can contribute significantly to the well-being of children if adequate resources are provided. Furthermore, this review support an activist view of child welfare services. Much good can and does result from intensive services. Children can thrive at home, in adoption, with kin and in guardianships, and in long-term foster care. We see no evidence to indicate that a minimal intervention—despite its countervailing virtue of respecting family privacy—is a priori the best one. Indeed, child welfare services now reach only the most troubled families. So few families reach the point at which they are entitled to receive child welfare services that they often need considerable service by then. Furthermore, they often welcome those services (Fryer et al., 1990). We can not yet indicate which child receiving which service will do best but only clarify which children stay in which settings for how long and which elements of service are best for children's optimal growth and development.

2

Growth in Child Abuse Reports and Child Welfare Services Caseloads

Policies creating the permanency planning revolution and accompanying practice changes appear to have resulted in different outcomes for children and families. Students of child welfare, at all levels, know that the impact of policies and practices depends mainly on the sociopolitical context. Indeed, a socioecological framework for understanding families dominates the child welfare field (Germain, 1979; Pecora, Whittaker, Maluccio, Barth, & Plotnick, 1992). Most often, researchers draw on this framework to generate practice implications.

In this chapter, we go back to Bronfenbrenner's (1979) original formulation that an ecological framework includes the influences of broad social trends and public policies. Just as these factors indirectly influence human development, they also influence the performance of families, social workers, and policymakers. Using county-level administrative child abuse and child welfare data, we demonstrate the power of an ecological model to explain growth in child abuse reports. This analysis provides provocative contextual information for an interpretation of permanency planning's success and limits.

At every level, sharp growth in caseloads causes concern. Among other consequences, substantial growth in caseloads means that fiscal costs are increasing. It suggests that more children are risking or experiencing harm and more families verge on dissolution. It also may reflect changes taking place in general population demographics or in child welfare system policies and practices. Furthermore, increases in the number of child abuse reports and foster care caseloads may reflect increases in the number of children in the general population, in child abuse and neglect incidence or seriousness, or changes in other socioecological developments, such as substance abuse, poverty or homelessness.

The focus of this chapter is on California's children receiving child welfare services under the four programs described in Chapter 1: Emergency Response (ER), Family Maintenance (FM), Family Reunification (FR), and Permanency Planning (PP). We first describe changes in those caseloads in recent years. Child abuse and neglect reports are described by using ER dispositions; that is, the number of decisions during the month regarding children who are leaving the ER program after their situations were investigated. Thereafter, attention is paid to trends in FM (in-home services) and to the foster care caseload and to a comparison of these trends.

The analytic section of the chapter is devoted to modeling and simulations. A time-series model is developed for ER dispositions between 1985 and 1991. The model is used for determining the extent to which selected external developments have an impact on the number of ER dispositions. The model is also used to forecast the consequences of external developments for ER caseload. The results of the forecasting exercises and policy recommendations are presented in the last section of the chapter.

REFORM OF CALIFORNIA CHILD WELFARE SERVICES

The Federal Adoption Assistance and Child Welfare Act of 1980 (P.L. 96–272) was an outgrowth of a child welfare service reform movement in California and other states (Ten Broeck & Barth, 1986). Senate Bill 14 was passed in 1982 as California's response to the federal law. The law restructured and expanded the existing child welfare system in California. This bill established the four child welfare service programs mentioned earlier: Emergency Response, Family Maintenance, Family Reunification and Permanency Planning. Senate Bill 14 incorporated four major goals for these services: (1) prevention of unnecessary foster care placements; (2) if possible, reunification of foster care children with their parents; (3) reduction in the number of long-term foster care placements by finding adoptive homes or guardianship placements; and (4) for those who remain in long-term foster care, assurance of stable and familylike placements (State of California Legislative Analyst Office, 1985). In order to accomplish these goals, SB 14 required that the number of court reviews of foster care cases increase and that the type of services provided to children and their families expand. Since their inception, the four programs have undergone many changes. The following sections describe changes in these programs' caseloads since the implementation of permanency planning.

TRENDS IN CALIFORNIA'S EMERGENCY RESPONSE DISPOSITIONS

The ER program is responsible for assessing and investigating child abuse reports and for determining the outcome of those reports. Counting child abuse reports is no simple matter, as some reports to ER are for information only, some are already open cases, some are judged as not needing a face-to-face response, and more serious calls require opening the case to ongoing services. Each county delineates its ER program activities related to each of these responses during the month and provides these data to the state of California in estimating, budgeting, and allocating funds for preplacement preventative services.

Prior to April 1988, the total number of ER dispositions recorded during any month included the number of children that left the program by transferring to the Family Maintenance, Family Reunification or Permanent programs and those who were investigated but were later determined to have an open child welfare services case already. Also included in the monthly ER dispositions were those cases requiring no further action.

A change occurred in the reporting system in 1988 that resulted in the counties' inclusion of a new definition of what constituted an ER case. Effective April 1988, the ER cases that are assessed and closed by the worker after being determined inappropriate for in-person response were also included. Overall, the number of total ER dispositions in any given month includes some of the referrals made to child protective services during that month but also includes some referrals made in prior months, as children may not leave the ER program the same month the referral is made. Most of the categories that make up the total number of ER dispositions in any given month are those regarding children who were provided with in-person response and who subsequently leave the ER program. As demonstrated in Chapter 3, about child abuse and referral process, the decision to further investigate, act on, or close a referral is defined as a case disposition, and the meaning of case dispositions vary.

This study focuses on growth in the number of ER dispositions, rather than on growth in the number of child abuse or neglect referrals received during the month, for two major reasons. First, counties record the number of families referred for abuse or neglect during a month, rather than the number of children. This number of referrals does not meet the needs

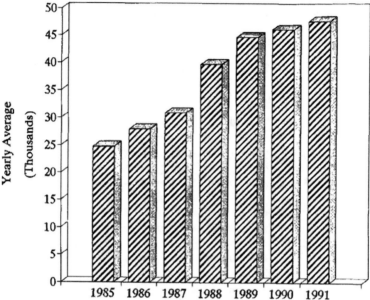

Figure 2.1. Emergency response dispositions.

of this study since its focus is on children, rather than families receiving protective services. Second, the total number of referrals received during any given month includes those families for which insufficient information exists, and consequently these referrals are not investigated beyond the initial complaint. For example, some of the complaints are prank calls, and others do not provide any information about the location of the alleged abuse or neglect situation. Hence, the number of child abuse reports received during the month is erratic, including events that might not necessarily reflect the actual occurrence of child abuse or neglect in the population.

The year-by-year growth in California's total ER dispositions since 1985 is shown in Figure 2.1. When examined on a monthly basis, these trends reveal considerable seasonality: total ER dispositions peak in the summer months and dip in the winter months. Calculations reveal that the average number of total ER dispositions per month in 1985 was 24,672, whereas the corresponding number in 1991 was 47,601. This is an overall growth of 93%. The average monthly growth rate differed substantially between three periods. For every month between January 1985 to December 1987, on average, there were 130 more dispositions than in the previous month. Between January 1988 to December 1988 there were about 980 more dispositions every month; and between January 1989 and December 1991 there were about 143 more dispositions every month.

TRENDS IN CALIFORNIA'S FAMILY MAINTENANCE CASELOAD

The Family Maintenance program is designed to help children remain with their families by providing them with various in-home social work and community services. As expected, the number of children served in the Family Maintenance program is substantially less than the number served in the Emergency Response program. Moreover, although the ER caseload has invariably increased during the study period, the picture for the FM caseload can be characterized as one undergoing stretches of sharp increases and decreases.

Yearly trends in California's Family Maintenance caseload since 1985 are shown in Figure 2.2. Whereas the average number of FM cases per month in 1985 was 31,017, the corresponding number in 1991 was 27,302, an overall decrease of 14%. Monthly analysis reveals that growth rates of the FM caseload differed substantially between four periods. Between January 1986 and April 1986, the number of FM cases rapidly subsided by 23%. Whereas in January 1986 there were 31,859 FM cases, the corresponding figure in April 1986 was 25,919 cases. The FM caseload continued to decline between April 1986 and January 1988, but only by 8%. The picture changed between January 1988 and July 1990, when the caseload rapidly grew by 28%. The caseloads declined by 11% between July 1990 and April 1991 and then stabilized.

TRENDS IN CALIFORNIA'S FOSTER CARE CASELOAD

California's foster care caseload comprises nearly one-fifth of the national foster care caseload; its growth needs to be described and analyzed. Figure 2.3 presents California's Welfare Supervised Foster Care caseload from 1985 to 1991 and incidence rate per 10,000 children. The caseload numbers are the cases open at the end of each month under social services supervision (that is, they exclude probation-supervised children in foster and group care). Looking at the figure, several salient features stand out. First, between December 1985 and December 1990, California's foster care caseload grew by about 83%, from 36,815 to 71,464 cases. This is a growth rate of about 15% per year. Second, the greatest increase in the caseload

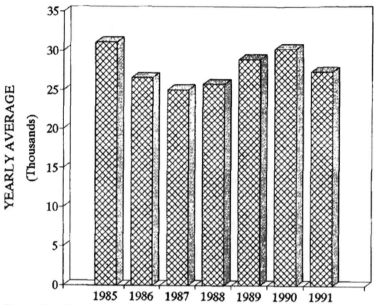

Figure 2.2. Family maintenance caseload.

occurred between March 1987 and February 1990: The caseload grew by close to 61%, from 44,786 to 72,237 cases. This is a growth rate of about 1% per month. Third, from February 1990 to November 1991, caseload growth abated. Fourth, every year from 1985 to 1991, a higher proportion of children under the age of 18 from the general population have participated in the foster care system. Whereas in 1986, on average 57 per 10,000 children in California were in foster care, the figure for 1991 was 93 per 10,000 children, an increase of about 60%. (See Appendix 2.A for variable sources.) This incidence rate has stabilized in 1990 and 1991.

Overall, California's foster care caseload grew substantially between 1985 and 1990, as did caseloads in other parts of the country. Although the surge in the size of the foster care caseload in the latter half of the 1980s was not unique to California, California's caseload grew more than twice as fast as the national caseload. Other large states, especially Michigan, New York, and Illinois also have experienced an increase in their foster care caseloads. In attempting to disentangle sources of this growth, several researchers examined total admissions, discharges, and net contributions in each of the three states. They claimed that prior to the mid-1980s, when the caseloads were not growing at a rapid pace, the levels of admissions were comparable to those of discharges. After 1986, the foster

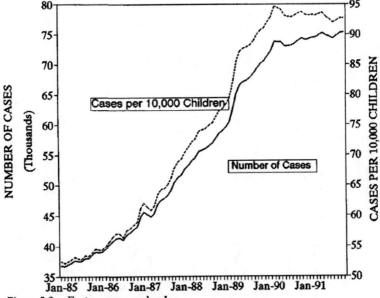

Figure 2.3. Foster care caseload.

caseload in these states also grew due to increasing admissions and declining terminations (Wulczyn & Goerge, 1990a). The surge in infant placements in the latter half of the 1980s may be one reason exit rates have also decreased in California. Infants, especially those under the age of 6 months, have longer foster care spells than their counterparts (see Chapter 5). Recent research (Wulczyn, 1991) has also demonstrated that, at least in New York state, reentry has played a significant role in exerting upward pressure on the foster care caseload. (Because we are using aggregate data for this analysis we are unable to analyze reentry rates.) The extent to which caseload growth in California resulted from increases in the number of openings or from decreases in the number of closing or both is addressed next.

Patterns of Change

Changes in the caseload from one period to the next are the result of adding new cases (admissions) and closing other cases (exits). The difference between admissions and exits during any month is the net contribution. Figure 2.4 presents the number of admissions, exits, and the net contribution for the foster care caseload from 1985 to 1991.

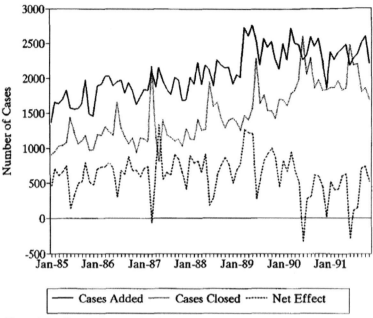

Figure 2.4. Foster care caseload.

On this graph, the large seasonal fluctuations make patterns difficult to discern. Several observations, however, can be drawn. First, from December 1985 to May 1990, the average net contribution was fairly constant at about 680 cases per month. Second, during the next six quarters net contribution fell by almost one-half to an average of 350 cases per month. Whether this drop is temporary or signifies a permanent abatement of caseload growth is unknown. Third, foster care openings and closing show some cyclical sensitivity: Both total admissions and discharges are higher during the summer months and lower in the winter months. Fourth, when the caseload was growing rapidly in 1987, 1988, and 1989, closings were about 66% of openings in each of these years. This produced a net gain of about 670 additional cases per month in 1987 and 1988. During this period the caseload continued to grow at an almost constant rate. During 1989 openings exceeded closings by 830 cases per month. This resulted in a somewhat steeper increase in the caseload during 1989. In a nutshell, in 1989 there were about 10,000 more openings than closings, whereas in 1987 and 1988 the corresponding figure was about 8,000. In 1990 and 1991, when the caseload stabilized, closings increased from 66 to 80% of openings. At the same time, openings leveled off at their 1989 level of about 2,400 per month. This stabilization of admissions, coupled with the higher number of exits, led to the abatement of caseload growth during 1990 and 1991.

COMPARISON OF TRENDS

Figure 2.5 provides for a comparison between the average yearly percentage of increases in the ER, FM, and FR/PP caseloads in California. In looking at the figure, we see three distinct periods stand out that have some implications for the relationships between the three programs. During the first period, 1986 and 1987, child abuse reports and foster care caseload increased, and in-home services declined. It was only during the second period, 1988 to 1990, that in-home services increased, as did the other two caseloads. During this period, however, the foster care caseload grew at a much faster rate than the family maintenance caseload, although it grew at a slower rate than the FM caseload in 1990. (The very sharp increase in the number of child abuse and neglect reports in 1988 was partially due to changes in reporting rules.) Finally, in 1991, the foster care and ER caseloads increased, whereas in-home services declined once again.

Overall, the hypothesized relationship between a wider provision of in-home services and a resulting reduction in foster care caseload is not observable here. In each of the years, whenever the family maintenance caseload grew, the foster care caseload grew at an even faster rate. This comparison of the caseloads suggests that no simple statements can be made about the relationships between child abuse reports, in-home services, and foster care. At present, it is not possible to validate the notion that in-home services are direct antidotes to foster family care. Although we take the following argument well beyond the graphed data and rely on our own impressions of what has recently occurred in the faltering family preservation movement in California, we would argue that the value of family maintenance services is limited to the willingness of communities to see them as a potential alternative to foster care. The findings and legal mandates for child abuse investigations and foster care are also much more stable than those for in-home services. We expect the availability of in-home services to be significantly affected by the availability of state and local funds. More definitive conclusions, however, about the general relationship between these caseloads cannot be made without support of a study that specifically tests these relationships while controlling for other external factors.

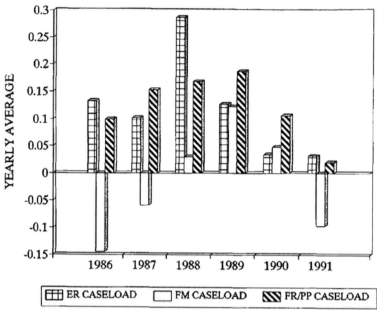

Figure 2.5.   Average yearly percent change ER, FM, and FR/PP caseloads.

USING TIME-SERIES ANALYSIS IN HUMAN SERVICES

Time-series analysis has been a popular and widely used analytic technique in the field of economics, and, as explained in Chapter 1, it has recently captured the attention of some social welfare policy analysts. Growth in the Aid to Families with Dependent Children (AFDC) caseload has been explained using time-series analysis. For example, Plotnick and Lidman constructed a multivariate model for the single-parent Aid to Families with Dependent Children caseload for Washington State using data for the years 1974 to 1983. Their model tracked actual AFDC caseload quite well and selected variables explained about 99 percent of the variation in the caseload (Plotnick & Lidman, 1987). Whereas Plotnick and Lidman specified a single model for the AFDC caseload, Albert (1988) modeled the AFDC caseload by decomposing the caseload into month-to-month changes in AFDC additions and AFDC terminations. Each component of the caseload is hypothesized to be a function of labor-market conditions, demographics, and welfare system characteristics. This work allowed for the calculation of the consequences of major national policy shifts for AFDC accessions, terminations, and the entire caseload. Overall, then, time-series analysis has been used to explain growth in the AFDC caseload or its components, additions, and terminations by incorporating three set of variables: labor-market conditions, AFDC program characteristics, and demographics. Time-series analysis, however, has not been used to explain growth in the foster care caseload or growth in the incidence of child abuse and neglect. The advantages of using this type of analysis in the field of child welfare are examined next.

MODELING THE NUMBER OF CHILD ABUSE REPORTS

While some research has been conducted in the area of foster care caseload dynamics, studies that explain growth in the incidence of child abuse and neglect are scarce (Ards, 1989; Garbarino, 1976). Available studies, however, are informative, because they provide for an understanding of how changes in select external developments may affect local child abuse rates; yet, because they are cross-sectional, they do not demonstrate how historical changes in external developments may affect changes in such rates. Moreover, these studies do not account for recent drug-related problems that undoubtably have contributed to the rise in the incidence of child abuse and neglect. In related social welfare fields, time-series analysis has been used successfully to explain historical changes in welfare caseloads. Time-series is used in the present study to explain ER caseload growth.

A model used to forecast child abuse and neglect reports must rest on some theoretical grounds about the relationship between the dependent variable, in this case the number of ER dispositions, and external factors. Aside from theoretical expectations, a model also should be based on what past research has concluded about the relationship between relevant variables. With a good model in hand, time-series analysis can be useful in child welfare in at least two major ways: (1) by enabling a determination of how and to what extent external developments such as the number of drug-related arrests affect the number of child abuse and neglect reports; and (2) by providing an opportunity to forecast the consequences for the ER caseload under alternative assumptions about external developments.

An important forecasting exercise is to determine the impact of changes in external developments on the dependent variable. In this study, such forecasting is performed to determine the impact of changes in the number of births. Another forecasting exercise determines the impact of major child welfare policy changes by estimating what would have occurred in their absence and by comparing these results with what actually occurred with the policy changes in effect. In this chapter, such forecasting is performed to determine the impact of changes in the CWS budget-allocation methodology on the ER caseload.

In order to engage in the desired forecasting exercises, we constructed a monthly time-series model for analyzing and simulating California's ER caseload. As no similar time-series analysis had been conducted before, the modeling efforts relied on available descriptive information about the characteristics of children receiving child welfare services and on the best judgment of the researcher.

Overall, the dependent variable in the equation consists of the total number of ER dispositions per month. The idea underlying the model is that month-to-month changes in the number of ER dispositions is a response to changes in various independent factors. These independent factors are listed in Figure 2.6.

As shown in Figure 2.6, the model incorporates seven independent variables. These variables directly affect both ER dispositions and the caseload. The following discusses the possible effects of selected variables on the ER caseload.

Demographic Factors

Births. Between 1985 and 1989, California experienced a dramatic rise in the number of children under 1 year admitted to the foster care system. Nearly 4,400 infants were in foster care in 1989, an increase of 235% in 4 years. As demonstrated by other research, children who enter foster care as infants tend to remain there for longer periods of time than older children (CWDA, 1990). All else being equal, this means that a surge in infant placements is bound to alter the dynamics of Child Welfare Services caseloads and in turn have fiscal ramifications.

Given the recent upsurge in infant foster care placements, the number of births in California in any given month can be expected to partially explain the size of the ER caseload and of the foster care caseload. Only the ER caseload is modeled, and this model contains the monthly number of births in California as an explanatory variable of the number of child abuse reports. From 1985 to 1991 the number of births shows considerable seasonality, with peeks in the summers and troughs in the winters. In 1985, the average number of live births in California was 39,235, whereas in 1991 the corresponding figure was 50,697, an increase of about 30%. (See Appendix 2.A for variable sources.)

When babies are reported to Child Welfare Services and perhaps placed in foster care, they are often placed soon after birth due to parental abandonment or inadequacy. The impact of births on the size of the ER

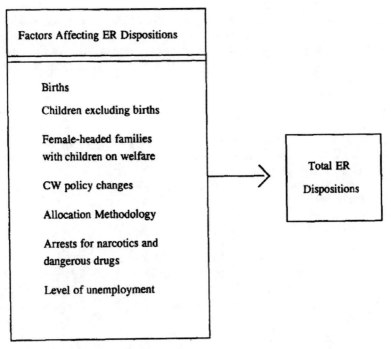

Figure 2.6. Model of ER dispositions.

caseload is expected to be immediate, since many infants are attended to by the child welfare system soon after birth. Since, it may take a while for the effect of births to show up in the number of ER reports, a 1-month lag in addition to no lag should account for most of the underlying effect of births on the ER care caseload. In other words, all else being constant, in any given month the size of the ER care caseload is a function of the number of births that occurred during that month and the month before. The extent to which the number of births influences the number of child abuse or neglect reports is a question that can only be answered after a model controlling for other factors is tested.

Children (Excluding Newborns). From July 1985 to July 1991, the total number of children in California's population increased by about 10% from 7,098,867 to 7,869,864. Throughout this 6-year period, Caucasian children constituted close to one-half of all children, while the corresponding figure for Latino children was about one-third. Corresponding figures for African-American and Asian children have been close to 9 and

10%, respectively. Some variation, however, has occurred during this time interval: The proportion of Caucasian children has decreased slightly, whereas the proportion of African-American and Asian children has remained virtually the same and the share of Latino children in California increased slightly, from 33 to 35%. (See Appendix 2.A for variable sources.)

As discussed more fully in Chapter 3, African-American children are disproportionately involved with the child welfare system. About one-half of all children referred for abuse or neglect are minority children. As Chapter 5 shows, about 58% of children entering foster care are identified as minority. Moreover, nearly two-thirds of children in out-of-home care in California are minority children.

Therefore, an increase in the number of child abuse reports should be predictable from an increase in the number of African-American or Latino children under age 18 in California. African-American and Latino children between 1 and 18 years old are also included in the model.

Female-Headed Families on Welfare. Female-headed families with children have a high propensity for experiencing prolonged poverty and welfare dependence (Albert, 1988). In California, from July 1985 to July 1991, female-headed families constituted about 10 to 11% of all families with children. During these years, about 65 to 70% of all female-headed families received AFDC subsidies at some time. (See Appendix 2.A for variable sources.)

Close to four out of five children placed in foster care in 1990 came from single-parent families, and close to two out of three children in foster care came from AFDC-eligible families. Consequently, any changes in the proportion of either female-headed families or those receiving welfare may affect the number of child abuse reports and, in turn, the foster care caseload. Since the two variables that capture changes in these types of families are highly correlated, only one variable representing the number of female-headed families with children who receive AFDC is used as an explanatory factor of child abuse and neglect reports. It would be expected that, as the number of female-headed families with children on welfare increases, so would the number of child abuse reports. A 1-month lag structure should account for most of the underlying effect of female-headed families on welfare on the ER caseload.

Social and Economic Factors

Drug Abuse. Drug abuse by a parent or guardian has become a major factor associated with out-of-home placement. A survey by California's Senate Office of Research in 1988 and 1989 revealed that over 3,150 children under the age of 1 were made dependents of the court as a result of substance exposure (CWDA, 1990).

The number of arrests for narcotic and dangerous drugs partially reflects the extent to which drug use or abuse occurs in California. This number is quite seasonal, increasing during the summer months and decreasing during the winter months. From January 1985 to August 1989, the number of narcotic and dangerous drug arrests climbed at a monthly rate of about two percentage points. From August 1989 to December 1991, it declined at a monthly rate close to one and one-half percentage points. In January of 1985, the number of drug arrests was about 6,200. By August 1989, the number of drug arrests for narcotics and dangerous drugs hovered around 13,600. The corresponding figure in December of 1991 was about 8,100. (See Appendix A for variable sources.)

The picture of drug-related arrests for females closely resembles the one we outlined. Drug-related arrests for females also began declining after August of 1989 at a monthly rate of about two percentage points per month. While in January 1985, drug-related arrests for females were 1,126 and in August 1989 the number was 2,587, the corresponding number in December 1991 was down to 1,365.

Since the number of drug-related arrests on the part of the parents and in particular on the part of the mother may result in the need for more child welfare services, the model incorporates a variable representing the number of monthly arrests for narcotics and dangerous drugs for females in California. It is expected that, as this number increases, so will the number of child abuse or neglect reports. A 1-month lag structure should account for most of the underlying effect of drug-related arrests on the ER caseload.

Unemployment. The state's economic conditions are features which are particularly relevant to the analysis of growth in child abuse dispositions. The state of California has experienced one major recession in the past 8 years. This recession began during 1990 and is still lingering in 1993. During the study period, 1985 to 1991, it produced maximum joblessness in 1991.

Past research has demonstrated that a rise in the number of children who are welfare dependent in California is linked to labor-market conditions (Albert, 1988). It also stands to reason to expect that poor labor-market conditions are associated with more children at risk of entering the CWS. It is hypothesized, therefore, that the number of seasonally unadjusted unemployed in California is a measure of the economy assumed to affect the number of children served by the ER program. Although levels marked by this general measure may probably understate unemployment in California and certainly understate the number of jobless among families that are at risk of being served by the Child Welfare System, it is quite possible that variations in the number of unemployed are highly correlated with variations in unemployment in the populations at risk of being served by the Child Welfare system. A 1-month lag structure for the seasonally unadjusted unemployed variable is incorporated into the model.

Child Welfare Policies and Practices

Previous ecological models to explain child abuse or foster care have not included the impact of public policy changes. Such changes are accounted for in our model.

Senate Bill 243. Senate Bill 243 (SB 243) passed in the fall of 1987 and was implemented in January 1988. This bill made major changes in the CWS system to further implement permanency planning. The first such major change since the 1982 legislation authorizing California's version of the AACWA. Of particular relevance to this study, the bill narrowed the definition of abuse for dependency proceedings. Due to SB 243, the decision to remove a child from the home or terminate parental rights is to be based on the immediate danger to the child. Previous law was broader, not focusing on immediate danger.

Senate Bill 243 has other provisions relevant to this study. Very important, it reemphasized the priority of relative foster care placement. It codified the public's intent that the foster care placement of choice should be with the child's relatives before other foster care placements are considered.

The way in which this bill has affected the size of the ER caseload is difficult to predict. On the one hand, it would be expected that, because the bill narrowed the definition of child abuse, fewer children would be considered appropriate for ER services. On the other hand, SB 243 may have slightly clarified the ambiguous situation of child abuse or neglect, in turn allowing more children who previously would have fallen through the cracks to receive ER services. A dummy variable accounting for the bill is incorporated into the time-series analysis in order to test the effect of the law on the size the ER caseload.

Changes in Reporting. As indicated, effective April 1988, child welfare workers were to include in the total number of reported ER dispositions the number of cases assessed but determined inappropriate for in-person response. In addition, the counties were to be held accountable for the accuracy of statistical data reported on the new system. In a letter dated January 28, 1988, the counties were told that the new reporting system should be accurate and represent the actual number of ER referrals and dispositions. As discussed in the subsequent section, it also was in 1988 that the state began to allocate monies to the counties for Child Welfare Services solely on the basis of their caseload sizes.

Although the new reporting system was to be implemented beginning in April 1988, the counties' caseloads began to increase substantially even earlier than that date, perhaps partially in anticipation of the changes in the reporting system. Only one dummy variable reflecting both SB 243 and changes in the reporting system is incorporated into the model, as both went into effect at the same time. It is expected that, all else being constant, these changes in the reporting system have led to a larger statewide ER caseload.

Budget Allocation Methodology for CWS. The extent to which California counties are able to adequately meet their CWS needs and legislative requirements and the degree to which these service needs are delivered in a satisfactory fashion largely depend on the allocation level they receive each fiscal year. Yearly county allocation levels for the CWS are determined by the California Department of Social Services (CDSS). During the past decade, the CDSS has used two criteria for distributing funds to counties for the CWS: one based on what is commonly known as "demographics," and the other on the basis of the county's historical caseload statistics. When resources were distributed to counties partially on the basis of demographics, the number of children in the AFDC program and the number of children under the age of 18 in the general population were used. In addition, caseload statistics for FR and PP were accounted for.

Overall, from FY 1984–85 to FY 1987–88, the CWS allocation formula was based on both caseload and population measures, with population measures having a decreasing proportional impact on the allocation methodology over time. Resources were distributed to counties on the basis of both demographics and caseload statistics in order to help counties make the transition from an allocation formula based on demographics to one based on caseload statistics. It is only since the beginning of FY 1988–89 that the CDSS allocated resources for CWS solely on the basis of caseload statistics. Thus, a "pure" caseload-driven formula has not been in place for a very long time, perhaps not allowing for its full effects to take place. The shift toward a caseload-driven methodology was made in response to SB 14 and to general dissatisfaction with the allocation criterion based on demographic factors. In short, the counties believed that they would be more fairly treated if they were funded on the basis of an estimate of the services they provided rather than the need in the county.

When allocations were based on the number of children in the general population and on the number of children receiving AFDC subsidies, it was assumed that these numbers would be proportional to the extent to which child abuse and neglect would prevail in a particular county. Thus, it was assumed that these indicators are related to the level of need for CWS in a particular county. This approach to allocating resources requires a clear definition and identification of the "potentially eligible" population for services in a particular locale.

In contrast to the criterion for allocating resources that is based on demographic factors, which rewards counties with the potential of having greater level of need, the criterion for allocating resources on the basis of caseload statistics rewards counties that can justify serving more children or that can justify a greater level of need based on historical counts. The caseload-statistics approach can become self-perpetuating, because counties with small caseloads may have greater unmet needs but more difficulty in justifying their need. Counties with insufficient staff may in fact be serving *needier* clients (Hasler, 1986).

Another problem associated with the caseload-driven approach to distributing moneys is that it creates the opportunity for local administrators to manipulate caseload statistics. The policies and practices for opening and closing cases in each locale affect the size of the reported caseload. Clearly, prompt openings of cases even in the absence of provision of services and delays in closing cases will affect caseload size and future allocation levels. This approach, however, does assure continuity of services and make unlikely an abrupt reduction of service resources and as a consequence the termination of services (Hasler, 1986).

Overall, while an allocation approach based on demographic factors is inherently more equitable, because it provides no incentives for manipulating caseload statistics, it may not accurately reflect a county's need for resources, nor may it guarantee the continuity of services. On the other hand, a caseload-driven approach ensures continuity of services but has the built-in disadvantage of maintaining the status quo.

Whether an increase in the size of California's ER caseload would be associated with the presence of a caseload-driven methodology is impossible to guess. On the one hand, it may be that in the presence of this methodology the size of the ER caseload is greater than it would have been had the demographic methodology remained in effect, because the system rewards larger county-level ER caseloads. On the other hand, this may not have occurred: Caseload statistics may not have been altered in order to benefit allocation levels. In order to determine the effect of changing methodology while controlling for other variables that also explain caseload growth, a variable reflecting the increasing percentage in caseload statistics was constructed and incorporated in the model.

Seasonality

Finally, we tested the commonly held idea that child abuse reports vary with the seasons. The ER caseload equation includes a set of seasonal monthly dummy variables. Although the variables discussed above cover some of the major influences on the ER caseload, other social factors also may affect growth in the caseload. To the extent that these factors systematically or seasonally change the caseload, a set of seasonal variables is appropriate. As some of these social factors are unknown, the sign of the coefficient of each seasonal variable is difficult to hypothesize. The seasonal variables are included in an additive, rather than proportional, form, since the model is in a linear functional form.

Summary of Variables

In the absence of any known previous time-series analyses in the field of child welfare, we selected the independent variables in the model on the basis of available descriptive statistics or anecdotal evidence that show that children with certain characteristics and problems are more apt to be involved in the Child Welfare system. Similarly, the lag structure of the equation was left solely to the judgment of the researcher. For the most part, a 1-month lag structure seems appropriate for predicting the incidence of child abuse or neglect by using total ER dispositions.

TIME SERIES RESULTS

The estimated equation for total ER dispositions is presented in Table 2.1. The independent variables in the regression equation explain about 96% of the variance in monthly dispositions. In addition, the results reveal that most of the variables in the equation have a significant impact on the number of decisions regarding child abuse and neglect reports received either during the same month or in the prior month. It should be noted that the key findings present other levels of statistical significance associated with some of the variables than the conventional statistical level of .05 for rejecting the null hypothesis. This level is quite difficult to attain in time-series analysis, because correlations between time and the independent variables often exist. The following summarizes key findings.

- The number of births, a highly seasonal variable, has a substantial impact on the number of child abuse and neglect reports finalized

Table 2.1. Regression Results

Total observations	83	Skipped/missing	0
Usable observations	83	Degrees of freedom	63
R**2	.97131280	RBAR**2	.96266111
SSR	.20601053E+09	SEE	1808.3165

Variable	Lag	Coefficient	Significance Level
Constant	0	6246.080	—
Births	0	1.392	.001*
Births	1	−.528	.001*
Non-white	1	−.016	—
AFDC-FG	1	.034	—
Drug arrests	0	3.286	.05
Unemployed	1	6.484	.06
Allocation	0	9007.531	.001
SB 243 and report- ing changes	0	4990.802	.001

A joint F test for multiple lags reveals $p < .001$.

Note: For variable definitions see Appendix A. Both the AFDC-FG and Non-white variables also reveal insignificant results.

during the month. The sum of the coefficients' signs is positive, indicating that a monthly increase of 1,000 births results in an increase of about 864 ER dispositions. (We explain this apparently surprising finding later in this chapter.) A joint F test on the lagged set of births reveals statistical significance ($p < .001$).

The sign of the coefficient associated with African-American and Latino children in California is negative, unexpected, and not significant. The sign of the coefficient suggests that, as the number of African-American and Latino children in the population increases, the number of ER dispositions decreases.

- Although statistically insignificant, the coefficient associated with the number of AFDC-Family Groups indicates that as this number increases, so does the number of ER dispositions.
- A monthly increase of 1,000 unemployed in the population results in an increase of about 6,500 more ER dispositions. The results show that this variable is almost statistically significant ($p < .06$).
- The number of arrests in California for dangerous or narcotic drugs among females has a great impact on the number of children in each month. This variable indicates that an increase of 1,000 drug-related arrests results in an increase of 3,300 total dispositions. This variable is statistically significant ($p < .05$).

With the onset of SB 243 and changes in the reporting system in 1988, total dispositions increased by about 5,000 per month. The coefficient is highly statistically significant ($p < .001$).

As allocations for child welfare services were based more and more on caseload statistics and less on demographic measures, total dispositions increased by about 900 per month for each hypothetical 10% increase in the proportion of caseload statistics in the allocation formula. In other words, as the weight given to caseload statistics increases from 50% to 60%, this is associated with an increase of about 900 statewide ER dispositions per month. The coefficient is highly statistically significant ($p < .001$).

SUMMARY AND IMPLICATIONS

Overall, the selected independent variables explain a large percentage of the variance in the monthly number of ER dispositions. Four variables in particular have a *substantial impact* on each of the dependent variables and are found statistically significant: (1) the number of births, (2) the number of arrests for narcotics and dangerous drugs, (3) the impact of SB 243 or reporting changes, and (4) the budget-allocation methodology.

When examining the effect of births during the month and in the prior month, one can see that their impact on ER dispositions caseload is sizable. The results suggest that 86% of any increase in the number of newborns in the population results in another child reported for child welfare abuse or neglect. In other words, for each increase in 100 newborns in the population there is an increase of about 86 child abuse and neglect reports. Either there is substantial error in these birth coefficients or some other explanation for these rather surprising results.

Because the set of lagged births yields a statistical significance level of .001, the results do not appear to show large error. The large impart of births may be explained in several ways. First, it may be that the arrival of a newborn triggers events for other children in the family. If one assumes that there are two children per family and that both children would be reported to the investigative agency, the present results suggest that about 40% of any increase in the number of newborns results in receipt of some child welfare services. Even so, this figure is still quite high.

A second explanation may be that some other variables unaccounted for in the model fluctuate in a similar fashion to births and contribute to the rise in ER dispositions. For example, births may be a proxy for young families with greater risk of child abuse. Another explanation may be that a rise in additional births in the population leads to problems in other families whose children wind up referred to the system. The more children in the population, the further existing social and educational services for children must be stretched.

The impact of the number of drug arrests on dispositions confirm anecdotal evidence regarding the impact of drug abuse on child welfare services. The impact of this variable on ER dispositions indicates that an increase of 1,000 drug-related arrests results in more than 3,300 ER dispositions. Again, this must be understood as an indicator of a cluster of factors associated with the major dishevel related to the major increase in maternal drug abuse. For every parent that experienced a drug-arrest, many more experienced a child abuse report.

Finally, the results reveal that child welfare policies do indeed have substantial impact on the number of child abuse and neglect reports. Although the unique contribution of changes in reporting rules and of SB 243 are unknown because these two system changes occurred simultaneously, the results show that a positive and large relationship between the dummy variable representing these changes and the variable representing total ER dispositions exists. In addition, the results reveal that the coefficient of this variable is statistically significant ($p < .001$).

The best explanation for the positive relationship between changes in reporting and ER dispositions is that with the onset of the new reporting system counties were not only counting ER cases that were not counted previously, but also, as asked by the state, they were more careful about accurately recording the ER caseload movement. A plausible explanation for a positive relationship between SB 243 and ER dispositions is that SB 243 helped to clarify the definition of abuse or neglect for dependent children, in turn letting more children be served in the system than otherwise would have been the case. It also could be that SB 243 restricted the definition of abuse or neglect thereby decreasing the number of ER dispositions, whereas the changes in reporting rules increased the number of ER dispositions to a much greater extent. Once again, without separately analyzing the unique contribution of changes in reporting rules and of SB 243, one never knows for sure.

The results further demonstrate that the type of allocation methodology the state of California uses to allocate resources to counties does effect the number of ER decisions the counties make. All else being constant, since the state has been allocating resources to the counties on the basis of historical caseload statistics, there have been close to 5,000 more dispositions reported per month than there would have been had the state distributed resources for CWS solely on the basis of demographics. It should be emphasized, however, that from the present findings we cannot ascertain whether an increase in the number of dispositions has meant that services also changed under the present system. Whether ER services reached more children who needed to be served, or perhaps whether children received better services under the caseload-driven system, is unknown from the present research. It is plausible that social workers simply began to record their child abuse investigations more assiduously.

Overall, the model of ER dispositions is designed to test hypotheses about the effects of independent variables, to simulate total dispositions, and to determine the impact of select variables on the ER caseload through several forecasting exercises.

THE SIMULATIONS

In this study, three simulations or forecasting exercises are performed. The first simulation is historical, the second estimates the impact of births and the third determines the impact of a caseload-driven budget-allocation methodology for the Child Welfare Services.

Historical Simulation

In time-series analysis, a model's ability to replicate actual data is not completely determined by the amount of variance explained by the independent variables in the regression equation nor by the statistical significance of its coefficients. The ability of the model to simulate actual series is very important. For a model to predict historical (actual) series well, the simulated series needs to track the historical series closely. An historical simulation, therefore, is performed in order to evaluate the present model's abilities to replicate historical data. The historical simulation begins in February 1985 and ends in December 1991. It begins in February 1985, rather than in January 1985, because the model has at most a 1-month lag. A graphic representation of the simulated and historical time series is presented in Figure 2.7.

Figure 2.7 shows that the simulated series of total ER dispositions replicates the historical series quite well. Every sharp increase or decrease is captured. The simulated independent variables oscillate through the historical values, and there is not much consistent overestimation or underestimation in the dependent variable.

Calculations show that, from March 1985 to December 1991, the mean and standard deviations of actual and simulated series were quite similar. The average monthly number of dispositions was 37,515; the corresponding figure for the simulated series was exactly the same. The standard deviations for the historical or actual series was 9,358; the corresponding

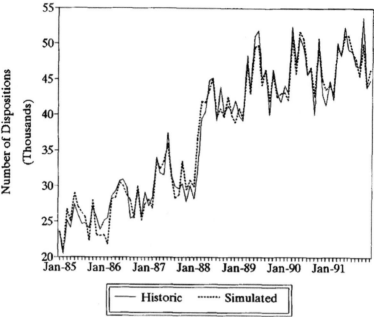

Figure 2.7. Historical and simulated dispositions.

figure for the simulated series was 9,223. In absolute terms and on average, the simulated series deviated from the actual series by about 1,280 dispositions per month, which is a 3.5% mean level of dispositions. Overall, total ER dispositions simulated values are close to the historical values, as further evidenced by the root mean square percentage error of less than 5%. This error is a common measure of accuracy in time-series analysis. Given the overall performance of this model and the statistical significance of the variables measuring births and the allocation methodology, the model can be used to determine:

The consequences for the size of the ER caseload if the number of births decreased by 20 percent.

The consequences for the size of the ER caseload if the budget-allocation methodology were solely based on demographic measures, rather than based on caseload measures or a combination of both.

Forecasting Births

For this exercise, the number of births is lowered by 20% along with the resulting decrease in the number of children in California's population.

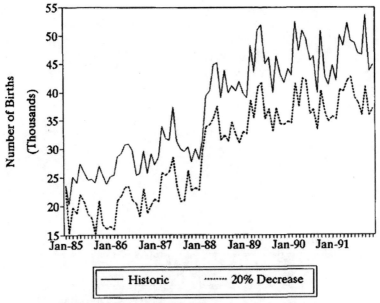

Figure 2.8. Effects of decreasing births.

This simulated series is compared to the historical series in Figure 2.8. The results of this exercise illustrate the key role that changes in the number of births plays in shaping the ER caseload. It is estimated that decreasing births by 20% would result in close to a 20% decrease in the ER caseload. As argued before, this figure must include the effects of more than one child becoming involved in the CWS or perhaps the impact of other variables unaccounted for in the model that fluctuate similarly to births. Overall, the effect of births on the number of child abuse and neglect reports is sizable.

The Impact of a Caseload-Driven Budget Allocation Methodology on ER Caseload

Initially, in order to analyze the effects of a caseload-driven allocation methodology on ER dispositions, we constructed a variable reflecting the proportion of caseload statistics that were accounted for in the allocation formula during the study period. In order to determine the size of the ER caseload in the absence of a caseload-driven methodology, this variable was set to zero. Thus, the simulated series estimates what would have

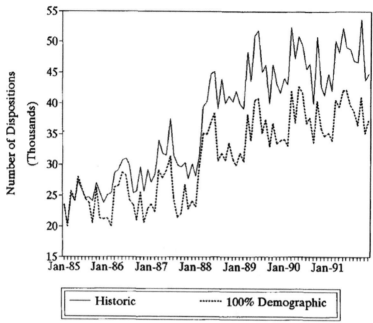

Figure 2.9. Caseload allocation methodology effects.

been the size of the ER caseload had only the previously used demographic measures for allocating resources been used during the entire study period. No other variables are altered for this exercise since all other variables in the model were not effected by changes in allocation methodology.

Figure 2.9 shows the ER caseload with and without a caseload-driven allocation methodology. The dotted lines represent the caseload in the absence of a caseload-driven methodology while the solid lines show the actual series. Over the entire study period, in the presence of an allocation methodology based solely on demographic measures, the ER caseload would have been about 17% lower. The gap between the actual caseload and the simulated caseload differs between each of the fiscal years in the study period. These differences are demonstrated in Table 2.2.

As Table 2.2 demonstrates, the gap between the actual and simulated ER caseloads increases with each fiscal year. In other words, as more emphasis was given to caseload statistics in the allocation formula, the difference between the actual and simulated caseloads grew. For example, when caseload statistics accounted for only 20% of the allocation formula in FY 1985–86, an ER caseload based solely on demographic statistics

Table 2.2. The Effect of 100% Caseload-Driven Formula on ER Caseload

Fiscal Years	Average Number of ER Cases		Percent Difference
	Actual Series	Simulated Series	
85–86	26,651	24,048	–9.8%
86–87	29,638	25,066	–15.4%
87–88	34,044	28,286	–16.9%
88–91	45,402	36,223	–20.0%
3/85–12/91	37,724	31,150	–17.4%
The Effect of 50% Caseload-Driven Formula on ER Caseload			
87–88	34,044	32,790	–3.7%
88–91	45,402	40,727	–10.3%
7/87–12/91	42,878	38,963	–9.1%

would have been about 10% lower than it actually was during this period. In contrast, when caseload statistics accounted for 75% of the allocation formula in FY 1987–88, an ER caseload based solely on demographic statistics would have been about 17% lower than it actually was.

Another related exercise was performed, and its results also are presented in Table 2.2. For this exercise, it was assumed that from FY 1987 until the end of the study period, the allocation formula was equally based on demographic and caseload measures. As the table shows, in FY 1987–88, when 75% of the actual allocation formula was based on caseload measures, the ER caseload would have been about 4% lower had only 50% of the formula been based on caseload statistics. From FY 1988 onward, when the allocation formula was solely based on caseload measures, the ER caseload would have been about 11% lower had only 50% of the formula been based on caseload statistics. Overall, if in the allocation formula only demographic measures were used, the model estimates that the ER caseload would have been substantially lower than if equal weights were placed on caseload and demographic measures in the allocation formula, and even lower if only demographic measures had been used.

SUMMARY, POLICY AND PRACTICE IMPLICATIONS

The Impact of External Factors on Child Abuse Reports

In this chapter we determined the impact of changes in external factors on child abuse or neglect reports, measured by the number of monthly ER

dispositions. Because California's share of the nation's children is relatively large, the consequences of changing external factors for California's
ER caseload have both state and national ramifications.

Evidence from other studies indicate that child abuse may be more
likely to follow unwanted births (Zuravin, 1991). Although the data used
for this study do not allow for the testing of such hypothesis, they,
however, did allow for the determination of the effects of total live births
on ER dispositions. Some of the findings from this study suggest that
trends in the infant subpopulation strongly influence trends in the ER
caseload. In a similar vein, the findings show that the number of arrests
for narcotic or dangerous drugs partially determine the number of child
abuse and neglect in any given month.

Thus, in part, the success of state or federal attempts to reduce the
incidence of child abuse or neglect will depend on the success of programs that reduce the birth rate and the drug abuse rate in the general
population. The success also will depend on the extent to which problems
accompanying single parenthood, poverty, and welfare are alleviated.
The relationship between these efforts must be understood. For example,
strategies to combat drug use that involve the arrest and incarceration of
parents should consider their impact on the incidence of child abuse or
neglect reports.

Three important policy implications may be drawn from the findings
presented in this chapter:

- State and federal efforts should focus on preventing unwanted or
  unplanned births. Ample and affordable family planning should be
  provided to women who are likely to face poverty and other hard-
  ships after giving birth.
- State and federal efforts need to continue to focus on providing aid
  to families in which drug abuse is known to exist. Programs that
  address the needs of parents incarcerated for drug abuse need to be
  expanded. These include arrangements for mothers to receive drug
  treatment while residing with their children in group care, foster
  care, or residential treatment (Barth, 1993a).
- State and federal efforts need to focus on further assisting poor
  female-headed families with children, so that fewer children from
  these families wind up in the child welfare system.

Implications for Changing Child Welfare Policies

This study reveals that the impact of SB 243 and of changes in reporting
rules on the number of monthly ER dispositions is substantial. Although
the unique impact of each of these variables is not determined, this

finding reveals the important consequences child welfare policies and reporting practices have for the child welfare system. Additional reexaminations or clarifications of the impact of changes in child abuse definitions on child abuse reports, child abuse investigations, family maintenance, and foster care remain necessary.

Overall, in attempting to understand and deal with problems of child abuse and neglect, the child welfare system needs to coordinate its intervention and research efforts with other public systems that aim to alleviate problems accompanying unwanted pregnancies, drug abuse, poverty and welfare dependence.

Implication for Allocating Child Welfare Resources

Because selected variables were found to be good predictors of child abuse and neglect reports, these variables or a similar array of variables may be incorporated to a budget allocation used to determine funding for county's Child Welfare Services. Using a set of demographic variables for the purpose of allocating child welfare resources to counties is under consideration in some states. At present, the state of California is examining the possibility of creating an allocation methodology for the ER program that would incorporate the demographic variables used in our study. The extent to which the model constructed for the present study can work on a county level is being studied.

Other states are also considering the use of demographic measures for allocating resources. For example, the state of Washington, which primarily uses child population figures to allocate child welfare resources to regions across the states, has recently examined the possibility to using various other measures for allocating funds, among them the region's AFDC caseload, child abuse reports, and single female-headed families excluding those on AFDC as indicators that reflect the potential of need for child welfare services (Washington Department of Social and Health Services, 1992).

The variables used in present study should be accounted for in a need-based allocation formula used to distribute resources to the ER program. An allocation formula based on demographic measures seems less valuable for allocating resources to such programs as foster care, because less ambiguity about case opening and closing exists in programs that are overseen by the courts. Since demographic variables incorporated in an allocation methodology exist outside of the Child Welfare system, these cannot be subject to any statistical manipulations. Overall, by using a demographic formula for distributing funds to the ER program, some of the built-in inequities inherent in a caseload-driven methodology may be eliminated.

Summary of Key Findings and Recommendations Regarding Growth in Child Welfare Services Caseloads

Finding	Recommendation
1. Trends in the infant subpopulation strongly influence trends in the ER caseload.	1. State and federal efforts should focus on preventing unwanted or unplanned births. Ample and affordable family planning should be provided to women who are likely to face poverty and other hardships after giving birth.
2. The incidence of arrests for narcotic and dangerous drugs partially determine the incidence of child abuse and neglect in any given month.	2. State and federal efforts need to continue to focus on providing aid to families in which drug abuse is known to exist. Programs that address the needs of parents incarcerated for drug abuse need to be expanded.
3. Child welfare policies such as SB 243, that altered the definition of abuse and neglect do affect the number of child abuse and neglect reports.	3. Additional reexaminations or clarifications of child abuse definitions within the child welfare system are still necessary.
4. The type of allocation methodology the state of California uses to allocate resources to counties does effect the number of decisions regarding child abuse and neglect reports in the ER program. Because the state has been allocating resources to the counties on the basis of historical caseload statistics, the number of dispositions per month have been substantially more than there would have been had the state distributed resources for CWS solely on the basis of demographics.	4. The demographic variables used in the present study or a similar array of variables should be accounted for in an allocation formula used to distribute resources to the ER program. Allocation formulas based on demographic measures are not recommended for programs, such as foster care, as less ambiguity about case opening and closing exists under court review.

APPENDIX
VARIABLE DEFINITIONS AND SOURCES

ER Disposition (t): The monthly numbers of Emergency Response dispositions were provided by California Health and Welfare Agency, Department of Social Services, Statistical Services Branch, SOC 291-Preplacement Preventative Services Caseload Movement Reports, Sacramento, 1/1985 to 12/1991.

Births (t):   Monthly live births taken from California State Department of Health, Birth Records Division, Sacramento, 1/1985 to 12/1991.

Non-white (t):   The number of African-American and Latino children under the age of 18 excluding births during month *t*. Yearly numbers of children under the age of 18 by race were provided by the State of California, Department of Finance, Population Research Unit. These numbers were linearly interpolated to monthly values.

AFDC-FG (t):   The number of Aid to Families with Dependent Children—Family Groups during month *t*. The monthly numbers were provided by California Health and Welfare Agency, Department of Social Services, Statistical Services Branch, Aid to Families with Dependent Children-Cash Grant Caseload Movement and Expenditures Report. Sacramento, 1/1985 to 12/1991.

Drug Arrests (t):   Monthly numbers of arrests among females for narcotics and dangerous drugs in California were provided by the State of California Department of Justice, Bureau of Criminal Statistics and Special Services, Sacramento, 1/1985 to 12/1991.

Unemployed (t):   Seasonally unadjusted number of unemployed during the month. Numbers were provided by the California Health and Welfare Agency, Employment Development Department, Report LF101, Employment Data and Research Division Estimates, Economic Research Group.

Allocation (t):   The variable accounting for the portion that caseload statistics were accounted for in the allocation methodology from Fiscal Year 1985–86 to Fiscal Year 1990–91.

SB 243 (t):   A dummy variable identifying the presence of Senate Bill 243 beginning in March 1988.

3

From Child Abuse Report to Child Welfare Services

The implementation of permanency planning has been concurrent with the explosion of child abuse and reporting. Child welfare services traditionally served parents of children in conflict and children with behavior problems in addition to abused, neglected, and abandoned children. The national concern about child abuse has resulted in a refocusing of child welfare services to address the needs of the nation's most vulnerable children. Although the child welfare service system continues to serve older and troubled youths, it most often follows a child abuse allegation and a child protective services (CPS) investigation. Kamerman and Kahn (1990) portray a dramatic, perhaps overly dramatic, picture of this trend: "Child protective services today constitute the core public child and family service, the fulcrum and sometimes, in some places, the totality of the service" (p. 8).

The CPS involvement has indeed become almost essential to receiving additional child welfare services, but many children who are the subject of a report of child abuse to the CPS do not receive additional services. Understanding the child welfare system requires, then, knowledge of the pathway between initial child abuse reports, subsequent child abuse reports, and receipt of additional child welfare services.

State child abuse and neglect laws require select professionals to report cases of suspected child abuse and neglect. The specific mandates of these laws, legal definitions of maltreatment, and actual incidents of maltreatment influence the number and types of child abuse or neglect reports received by an investigative agency. Whatever the origins of initial reports, the goal of the service response is to reduce the risk of subsequent harm. The extent to which children are repeatedly referred to the system is partially determined by the extent to which an agency is successful in providing appropriate services to referred children and their families.

The analyses in this chapter focus on identifying the characteristics of children referred for abuse and neglect, exploring the types and frequency of referrals for these children, and examining the dispositions of these referrals. The findings will allow us to identify those children at risk of being referred for selected types of maltreatment. It also raises issues regarding definitions of maltreatment and public awareness of abuse and neglect. Perhaps most important, the findings provide us with some understanding of the degree to which efforts have been successful in preventing the reoccurrence of abuse and neglect.

SAMPLE SELECTION AND CHARACTERISTICS

California, like most other states, has no statewide on-line management information system (MIS) for child abuse and neglect reports. Most available child abuse data are collected as end-of-month summaries, and these do not include descriptions of the process of referral. Several California counties, however, have instituted child abuse MISs. This study draws on data from San Diego, Santa Clara, and San Mateo counties, which use a similar system called the Social Service Reporting System (SSRS).[1] These counties were selected for analysis, because their SSRSs collected fairly uniform information and because their data extended the furthest back in time.[2]

Sample Selection

To ensure that the best and most representative sample is used for analysis, a sample of 26,506 children whose first referral occurred between January 1991 and September 1991 was extracted from the three SSRS databases.[3] As expected, the majority of children in the sample were from San Diego county (61%), because San Diego county is the most populated sampled county. Close to 27% of the sample was from Santa Clara county, the next most populated county, and the remainder (12%) was from San Mateo. Statistical analyses were performed for the sample as a whole.

San Diego county has the second largest child population in the state of California, with 24% of its residents under the age of 18 (*Children Now*, 1991). Santa Clara has the fifth largest child population in the state, and San Mateo the thirteenth. Taken together, the three counties have a population of nearly 4 million, which would make them the 23rd largest state. Table 3.1 provides a breakdown of the ethnic mix of children in each of the counties in 1990. As the table shows, counties are roughly similar in ethnicity, in spite of San Diego county's proximity to the Mexican border. Using median income as an indicator of family wealth, we find that San Diego has a median income of $41,300, San Mateo is somewhat better off at $49,900, and Santa Clara county's median income is comfortable at $57,700. Using the percentage of families receiving AFDC subsidies in each of the counties as an indicator of child poverty, we find that the poverty rate in San Mateo county is the lowest (6% of families used AFDC in 1990). Twelve percent of Santa Clara county's families received AFDC, and 15% of families in San Diego were AFDC recipients. These are, then, three relatively well-to-do counties that, by national standards, have relatively high Latino and Asian populations and relatively low African-American and Caucasian populations.

Children's Characteristics and Household Information

The sample of 26,506 children consisted of 52% females and 48% males. The children in the sample were of varied ages. The average age was 7.43 years. About 25% of children were under 2-years-old, 20% were from ages 2 to 5, 34% were from age 5 to 12, 12% were from 12 to 15, and the remaining 9% were over 15 years old.

Children in the sample were of varied ethnic and racial backgrounds. The most common were Caucasian (50%), Hispanic (28%), and African Americans (14%). Children of diverse Asian backgrounds were included in the sample, but each ethnic group constituted at most 1% of the total sample. Often, the child's language spoken in the country of origin was the one spoken in the home. As expected, English and Spanish were the most frequently spoken languages.

Children's ethnic and racial backgrounds varied significantly across the three counties ($\chi^2 = 623$, $df = 6$ $p < .001$). Hispanic children were referred more frequently in San Mateo and Santa Clara counties (about 33%) than they were in San Diego county (about 25%). Children of African-American descent were referred more frequently in San Mateo and San Diego counties (about 17 and 15%, respectively) than they were referred in Santa Clara county (about 10%). Whereas relatively more children falling under the "other" category (mostly Asian children) resided in San Mateo and Santa Clara counties, the corresponding figure for San Diego county was only 6%.

Overall, three demographic characteristics were available for almost all children in the sample: age, gender, and racial or ethnic backgrounds.

Table 3.1. Ethnic Composition of San Diego, San Mateo, and Santa Clara
    Counties (%)

	San Diego	San Mateo	Santa Clara
Caucasian	53	48	47
Latino	29	25	29
African-American	7	7	4
Asian/Other	10	20	20

Information about other household members was quite limited. Information about various aspects of the referral process, including the type of referrals, referral sources, and disposition reason was available for a large percentage of the sample. Limited information was available in the data base regarding nonreferred children who resided in the same household as the referred child. Information about the adult who was suspected of abuse was virtually nonexistent. Some, yet questionable, information was available about the nonsuspect adults living in the household.[4]

THE REFERRAL PROCESS

The first step in a referral process is for someone to refer a child suspected of being abused or neglected to the proper authorities. Fairly soon after a referral is initially investigated, a decision is made over whether the referral needs to be further investigated, acted on, or whether it should be closed. In this chapter the outcome of this decision is called the disposition of the case. In Chapter 2, the definition of ER disposition is taken from the SOC 291 report.

Thus, at intake some referrals are opened or activated and others are closed. Most of the time, for those referrals that are activated, ER services are provided to the child and family. In some instances, the child is transferred to other programs, such as Family Maintenance, Family Reunification, or Permanency Planning soon after the referral has been made. All referrals recorded in the SSRS have disposition dates, because some type of decision takes place in response to each referral. Disposition reasons, however, are only recorded for those referrals that are closed soon after the referral is made. Figure 3.1 summarizes the referral process.

As seen in Figure 3.1, the referral process may be thought of as having three major components: receipt of referrals, closing of referrals, and activating cases. Although these components are identical across the three participating counties, the criteria used for screening referrals may vary.

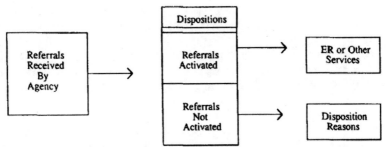

Figure 3.1. Referral process

The three counties are required to meet some statewide regulations for screening referrals. These are stated in the Division 30 regulations, the Welfare Institutions Code and the Penal Code. The counties, however, are given latitude with respect to the type of questions that are asked in order to determine whether the child is actually at risk of abuse or neglect. All three counties' workers fill out a form after a referral has been made. According to county officials, the questions on the form are general and may vary from county to county, leaving some discretion to an individual worker.

Counties' screening practices may differ in several other ways. For example, San Diego county was not investigating complaints about latchkey children even prior to 1990 when Division 30 regulations stated that these types of complaints should not be investigated. Given San Diego's screening practice prior to 1990, it may be that presently this county is more rigid about screening out these types of referrals than the other two counties. Procedures used to screen out multiple referrals may also vary from county to county.

TYPES AND SOURCES OF REFERRALS

Referrals to ER in our sample were a result of suspected sexual abuse, physical abuse, severe neglect, general neglect, emotional abuse, exploitation, and caretaker absence or incapacity. Definitions and data collection among these categories are common across the counties. Drug-related referrals were recorded for children residing in San Diego County under numerous drug-related codes. Santa Clara county also used several drug-related categories, but fewer than those found in San Diego county. In contrast to both of these counties, San Mateo has chosen not to code drug-related maltreatment separately from other problems. (This recordkeeping tends to skew drug-related referrals away from San Mateo and to the other two counties.)

Referral sources fall under eight major categories: (1) social services, (2) law enforcement, (3) school or daycare, (4) medical profession, (5) relatives, (6)nonrelatives, (7) public agencies besides social service agencies, and (8) others. Referrals from social services include those from the child welfare system, residential treatment, welfare, licensing, and transfers from other counties' social service agencies. Law enforcement includes probation and police departments. The medical profession includes private physicians, hospitals, and public health nurses. Relatives include those living in the home of the child and those who do not. This category also includes self-referral by the child. Nonrelatives include acquaintances, such as neighbors and friends. Public agencies excluding the social service agencies listed earlier include community-based agencies, and mental health and family services. Others include anonymous referral sources and those simply coded as others. Some of the findings regarding referral types and sources follow. For the most part, the analyses consider the last or most recent referrals, because the vast majority of children had only one referral.

Types of Referrals

When drug-related and non drugrelated referrals were aggregated, the findings revealed that the most common referral reason was physical abuse and that the least frequent reason was exploitation. The data show that 32% of the referrals were for physical abuse, 25% for general neglect, 20% for sexual abuse, 11% for caretaker absence or incapacity, 8% for emotional abuse, 4% were for severe neglect, and 0.3% were related to exploitation.

About eight out of 100 referrals were identified as drug related, and over one-half of these fell under the broad category of general neglect. Separate drug-related categories are mainly used in San Diego county, but the other two participating counties may incorporate these types of referrals under broader categories of abuse and neglect. Consequently, the figure of 8% of drug-related referrals is very likely to be an underestimate of the actual percentage of drug-related referrals made in the three counties. About 12% of the drug-related referrals falling under general neglect consisted of those related to lack of supervision. Drug-related referrals falling under each of the other categories constituted from less than 1 to 10 of the total drug-related referrals.

Only a very small number of children were referred because of homelessness (28 children, or 0.1%). As in other instances, however, this figure may not reflect the actual incidence of homelessness as a reason for referral, because only San Diego county designated separate codes for this type of referral and the other two participating counties did not and coded these under broader categories.

When considering drug-related categories and homelessness in San Diego County alone, it was found that 2,134 (13%) of referrals fell under these categories (about 96% of all the drug-related and homelessness referral reasons for the total sample in 1991). Of the 2,134 drug-related and homelessness referrals, 58% were associated with general neglect. Only seven children were considered homeless because of drug-related reasons. Only 21 children were considered homeless for other reasons. Drug-related referrals associated with either physical abuse or severe neglect, each constituted about 10% of all drug-related referrals. Corresponding figures for drug-related referrals associated with emotional abuse or caretaker absence or incapacity were 16 and 7%, respectively.

In Santa Clara county, 83 children were referred for drug-related reasons during the nine-month study period (about 4% of all drug-related and homelessness referral reasons for the total sample). For 63 of these children, drug-related referrals were associated with general neglect. Twenty-three babies were considered severely neglected because of positive toxification. Although none of the children in Santa Clara were considered homeless, some of the homeless may have been included under another category, very possibly the subcategory under general neglect, which is called inadequate care to the child, such as food or shelter.

Table 3.2 compares reasons for referral for children of diverse ages, sex, and race or ethnic backgrounds for the total sample. As the table shows, types of child abuse and neglect reports were unequally distributed among children with different racial and ethnic backgrounds. A larger percentage of Caucasian children were referred because of suspected sexual abuse than their counterparts (24%). Physical abuse was a slightly more common referral type among those classified as "other" (mostly Asian children). Severe and general neglect were relatively more frequent referral reasons among children of African-American descent than among their counterparts (36% of African-American children were referred for these reasons). Similarly, caretaker absence or incapacity was a more frequent referral reason among children of African-American descent (15%) and least common referral reason among Caucasian children (9%). Although emotional abuse was about equally common as a referral reason among all groups (about 6 to 9%), it was a slightly more common referral type among Caucasian children (9%). Exploitation was a very infrequent referral reason among all ethnic or racial groups (about 0.3%).

Table 3.2. Referral Type By Age, Race and Sex

Variables	Sexual Abuse	Physical Abuse	Severe Neglect	General Neglect	Emotional Abuse	Exploitation	Caretaker Absence or Incapacity	Total
Race/Ethnicity								
African-American	501 (15%)	948 (28%)	202 (6%)	1027 (30%)	234 (7%)	6 (.17%)	516 (15%)	3434
Latinos	1374 (19%)	2318 (33%)	290 (4%)	1744 (25%)	441 (6%)	20 (.28%)	903 (13%)	7090
Caucasian	3036 (24%)	3967 (31%)	402 (3%)	2976 (24%)	1076 (9%)	45 (.36%)	1130 (9%)	12,632
"Other"	331 (17%)	750 (39%)	51 (3%)	382 (20%)	137 (7%)	6 (.32%)	247 (13%)	1904
Age								
<2	997 (15%)	1709 (26%)	558 (8%)	2072 (31%)	510 (8%)	21 (.32%)	785 (12%)	6652
2–<5	1095 (21%)	1454 (28%)	187 (4%)	1560 (30%)	404 (8%)	10 (.19%)	577 (11%)	5287
5–<12	2044 (23%)	3121 (35%)	172 (2%)	2125 (24%)	724 (8%)	19 (.21%)	840 (9%)	9045
12–<15	820 (26%)	1248 (39%)	46 (2%)	482 (15%)	211 (7%)	11 (.35%)	356 (11%)	3174
15–18	599 (27%)	841 (38%)	19 (.9%)	276 (12%)	154 (7%)	17 (.76)	335 (15%)	2241
Sex								
Females	3610 (27%)	4021 (30%)	456 (3%)	3083 (23%)	1003 (7%)	46 (.34%)	1359 (10%)	13,578
Males	1903 (15%)	4265 (34%)	517 (4%)	3284 (26%)	973 (8%)	32 (.26%)	1509 (12%)	12,483

Note: Chi-square statistics are provided in text.

Overall, a chi-square measure of association between race or ethnicity and type of referral revealed statistical significance ($\chi^2 = 482$, $df = 18$ $p < .001$).

Looking at Table 3.2 one is struck by three findings. The first is that general neglect was a relatively more common referral reason among those under the age of 5, whereas physical abuse was a relatively more common referral reason among children over the age of 5. The second is that sexual abuse was a relatively more common referral reason among older children. In contrast, severe neglect was a relatively more common referral reason among very young children. The third observation is that caretaker absence or incapacity was a relatively more common referral reason among those over the age of 15, whereas emotional abuse or exploitation constituted about the same percentage of referrals among each of the other age groups. As in the case of race or ethnicity, a chi-square measure of association between type of referral and age revealed statistical significance ($\chi^2 = 1,481$, $df = 24$ $p < .001$).

As demonstrated by Table 3.2, some of the differences between male and female children with respect to reasons for referral are not very pronounced. Referrals about sexual abuse involved more females than males, (27% and 15%, respectively). In contrast, referrals regarding severe neglect and caretaker incapacity or absence involved about the same percentages of male and female children. Overall, the chi-square measure of association between gender and reason for referral was statistically significant ($\chi^2 = 512$, $df = 6$ $p < .001$).

Referral Sources

The findings revealed that schools, daycare centers, and referral sources classified as "others" made relatively more referrals than their counterparts (17% each). The percentage of referrals from law enforcement agencies, the medical profession, and relatives was about 12% each. Referrals from nonrelatives and public agencies constituted 10 and 11%, respectively. The fewest referrals came from social service agencies.

These findings corroborate evidence from other studies that suggest that school personnel are the most active professionals in exercising their obligation to report suspected abuse and neglect (Finkelhor, Gomez-Schwartz, & Horowitz, 1984). In fact, other studies have examined the reporting behaviors of medical and mental health professionals (James, Womack, & Stauss, 1978; Kalichman & Craig, 1991; Muehleman & Kimmons, 1981; Zellman, 1990). Clinicians in one study were less likely to report suspected abuse if they were not fully certain that abuse had occurred (Kalichman, Craig, & Follingstad, 1991). Studies of Head Start personnel also suggest that reporting behavior may be influenced by the reporter's relationship with the family as well as the form of maltreatment in question (Nightingale & Walker, 1986). Information available through the American Humane Association describes another picture of teacher's reporting behavior. Their 1980 data show that school personnel nationwide reported suspected abuse in 18% of cases. These data closely parallel our findings (American Humane Association, 1989).

Our results further show that the most frequent referral sources vary for a particular referral reason. Whereas the number of sexual abuse reports were about equally distributed across the different types of referral sources, most of the other types of referrals came from one to three different sources. The most common referral sources for children suspected of being physically or emotionally abused were the school and daycare system (28 and 18%, respectively). Referrals concerning physical or emotional abuse were also frequently made by anonymous agents (16 and 18%, respectively).

Children referred for severe neglect were most frequently referred by the medical profession (50%), whereas those referred for general neglect were most often referred by those classified as "others" (23%). Referrals regarding caretaker absence or incapacity were more frequently made by probation and police officers than by any other sources (28%). Of the relatively few referrals made regarding exploitation, 22% were from anonymous agents.

The findings further reveal that the most common referral reasons vary by their particular referral source. About one-half of the referrals from probation and police concerned physical abuse and caretaker absence or incapacity. About one-half of all referrals made by the school and daycare systems regarded physical abuse. Medical professionals most frequently referred sexual abuse (24%), physical abuse (25%), and general neglect (22%). Similar figures were found for relatives' referrals. Neighbors' and friends' referrals mostly concerned general neglect (40%), and professionals in public agencies such as mental health most frequently referred physical abuse (40%). Almost two out of three referrals made by "other" individuals were for physical abuse and general neglect.

Social services employees and relatives made relatively more multiple referrals than other referral sources. During the study period, 22% of all social service workers' referrals and 17% of relatives' referrals were multiple referrals. With the exception of referrals made by schools and daycare centers, 12% to 14% of the total number of referrals made by all other sources were made more than once. Referrals by school authorities most commonly resulted in a single referral (93%). This may have been the result of school authorities' knowledge of the child's living conditions or physical evidence of abuse.

REFERRALS: NUMBER AND LENGTH OF TIME BETWEEN REFERRALS

An initial complaint to an investigative agency about a suspected child abuse or neglect incident sometimes occurs with no immediate action taken. Subsequent complaints about a particular child may occur. These later reports about a particular child may be for the same or different types of maltreatment. For example, initially, a child may be reported for neglect. Subsequent reports may concern physical abuse, abandonment, or other problems. Only one type of abuse or neglect may be recorded at one time.

The number of child abuse and neglect complaints about a single child within a finite period of time may be unequally distributed among children of different racial, ethnic, and social groups. These numbers also may vary between referral sources. Child maltreatment reporting laws require that select professionals report a suspected child abuse or neglect incident to the proper investigative agency. Thus, given this legal requirement and given the fact that certain individuals are closer to the alleged victim, it would be expected that the number and frequency of complaints over a single incident or related incident differ between referral sources. Our findings reveal that some variation exists between the number of referrals received for a single child and various factors including referral types, sources, and ethnic or racial groups.

Number of Referrals

Child abuse and neglect referrals are seasonally sensitive. Referrals most frequently occurred in the spring and summer months. Only 5,949 children were referred from January to April (a total of 22.4%). About 15 to 17% of the children were referred each month between May and August of 1991 (a total of 47%).

Multiple referrals for a child during a finite time period may reflect a single incident or multiple incidences. Multiple referrals were relatively uncommon during the 9-month study period. None of the 26,506 children in the sample had as many as 10 referrals, and very few had more than four referrals. The majority of children were referred once (87%), and 97% were referred no more than twice. Still, 123 children (2%) had four referrals, and the remainder (less than 1%) had four or more. Perhaps the recidivism rate found in the present study would have been greater had referrals been followed for a longer time period. Another study that examined reports made to CPS for about 10 years found that at least one-half of the children were referred twice. In that study, about 10% of second reports were made during the first 6 months of the first report, and about 15% of third reports were made within 2 years of the first report (Knudsen, 1988).

Multiple referrals within the 9-month period were more common among children of African-American and Caucasian children than among their counterparts from other racial or ethnic groups. Close to 16% of referred children of African-American descent and close to 14% of referred Caucasian children had multiple referrals in the nine-month period. Multiple referrals among "others" who are mostly Asian children and among Latino children were about 11% each. Relatively more of the children referred for caretaker absence or severe neglect had multiple referrals than those referred for other reasons. Of those children referred for caretaker absence or severe neglect, about 18% were referred more than once in 1991. Multiple referrals in 1991 occurred more frequently among referrals concerning sexual abuse (11%), emotional abuse (11%), physical abuse (10%), and exploitation (8%).

Table 3.3 shows reasons for referral among children with at least two referrals within the study period. As the table demonstrates, some of the children with multiple referrals were not referred for the same reason each time. Of those children whose last referral was sexual abuse and who had at least two referrals (628 children), about one-half were previously referred for sexual abuse, but 19% were previously referred for physical abuse, and 13% were previously referred for general neglect. Of the 867 children whose last referral was physical abuse and who had at least two referrals, 50% were previously referred for physical abuse, while 12% were previously referred for sexual abuse, and 17% were previously referred for general neglect.

Other results show that of the 167 children whose last referral was severe neglect and who had at least two referrals, 42% were previously referred for general neglect and 13% for caretaker incapacity or absence. This may indicate that neglect that goes untreated may become more serious over time. Of the 888 children whose last referral was general neglect and who had at least two referrals, 17% were referred for physical abuse, and 12% were referred for caretaker incapacity or absence on the referral prior to the most recent one.

Length of Time Between Referrals

The number of weeks between successive referrals for children with multiple referrals was also examined. The findings reveal that most subsequent referrals for a single child were made within the third month

Table 3.3. Last Two Referral Reasons for Children Referred in 1991

Last 1991 Referral Reason	Sexual Abuse	Physical Abuse	Severe Neglect	General Neglect	Emotional Abuse	Exploitation	Caretaker Absence or Incapacity	Row Total
Sexual Abuse	336 (54%)	118 (19%)	12 (2%)	82 (13%)	33 (5%)	1 (.2%)	46 (7%)	628
Physical Abuse	101 (12%)	474 (55%)	15 (2%)	149 (17%)	71 (8%)	0 (0%)	57 (7%)	867
Severe Neglect	11 (7%)	15 (9%)	43 (26%)	70 (42%)	7 (4.2%)	—	21 (12.6%)	167
General Neglect	60 (7%)	147 (17%)	47 (5%)	452 (51%)	71 (8%)	4 (.5%)	107 (12%)	888
Emotional Abuse	38 (17%)	58 (26%)	7 (3%)	52 (23%)	52 (23%)	—	19 (8%)	226
Exploitation	—	3 (50%)	—	—	—	2 (33%)	1 (17%)	6
Caretaker Abuse or Incapacity	33 (6%)	85 (16%)	36 (7%)	140 (26%)	38 (7%)	—	205 (38%)	537

following the preceding referral. At least 80% of the multiple referrals were made by the end of the third month following the previous referral. For example, there were 3,321 children who had at least two referrals. About 5% of the children were referred twice during the *same day*. For 16% of the children, the last referral was made during the *same week* as the previous referral. For 25% percent of the children, the last referral was made between the *second and fourth week* after the previous referral. For 44% of this pool of children, the last referral occurred *within 1 month* after the previous referral and for 36% the last referral was made within the *second or third months* after the previous referral.

Of the multiple referrals made within the *same day* as earlier referrals, the most common referral reason was physical abuse. Close to 30% of the referrals made within the same day as earlier referrals concerned physical abuse. Sexual abuse and general neglect each constituted about 20% of the referrals made within the same day. The corresponding figure for severe neglect was 11%, and it was only less than 1% for emotional abuse or exploitation. About 15% of referrals made within the same day as preceding referrals were over caretaker absence or incapacity. Similar findings apply to the percentage of referrals received during the remainder of the week or the remaining first month.

Our findings also reveal that general neglect was the most common referral reason made after the *first month* of the earlier referral. Close to 30% of last referrals made *at least 1 month after* the previous referrals were because of general neglect. A small but striking percentage of last referrals made at least 1 month after the previous referral concerned severe neglect (8%) and exploitation (1%).

DISPOSITION REASONS

Once a referral is received by the investigative agency, a decision is made as to whether the referral should be activated and receive additional services. When a referral is not activated following an investigation, a disposition reason is recorded. The two most common reasons cases did not receive additional services were insufficient evidence (41%) and the absence of present danger to the child (35%). The findings revealed that there were 22,536 disposition reasons, or cases closed upon investigation. As there were 26,506 children in the sample, all having at least one referral, at least 85% of the 1991 referrals were not activated. This percentage may be a slight underestimate, because some disposition reasons may not have been recorded.

Of the 22,536 cases closed following investigation, 76% were of insufficient evidence or absence of any current danger to the child. The remaining reasons included: already served (7%), inappropriate referral (7%), unable to locate the child (3%), out of county (3%), referred to public agency (3%), only assessment was necessary (0,8%), and a status offense case (0.2%). ("Assessment" that did not result in a full investigation was recorded separately only in Santa Clara county, whereas in the other counties this type of activity is incorporated under a broader category.)

Table 3.4 presents disposition reasons by type of referral. Insufficient evidence and absence of current danger as disposition reasons varied by type of referral. Insufficient evidence was the most common disposition reason for children referred for exploitation (67%); this figure is higher than the one for other referral types. Insufficient evidence was also a very common disposition reason among those referred for emotional abuse (48%) and general neglect (48%). It was the least common reason for closure among those referred for caretaker absence or incapacity (27%).

"No longer in danger," a subcategory of "Not in Danger," was most frequently found among those referred for sexual abuse (25%), whereas "no demonstrated danger," (another subcategory of "Not in Danger") was the most common reason among those referred for severe neglect (20%). It was also a common disposition reason among those referred for physical abuse (20%) or caretaker absence (19%). Whereas "no demonstrated danger" was the most common reason among those referred for severe neglect (20%), it also was a quite common reason among those referred for general neglect (18%) or emotional abuse (18%). Overall, statistical analysis using chi-square measures of association between disposition reason and referral reasons revealed statistical significance ($\chi^2 = 1,613$, $df = 54$ $p < .001$).

Although disposition reasons vary by referral reasons, they also may vary by personal and professional characteristics of the ER workers. In other words, it is very likely that the type of decisions workers make about the validity of a particular child abuse or neglect complaint or about the extent to which a complaint deserves investigation depends on the workers' characteristics and background. Relevant workers' characteristics include degree of knowledge and experience with definitions of abuse and neglect, personal experiences with abuse or neglect, values and code of ethics, and level of formal education. The more ambiguous the definition of a maltreatment, the more likely the worker to assess a child's situation on the basis of personal values. It would be expected that, all else being constant, the more a worker is trained to evaluate the risk of a child being abused or neglected the more likely appropriate referrals will be investigated. According to related literature, among other things, the decision to investigate by the worker may be influenced by workers' perceived level of seriousness of the situation, degree of knowledge about

Table 3.4. Disposition Reasons by Referral Reasons

Disposition Reasons	Sexual Abuse	Physical Abuse	Severe Neglect	General Neglect	Emotional Abuse	Exploitation	Caretaker Absence or Incapacity	Row Total
Insufficient evidence	1647 (17.84%)	3055 (33.08%)	223 (2.41%)	2801 (30.33%)	855 (9.26%)	45 (0.49%)	608 (6.58%)	9234 (41.11%)
Not in danger	1804 (22.80%)	2655 (33.56%)	280 (3.53%)	1750 (22.12%)	579 (7.31%)	15 (0.19%)	828 (10.47%)	7911 (35.22%)
Already served	272 (18.12%)	372 (24.78%)	113 (7.53%)	254 (16.92%)	71 (4.73%)	1 (0.07%)	418 (27.85%)	1501 (6.68%)
Inappropriate referral	304 (20.42%)	451 (30.29%)	39 (2.62%)	482 (32.37%)	82 (5.51%)	2 (0.13%)	129 (8.66%)	1489 (6.63%)
Assessment only	74 (25.78%)	70 (24.39%)	4 (1.39%)	86 (29.97%)	19 (6.62%)	0 (0.00%)	34 (11.85%)	287 (1.28%)
Referred to public agency	221 (34.32%)	195 (30.28%)	15 (2.33%)	87 (13.51%)	64 (9.94%)	1 (0.16%)	61 (9.47%)	644 (2.87%)
Others	316 (22.61%)	367 (26.27%)	33 (2.36%)	390 (27.91%)	112 (8.01%)	3 (0.21%)	176 (12.59%)	1397 (6.22%)
Total	4638 (20.65%)	7165 (31.90%)	707 (3.15%)	5850 (26.04%)	1782 (7.93%)	67 (0.30%)	2254 (10.03%)	22463 (100%)

Note: Chi-Square statistics are provided in the text. Also, Others include "unable to locate," "out of county" and a few other categories where only several children were counted.

a situation, and perception about appropriate child care (Knudsen, 1988). The extent to which workers' characteristics influence the type of decisions made about whether to investigate select referrals of maltreatment is left to future empirical research.

SUMMARY AND POLICY OBJECTIVES

The child abuse and neglect referral process involves many parties and quite a few decisions. Without a doubt, some of these decisions are rather arbitrary (Lindsey, 1991; Wells, 1991). The parties included in the referral process are diverse. Often, school authorities, medical personnel, investigative agents, and relatives or friends are involved. The decisions involve whether to activate a referral and what type of services to provide a child once it is determined that services are needed. Preconceptions about a particular maltreatment, legal requirements, degree of knowledge about a specific situation and training or background of the worker, all affect the outcome of a particular referral.

This chapter does not allow us to gain an understanding of why certain decisions are made in the referral process or to what extent these decisions are appropriate. It does, however, allow us to gain an understanding of the types of referrals received, those that are activated, and their corresponding referral sources. The following summarizes some of the major findings and provides policy recommendations where appropriate.

Definitions of Maltreatment and Public Awareness

In this chapter we have demonstrated that certain types of maltreatment, such as physical abuse, general neglect, and sexual abuse, were referred more frequently than other types of maltreatment in the three selected counties (from 20% to 35%). Maltreatments such as emotional abuse and exploitation were referred quite infrequently (8% and .3%, respectively). These findings confirm national findings, which indicate that about 56% of child abuse reports involve various types of physical abuse and that the remainder involve various forms of neglect (U.S. DHHS, 1988). The findings also reveal that once some of the referrals were given a disposition reason, the most common reasons for not activating a referral were insufficient evidence and the absence of danger to the child (76%). Insufficient evidence was a much more prevalent disposition reason among those referred for exploitation (67%), emotional abuse (48%), or general neglect (48%) than among the other referral types.

The data suggest that perhaps physical abuse, general neglect and sexual abuse were referred relatively more frequently than emotional abuse or exploitation because the former are easier to identify than the latter or because they are relatively more widespread. Another plausible explanation is that the public is more aware or sensitive to the problems of physical abuse, general neglect, and sexual abuse than they are to other types of maltreatment. The public may also regard these problems as relatively more severe.

Our findings show that insufficient evidence is a more common disposition reason for referrals made regarding emotional abuse or exploitation. This may suggest that these forms of maltreatment are not easily assessed by outside authorities or, as other authors have suggested, that they are not well defined by the child welfare or legal systems (Bailey & Bailey, 1986; Garbarino, Gutman, & Wilson, 1986). The fact that general neglect is referred fairly frequently but that one-half of the cases result in insufficient evidence may indicate that although this problem may be identifiable by the public, it is rarely of such severity that social services personnel feel the need for agency involvement. Certainly, as the definitions for abuse and neglect become narrower due to funding constraints, the threshold for action in cases of neglect will rise. Overall, given our present findings, it appears that efforts should focus on increasing public awareness and sensitivity to all types of maltreatment.

Prevention

The findings suggest that child welfare services should be targeted toward children identified as being at risk for multiple referrals. Given the constraints of the database, it is not possible to provide a broad picture of the children's household environment or of the circumstances that may have led to a particular form of maltreatment. However, in this chapter we have shown who is likely to be referred for a particular maltreatment and who is likely to be referred more than once. It shows that children of color, especially children of African-American descent are disproportionately represented in the number of referrals received by the system. Moreover, the study reveals that types of maltreatment are unequally distributed across racial or ethnic groups. As is demonstrated by these data, sexual and emotional abuse are more frequently found among Caucasian children. Severe neglect, general neglect, and caretaker absence or incapacity are more frequent referral reasons for children of African-American descent. Because the causal link between neglect and poverty has been well documented (Pelton, 1989; U.S. DHHS, 1988), the types of prevention services appropriate to the reduction of child neglect might be quite different from prevention efforts focused on other forms of abuse.

This chapter has also revealed some interesting facts regarding recidivism. First, about 13% of the most recent reports in 1991 involved children who were previously reported during the same year. Perhaps this percentage would have been larger if the children were followed for a longer period of time. Second, relatively more of the children referred for severe neglect and caretaker absence or incapacity had multiple referrals than those referred for any other reasons (18%). Third, children of African-American descent have relatively more multiple referrals than their counterparts, possibly because they are more likely to be referred for neglect, caretaker absence, or caretaker incapacity. Fourth, a fair percentage of children with multiple referrals are not referred for the same reason each time: At least 10% of the children in this study were referred for a different reason than in the past.

Forms of maltreatment such as physical abuse, general neglect, and caretaker absence or incapacity are common prior referrals among children whose last referral was not for any of these reasons. Very important, of 167 children whose last referral was severe neglect and who had at least two referrals, 42% were referred for general neglect and 13% were referred for caretaker incapacity or absence on the prior referral. This finding would strongly indicate the need for preventive services targeted toward children who are reported for general neglect. Often, these children and their families are struggling; however, their difficulties have not become so severe that child welfare agencies see the need to become involved. Nevertheless, these problems may be exacerbated over time if the initial referral is dropped. Programs that provide early community-based intervention services to general neglect families could have a significant impact on this population if services were targeted and narrowly defined for these particular families.

Summary of Key Findings and Recommendations Regarding Child Abuse and
Neglect Referral Process

Finding	Recommendation
1. Select maltreatments, such as physical abuse, general neglect, and sexual abuse, are referred more frequently than other types of maltreatment.	1. Efforts should focus on increasing public awareness and sensitivity to all types of maltreatment.
2. Types and number of maltreatment are unequally distributed across racial or ethnic groups. Children of African-American descent are disproportionately referred to the child welfare system. Severe neglect, general neglect and caretaker absence or incapacity are more frequent referral reasons for children of African-American descent.	2. Child Welfare Services should be targeted toward children identified as being at risk of having select types of referrals. Prevention efforts should differ between types of maltreatment. For example, prevention efforts aimed to reduce child neglect need to be different than those that focus on other forms of abuse since there is a causal link between neglect and poverty.
3. Children of African-American descent or those referred for neglect or caretaker absence or incapacity have relatively more multiple referrals than their counterparts.	3. Child Welfare Services should be targeted toward children identified as being at risk for multiple referrals.

NOTES

1.   Electronic Data Systems (EDS), a private corporation, developed SSRS in conjunction with social service departments. Typical output from a SSRS does not include the analyses of relationships between variables. Working with the University of California at Berkeley, EDS has designed an output file that extracts longitudinal data for each child reported as abused or neglected since 1988 from San Diego, Santa Clara, and San Mateo counties.

2.   For the most part, the type of information provided by the three counties does not differ substantially. Some differences between the type or amount of information each of the counties maintains do, however, exist. For example, San Diego County gathers much more detailed drug-related referral information than its counterparts. Given differences in coding practices between the three counties, the results may slightly underestimate actual facts.

3.   EDS created a record for each child designated as a victim since 1988. For the most part, the three participating counties did not use the victim code until 1991.

4.   Information about the demographic characteristics of children who entered the foster care system across the state sometime between January and September

1991 revealed that, as in the case of children referred to ER in the three counties, about one-half of the children who entered the foster care system statewide between January and September 1991 were females (54%). For the most part, the age distribution of the two samples is comparable. However, the percentage of those falling between the ages of 5 and 12 differ between the two groups: Whereas about 34% of children in the SSRS sample were between the ages of 5 and 11, the corresponding figure for those entering foster care across the state was 29%. Some differences also were found between the ethnic and racial compositions of the statewide foster care group of children and those from the present sample. Of greatest significance was the difference found between the percentage of African-American children referred to ER in the three counties and the percentage of African-American children entering foster care in 1991: The former figure was 14%, whereas the latter was 29%. Clearly, we cannot assume that the percentage of African-American children in the present SSRS sample reflects statewide percentage.

II

Analyzing Foster Care Pathways

4

Rethinking and Researching Length of Stay in Foster Care

It is difficult from the research available to date to answer basic questions regarding the length of time children remain in foster care. Despite decades of study, we continue to learn what factors are associated with the length of time children spend in foster care prior to being returned to their parents. Discussion of the limitations of previous research regarding this issue helps to clarify the need for the advances in the analysis of foster care we advocate.

It might appear that a thorough review of the research literature pertaining to the length of stay in foster care is an unnecessarily narrow undertaking, considering the broad scope of this volume. An in-depth analysis of length of stay is appropriate, however, for three reasons. First, as shown in Chapter 1, length of stay in foster care has long been used as an indicator of child welfare services success. Indeed, the permanency planning era began because of research on foster care limbo and drift (Maas & Engler, 1959). Second, all previous studies of duration in care at least implicitly involve a study of family reunification, as a child's return home is generally the most likely reason for termination of a stay in foster care. Thus, any study of factors associated with duration in foster care is to some extent a study of the factors related to family reunification. Third, a broader research review helps to illustrate the methodological strengths and weaknesses of previous work and to justify the analytic approach in Part II and to provide direction for future research efforts.

PREVIOUS RESEARCH ON DURATION OF FOSTER CARE

Interest in the length of time children and youth spend in the foster care system is long-standing. This concern has been reflected in a number of studies since the 1950s that have included length of time in care as an object of inquiry. This review groups existing research on length of time in care into broad categories: (1) cross-sectional or point-in-time studies of length of time in foster care, (2) longitudinal studies that employ methods other than event-history analysis, and (3) studies that make use of event-history methods.

The review of the literature is meant to be comprehensive in the sense that it is a critique of various *methods* used to examine length of time in foster care. It is not, however, a complete discussion of all studies of length of time in care or even an exhaustive presentation of the findings of many of these studies. The limitations of most previous studies render their conclusions of limited value. Many of them rely on biased samples or employ analytic techniques that are so ill-suited to the study of timing of events that their findings cannot be considered valid. In other cases, restrictions on the population studied (e.g., exclusion of infants, exclusion of those in short-term foster care) severely limit the generalizability of findings. Thus, the present discussion will focus primarily on inherent methodological strengths and weaknesses of previous studies, and discuss substantive findings of problematically designed studies in detail only when they have played a significant role in developing child welfare policy.

CROSS-SECTIONAL POINT-IN-TIME STUDIES

The study by Henry Maas and Richard Engler (1959) reported in the book *Children in Need of Parents*, must be considered the first call to arms against "foster care drift." It is also the most prominent cross-sectional study of length of time in care. Maas and Engler studied the experiences of foster children in nine urban and rural communities, gathering information in 1957 and 1958 from all 60 child welfare agencies serving the children in those communities. They relied on a sample of children who were in foster care as of April 1, 1957, and another sample of children who left care for any reason within 3 months, before or after, of that date. Comparisons were made between the children who were in foster care and those who had returned home, been adopted, or left care for other reasons. Children who had been in care less than 30 days on April 1, or who were not in foster care for at least 90 days, were not included in the analysis. Their sample totalled 882 children.

Maas and Engler found that the median time in foster care for the children in their study was 3 years for children in foster homes and 2.7 years for children in institutions. Moreover, 28% of their subjects had been in care more than five and a half years. Their findings suggested that a number of factors (e.g., ethnicity, time in care, parental visiting, region of placement, and reason for placement) were related to the probability that a child would return home to his or her parents. They concluded, therefore, that a child who remained in care for more than one and a half years was very likely to "grow up" in foster care (p. 421). Not surprisingly, then, they expressed great alarm that large numbers of children were being raised to adulthood in foster care.

Indeed, Maas and Engler's study created the first major wave of concern on the part of the child welfare policy community as a whole regarding the problem of "foster care drift." Foster care drift refers to the perception that, once children have been in foster care for some (e.g., 18 months according to Maas and Engler), they are likely to remain in care without being returned home or placed in another permanent home. The significance of the 18-month figure, arrived at in the late 1950s, should not be underestimated. As Goerge (1990) has noted:

> The year-and-a-half figure has been used in congressional testimony and cited in the literature since 1959 to justify timely interventions on behalf of foster children who are at risk of drift. This figure has provided a general guideline as to when children should have left foster care. (p. 425)

As others have noted, however (Fanshel & Shinn, 1978; Goerge, 1990; Kadushin, 1978), cross-sectional point-in-time studies suffer from a methodological limitation that makes them inappropriate methods for the examination of length of time in foster care. As these studies include only those children who are in care at a particular point in time, they tend to overrepresent those members of prior-entry cohorts who stay in care for a relatively long time. Figure 4.1 illustrates this phenomenon: T_0 is the time children entered care and T_1 is the time the hypothetical child welfare researcher conducted a cross-sectional study. Of the five children entering care at time T_0, only children A, D, and E will be observed at hypothetical study time T_1 and so have their lengths of time in care measured. In contrast, children B and C, with relatively shorter stays in care, will not be observed in care at time T_1. Obviously, any mean or median measure of length of time in care can be biased by this method of analysis. Furthermore, the greater the time difference between T_0 (the entry to care time of the earliest entry cohort observed) and T_1 (the time at which length of

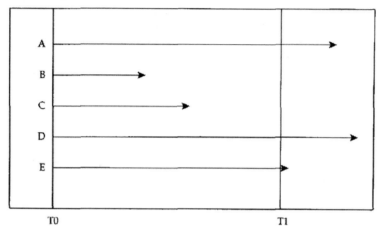

TO: Date of Entry of Entry Cohort Including Subjects A, B, C, D, and E.
T1: Date of Point-in-Time Study   ➤ : Discharge Date for Subject

Figure 4.1. Illustration of selection bias in point-in-time estimation of
length of time in foster care.

time in care is measured), the greater the upward bias in mean or median
measures of length of care will be, because the only representatives of the
earliest cohorts who will be measured at time T_1 are those with the
longest lengths of time in care.

This problem is particularly acute when the investigator simply includes all children in care at the time of a study in the population to be
studied. Such an approach would include those members of entry cohorts
from many years earlier who had spent virtually their entire childhoods
in foster care, while unwittingly excluding all those who had left care
many years before.[1] Nevertheless, in spite of the fact that it has long been
known that point-in-time estimates of duration in social processes exhibit
bias, such measures continue to be used in child welfare research. Two
examples illustrate this point. Jenkins, Diamond, Flanzraich, Gibson,
Hendricks, and Marshood (1983) used data collected by the U.S. Office of
Civil Rights to examine ethnic differentials in length of foster care placement, legal status, type of placements, and location of placement (dis-
tance from the child's home) for a national sample of children in foster
care in December of 1979. They concluded that a child's ethnicity was
related to all four outcome variables. In particular, they found that the
median time in care for all children was 25 months, but that there were
marked differences in time in care between African-American children
(median = 32 months) and Caucasian children (median = 20 months).

The discussion argues for cautious interpretation of the overall median figure derived by Jenkins et al. for the length of time in foster care. Ethnic differences in length of time in care inferred from their study are also questionable. The observed differences may be a reflection of relative differences in the proportions of the various ethnic groups that stay either a very short time in care (and are thereby undersampled), or a very long time in care (and are thereby oversampled). Furthermore, the other dependent variables in the study (i.e., legal status, type of placement, and location of placement) could be strongly associated with length of time in placement. For example, the probability that a child is placed out of county or in an institutional setting may increase with time in care. If this is the case, then the oversampling of those members of the population who stay in care relatively long, which is typical of point-in-time methods, could also explain or confound any observed ethnic differentials in these other outcomes.

Seaberg and Tolley (1986) tried to push the cross-sectional, point-in-time approach even further by conducting a multiple regression analysis of factors associated with length of stay in foster care. For their study, the researchers employed a national probability sample (Shyne & Shroeder, 1978) of children receiving public social services, focusing on those children who were in foster care on the survey date early in 1977. They concluded that a number of variables were related to the length of time children spend in foster care, including service, child, and family characteristics. Although the argument can be made that the multiple regression approach better identifies the unique contributions of explanatory variables to length of time in care than do the bivariate methods employed in earlier analyses, this does not overcome the inherent limitations of the point-in-time approach. Lindsey's (1991) more recent use of these data in employing an odds ratio approach to understanding the foster care placement decision suffers from the same limitations.

In summary, regardless of other methodological problems they might exhibit, point-in-time analyses of foster care outcomes, including length of stay, are of questionable utility for two primary reasons: (1) measures of time in care derived from these studies exhibit biases that cannot be assessed or corrected with point-in-time data; and (2) any interactions between population characteristics and length of time in care are impossible to assess, even by using multivariate methods, due to the biases mentioned above.

RETROSPECTIVE OR LONGITUDINAL STUDIES USING NON-EVENT-HISTORY METHODS

There have been other efforts to examine how long children spend in foster care and what factors are associated with their length of stay. Many of these have attempted to avoid the pitfalls of point-in-time estimates, relying instead on longitudinal scrutiny of a cohort of children as they move through foster care or retrospective examination of the paths through care of an entry cohort. The most important distinction between the point-in-time analyses and the studies to be examined presently is the fact that the latter do not involve an inherent uncertainty regarding which members of previous entry cohorts are systematically excluded from the study population. Theoretically, all members of a particular entry cohort are equally likely to be included for study, except in the case where explicit restrictions are placed on the sample (e.g., only children above a certain age at entry to foster care will be included). These studies are quite varied in the analytic approach used, methodological strengths and weaknesses, and generalizability of findings.

The most obvious limitations of many of these studies is that they were conducted prior to the implementation of permanency planning. To the extent that permanency planning was intended to decrease foster care drift, foster care length of stay was expected to decrease after implementation. Thus, it would not be expected that estimates of foster care duration made prior to 1980 would accurately reflect length of stay in foster care today.

Oddly, only one longitudinal study of foster care that considers foster care duration as a dependent variable does so in a manner that is not plagued with significant methodological limitations regarding the population studied. Over twenty-five years ago, Jenkins (1967) followed the progress of 921 New York City foster children, who entered care in 1963 for a period of 2 years. The population was a valid representation of children in foster care at that time in New York, with the exception that infants under 6 months old at entry to foster care were excluded from the analysis, because they "represented primarily out-of-wedlock births rather than family breakdowns resulting in foster care" (p. 450).

Jenkins's findings contrasted with Maas and Engler's because over one-half of her sample had left care within 3 months, and fully 75% had left after 2 years. She also perceived a trend in discharges—a declining probability of reunification—that would be noticed again years later (Goerge, 1990):

> The decrease of discharge over a period of time for children in the sample is apparent when one compares the percentage leaving care over successive periods. Approximately the same percentage of children leave care during the first week of placement as leave care during the next three weeks, and again during the next two months. For children who remain in care three months or more, approximately the same percentage leave care in the next three months, during the subsequent six months, and again in the final year. The hard core of placement cases—the remaining 25 percent—may well be

children who grow to their majority in social agency care. (Jenkins, 1967, pp. 451–452)

Thus, while Jenkins found a much smaller proportion of children remained in foster care than did Maas and Engler, she agreed that the longer a child remained in care, the lower the child's chances of exiting at all (at least prior to discharge at age 18).

Jenkins examined the relationship between several child and family characteristics and length of time in foster care by conducting a contingency table analysis of the number of children remaining in care under 3 months, between 3 months to 2 years, and 2 years and over. Nonwhite children generally remained in care a shorter time than white children, and children under 6 years old were more likely to leave care quickly than were older children. Children whose parents had no knowledge of placement and therefore did not participate in the decision to place them— were more likely than expected to experience short-term placement (under 3 months) than long-term placement. Children from one-parent families or whose families had two or more children placed were also more likely to experience short-term placement. Receipt of public assistance or living in a room as opposed to an apartment or private house were also associated with an increased likelihood that a family would have their child returned after a relatively short stay in placement. Jenkins summarized the implications of the relationship between family characteristics and length of stay as follows:

> For the five family variables, there appears to be a common pattern. The combination of characteristics representing typical social problems, such as one parent in the home, dependence on public assistance, and living in rooms tend, to be most prominent in the short-term placement group. They persist, but to a proportionately smaller extent, for families with children in long-term care. Thus the urgent environmental pressures bring more children into care, but do not necessarily mean they will remain in care. Situations that result in long-term care may well reflect other variables. (p. 454)

On the other hand, Jenkins's analysis of the relationship between reason for placement and duration of foster care suggested that more entrenched problems led to longer foster care stays. Children with emotional or personality problems or from families with problems such as "conflict between parents, incompetence, alcoholism, drugs, or desertion" tended to remain in care longer than those placed for other reasons (p. 455).

Although limited by the short time span of the study, the highly urban population studied, the time that had passed since its completion, and the dated statistical techniques that were employed, Jenkins's study contributes some of the most valid and generally instructive information on foster care duration provided by any research conducted through the late 1980s. In particular, her use of a minimally biased sample (excluding only infants under 6 months old) provided the first empirical support for a picture of foster care as a primarily short-term phenomenon. Only a relatively small proportion of foster children in her study were in care long enough to suggest that they might have been "adrift" in the system. The findings of the contingency table analysis should be regarded with some caution, however, in that no attempt was made to account for relationships between explanatory variables that might have confounded the effects of these variables on observed length of time in care.

In what remains the most in-depth longitudinal study of foster children, Fanshel and Shinn (1978) conducted a 5-year study of 624 New York City foster children who entered care in 1966. The subjects in the study had never been placed in foster care before, were under 12 years of age at the time of placement, and had been in foster care for at least 90 days. Although the results of the study were not reported in a manner that allowed for establishing a median duration in care, over one-half of the sample were still in care after 3 years, and approximately 36% were still in care after 5 years.

Using contingency table and correlational methods, Fanshel and Shinn concluded that a number of factors were associated with whether or not a child returned home after being placed into foster care. Age played a factor in discharge status, with younger children having a lower probability of returning home than older children. Minority children were more likely to remain in care than Caucasians. Reason for placement had an interesting relationship to discharge status. When discharge status at the end of the 5-year study was treated as a dichotomy (in care vs. discharged), reason for placement was significantly related to discharge status. Children placed for reasons of abandonment, neglect, or abuse were the group most likely to remain in care, with over one-half still in care after 5 years. On the other hand, those placed because of the physical illness of a parent or child-rearing person were more likely to leave care, with 43% leaving care within 1 year. Children placed for reasons of their own behavior showed the smallest proportion leaving care during the first year (under 8%) of any group. By the end of the 5-year period, however, over three-quarters of these children had been discharged. Fanshel and Shinn assert that the fate of this last behaviorally disturbed group results from the longer span of time required to affect behavior change in the children (over 1 year in the vast majority of cases) and that the intact home that was more often available to these children than to others may have resulted in better long-term outcomes.

Significantly, Fanshel and Shinn also find their data to conflict with the conclusions of Maas and Engler: "Our data tend to contradict the notion originating from earlier research that unless children leave foster care within the first or second year of entry, they are doomed to spend the remainder of their childhood years in care" (p. 119). They note that nearly 25% of their sample left foster care after 2 years in care but under 5 years after entry. They argued that the practice implications of their findings were obvious: "Even three, four, and five years after a child's entry into care, one need not relinquish hope of his eventual return to his own home or to the home of relatives or friends" (p. 119).

Unfortunately, the significance of the finding that a large proportion of children went home after 2 or more years is difficult to gauge. The proportion of the total entering foster care cohort in 1966 that was over 12 years old at entry into foster care or who spent less than 90 days in care was probably fairly large. For example, 22% of the 2,720 children who met the age criteria of the study and entered care during the January-to-August period of sample selection spent less than 90 days in care. Moreover, 18% of children in foster care in New York City at that time were 12 years or older. Although it is not possible to provide an exact figure for the entire entry cohort in 1966, Fanshel and Shinn likely overestimated to a large extent the proportion of all entering foster children who return home within 2 to 5 years after entry.

In general, the longitudinal approach used by Fanshel and Shinn, combined with the collection of a rich background of qualitative information on children, families, and service characteristics, still stands as the most promising approach to the examination of foster care outcomes, including factors associated with length of time in care. However, even though the New York study sheds much light on the experience of foster children, its findings pertaining to length of time in foster care are of limited generalizability. First, it is very dated at this point, reflecting an entry cohort from 1966, over 25 years ago. Many policy changes have taken place since then, not the least of which was the enactment of P.L. 96–272 and ensuing permanency planning efforts. Second, the exclusion from the sample of all children who remained in care less than 90 days has the unfortunate effect of biasing upward any estimates of length of stay. It also negates the possibility of examining differences between these short-term members of the foster care population and those who remained in care longer. Third, the exclusion from the sample of youths over 12 years of age at the time of the study precludes comparing entering adolescents and younger children in terms of relative time spent in care.

Lawder, Poulin, and Andrews (1986) studied the foster care outcomes for a cohort of 185 children who entered care with the Children's Aid Society of Pennsylvania between June 1, 1978, and May 31, 1979. During mid-1984, approximately 5 years after the children were initially placed, a team of professional social workers read the case records and completed structured case survey forms for each child in the study. The survey collected information regarding a number of child, family, and placement variables.

The researchers found that 34% of the children in the study left care within 3 months, over one-half had left within 1 year, and that 70% of the study population were in care 2 years or less. The study also considered length of time in care by dispositional status (e.g., return home, adoption). For children reunified with their families during the 5-year study period, nearly 49% did so within 3 months, 73% within 1 year, and 89% within 2 years of entering placement.

Lawder et al. also performed a regression analysis to examine the relationships between several explanatory factors and the child's dispositional status at the time of the study: The children either returned home to parents or continued in foster care. Six variables were found to be related to dispositional status. The number of family visits was positively correlated with return home. Conversely, the number of behavior problems exhibited by the child was negatively associated with return home. Placement into foster care for reasons of parental neglect, parental mental health problems, or a teenage parent decreased the likelihood that a child would return home during the study period. On the other hand, placement because of a family crisis or emergency was associated with a return home in the short term.

The findings of the regression analysis are called into question, however, because they treat dispositional status as a dichotomous variable. Technically, the sampling variances obtained using ordinary least-squares methods with a categorical dependent variable are incorrect, and any hypotheses tests based on these variances are invalid (Aldrich & Nelson, 1984; Goodman, 1978). A logistic regression analysis of the data would have eliminated this problem. The fact that the Pennsylvania data reports on the foster care experiences of children placed with only one agency (Children's Aid Society) also limits the utility of the findings from this study.

The study by Lawder et al. is important to this review primarily because it allows for comparison with the work of Jenkins. Using similar longitudinal methods, both studies found that only a relatively small proportion (25–30%) of foster children stay in care beyond 2 years. Furthermore, both the New York data and the Pennsylvania data suggest that the probability of family reunification is greatest immediately following placement and begins to decline fairly rapidly after only a few weeks have elapsed.

Another study is noteworthy because of its anticipation of later efforts to examine factors associated with foster care duration. Magura (1979) performed a time-series analysis of trends in the length of stay in placement of foster children who entered care in New Jersey between 1973 and 1978. The sources of his data were six consecutive annual cross-sectional reports on the characteristics of foster children, obtained from computerized files maintained by the New Jersey Division of Youth and Family Services. The study population excluded children in institutional care and children whose caregivers were not eligible for AFDC foster care funds (e.g., many relative caregivers). The cross-sectional data included information on how long any child had been in care on December 31 of each base year, as well as whether or not the child had left care. (Reasons for leaving care were not distinguished, but Magura noted that about 85% of exits were due to family reunification, adoption, or a move to independent living.)

Magura compared the percentages of children who remained in care for an additional year stratified by prior length of stay in foster care (under 1 year, 1–1.9 years, 2–2.9 years, etc.) as measured on December 31 of each base year. For example, in his study, 51.6% of the children who had been in placement less than a year on December 31, 1973, remained in care until at least December 31, 1974, whereas only 45.9% of those who had been in care less than a year on December 31, 1977, remained in care for at least an additional year. He concluded that, overall, there was a statistically significant linear decrease in the proportion of children remaining in care from one year to the next between 1973 and 1978.

Magura used this method of analysis to examine the relationships between prior length of stay and the probability that a child would go home in any given year. He concluded:

> One finds that the longer children have already been in foster care, the more likely they are to remain in care for an additional year. However, this relationship is not linear; the percentage remaining in care increases with prior length of stay, but it does so at a declining rate. (p. 32)

This is similar to the findings of Jenkins and Lawder et al.

By simultaneously accounting for prior length of stay and age at entry to foster care, Magura was able to examine the effect of age on remaining in care. For children who had been in care over 2 years, there was no significant relationship between age and remaining in care. On the other hand, for those who had been in care less than 2 years, children who entered foster care between the ages of 4 and 10 years old stood a greater risk of remaining in care than those older or younger at entry. This was particularly true for the group that had been in care less than 1 year.

Magura's study is interesting as a further confirmation that children generally exit foster care at a fairly rapid rate and that few remain for an extended period. Indeed, only 12.5% of those children in his study who entered care in 1973 remained in care at least 5 to 5.9 years. The analysis of trends in the aggregate characteristics of the foster care population (e.g., ages, average stay in care, yearly entries, yearly exits) is also useful because of its potential for evaluating the effect of changes in child welfare policy over time. In this sense, Magura's work foreshadows the more recent efforts of Robert Goerge and Fred Wulczyn and their colleagues (Wulczyn, 1991; Wulczyn & Goerge 1992; Wulczyn, Goerge, Hartnett, & Testa, 1986).

The longitudinal studies of foster care mentioned are limited in terms of the populations studied. Fanshel and Shinn's (1978) study excludes such a large proportion of the entering foster care population that it is, in effect, a study of "long-term" foster care for relatively young children (under 12) only. Jenkins (1967) does not include infants under 6 months old in her sample but later concludes that age is related to time in care. Recent studies of foster care indicate both that there are large numbers of infants entering care today and that age may be related to foster care duration (Goerge, 1990; Wulczyn & Goerge, 1992). Lawder et al. (1986) restrict their analysis to children who were placed with a particular foster care agency. It is unclear how representative this group was of Pennsylvania's foster children at that time, let alone of foster children in general. Magura's (1979) trend analysis does not include children in institutional or kinship care.

Furthermore, the statistical methods used in previous studies to gauge the relationship between explanatory factors and foster care duration were either inappropriate or limited in their ability to identify the unique effects of a particular factor while holding others constant.

Perhaps the most significant qualification that must be raised against the conclusions of these studies regarding foster care duration today is the fact that they are all based on information gathered prior to the enactment of Public Law 96–272. Although there was concern about foster care drift prior to the implementation of this legislation, there did not exist the federal guidelines regarding court review and timely decision making through permanency planning that have been put in place since 1980. To the extent that these policy initiatives were partly intended to move children out of foster care (through family reunification or into adoptive homes) in a timely manner, it is not unreasonable to expect that foster care duration may have changed since the early 1980s.

EVENT-HISTORY ANALYSIS OF LENGTH OF STAY iN FOSTER CARE

Nearly all research conducted after 1980 into foster care duration has employed event-history analysis. Goerge summarizes the purpose of event-history analysis in the following way:

> The central idea of event-history analysis is that, instead of statistically modeling observable variables directly, such as duration of foster care or the odds of a child's returning to parental custody, one models an unobservable or latent variable, commonly called a hazard rate or hazard function. This is posited as controlling an event's occurrence as well as the length of time preceding its occurrence. (p. 428)

Thus, in general, researchers in the past decade have modeled the *hazard rates* of children returning home or leaving foster care in some other way (e.g., adoption), rather than measuring the proportion of children exiting in any particular period (e.g., the first 2 years of care).

Intuitively, the hazard rate can be understood to be the probability that an individual will experience an event or make a transition (e.g., from foster care to the home of a parent) at a particular point in time (continuous-time hazard rate) or during a specified interval of time (discrete-time hazard rate), given that the individual has not yet experienced such a transition. Thus, when Jenkins noted that the proportion of children leaving foster care during a given time interval decreased the longer a child was in care, she was implicitly stating that the hazard rate decreased over time. Similarly, her finding that a higher proportion of children of color than Caucasian children left care early suggests that the two groups may have had differing hazard rates for foster care exit.

Event-history models have a number of advantages over methods previously used to examine foster care duration and other outcomes of foster care (Allison, 1984; Tuma & Hannan, 1984; Yamaguchi, 1991). The most important of these for the purposes of this study are the ability to make use of "incomplete" data on foster care duration and the availability of regression models that allow for the simultaneous analysis of the effect of multiple explanatory factors on foster care length of stay.

For example, in the study of life events, such as the transition from "foster care" status to "reunified" status in this study, the researcher often encounters the problem of how to deal with events that have not yet occurred at the time the data are collected. In the present study, about half of the children in the study had not left foster care at the time of the creation of the database. The event times for these children are considered "censored" in that we do not know their true value, only that they occurred after a particular point in time.

If one tries to construct an ordinary least-squares regression model with the time from entry to foster care to family reunification as the dependent variable, these censored observations would pose significant problems. One could be tempted to exclude these observations from the analysis, but that would waste valuable information and could result in substantial bias in the estimates of the regression model if these children varied from the others in significant ways. On the other hand, one could simply assign the time from foster care entry to the date of the study (as was done in many previous studies) for those children who had not returned home and use these event times in constructing a model. Unfortunately, this approach would clearly result in an underestimate of the time from foster care entry to reunification for this group, not to mention that it would require some type of assumption regarding whether or not these censored foster care spells ultimately end in return home. Fortunately, event-history models can make use of the information available from censored observations without biasing estimates of hazard rates.

Another advantage of event-history analysis over the largely descriptive studies of foster care duration conducted previously is the ability to simultaneously control for the effects of explanatory factors. Many models express the hazard rate (usually transformed into the logarithm of the hazard rate) in a regression format as partly a function of a set of independent variables (Allison, 1984). In the present context, this allows for a much more rigorous examination of the effect of child, family, and child welfare services characteristics on duration in foster care than was possible using the methods available to previous researchers.

It is possible to examine event-history data by using methods that make no assumptions about how hazard rates change over time. These methods generally use log-rank tests or a generalization of the Wilcoxon and Kruskal-Wallis tests to assess whether the distributions of event times (with or without censored data) differ between two or more groups (Lawless, 1982). For example, one might test whether the event times for African-American and Caucasian foster children making the transition home come from the same underlying distribution without making any assumptions about the form of that distribution. Although these methods have been used extensively in biostatistics, they have been used infrequently by child welfare researchers.

To date, event-history analyses of foster care duration have employed regression modeling of hazard rates. These studies involve varying assumptions about the relationship between duration in foster care and the hazard rate for exit from foster care. Testa (1985), Benedict, White, and Stallings (1987), and Benedict and White (1991) all employed a Cox Proportional Hazards regression model in examining the transition rates of children leaving foster care (Cox, 1972; Selvin, 1991; Tuma & Hannan, 1984). This model assumes that only hazard rates among subgroups of a population are proportional over time (i.e., the ratio between rates remains essentially unchanged) without specifying whether the rates increase, decrease, or remain the same as duration in a particular state changes. Cox's model is said to be partially parametric in that it allows for the estimation of parameters reflecting the effects of covariates on hazard rates, while leaving the underlying hazard function undefined.

Goerge (1990) and McMurtry and Lie (1992), on the other hand, tested fully parametric models in attempting to explain exit rates from foster care. Their models include a specification of how the underlying hazard rate for an individual child changes with duration in foster care independent of other explanatory factors. An investigator who assumes that there is a specific relationship between duration in a state and the probability of exiting that state is assuming that *duration dependence* exists in the hazard rate for that event.

Using administrative data from the Illinois Department of Children and Family Services, Testa (1985) studied children who entered foster care in Illinois between 1978 and 1983. He focused on length of stay in foster care and the effect of race and region of placement on this variable. His study suggests that there is an interaction between race and region in terms of their effects on length of stay. In Chicago, he found that there was a statistically significant difference in transition rates out of foster care between African Americans and Caucasians, with the median for African Americans being 17.4 months versus 12.2 months for Caucasians. On the other hand, although transition rates were much slower in general outside of Chicago, there were no statistically significant differences between Caucasians (median length of stay = 4.1 months) and African Americans (median length of stay = 7 months) in outlying counties.

Benedict et al. (1987) and Benedict and White (1991) reported the results of a longitudinal investigation of the foster care experiences of 689 children who entered care for the first time within three separate jurisdictions in Maryland between January 1, 1980, and December 31, 1983. The random sample was identified after stratifying for race (African American versus Caucasian), age at placement, and jurisdiction. Information was obtained on these children through review of their Department of Social Service case records from the time they entered care until June of 1986. Thus, the maximum observation period extended from two-and-a-half years for children admitted to care at the end of 1983, to up to 6 years for those who entered care at the beginning of the study period. At the time of the study, 93 children remained in care (i.e., were "censored" observations). For the purposes of this study, length of time in foster care was measured from the date of foster care placement to exit from foster care via return to the biological family, placement in an adoptive home, or adoption by foster parents.

The researchers found that 50.8% of the children in their study remained in foster care 6 months or less, and that 29.8% left care within a month. Slightly more than one-quarter of the sample remained in care 2 years or more. The median length of stay for the total population was 6 months.

Benedict and White were primarily interested in the effects of a number of factors on the hazard rate for discharge from foster care via reunification and adoption. They developed a proportional hazards regression model of foster care length of stay by using the Maryland data that included child, maternal, and agency characteristics as explanatory covariates. Interestingly, sex, race, and age at placement were not found to be related to length of stay. Developmental delays and poor school grades decreased the hazard rate of foster care exit (lengthened foster care stays) for children in the study. Children placed with relatives were also likely to stay in care longer. Family characteristics associated with a lower hazard rate for foster care exit included previous CPS referrals, an uncooperative relationship with child protective services personnel, the social worker's perception of need for parenting education, and the perceived need for regular visiting on the part of the parents. On the other hand, children from families who were characterized as wanting their children back generally exhibited a higher transition rate out of foster care, other things being equal. The need for the agency to obtain guardianship (an indicator of adoption planning) decreased the hazard rate for exit.

Working with a longitudinal database of the foster care experiences of children going back more than a decade in Illinois, Goerge (1990) examined how the probability of a child's reunification with his or her natural parents changes with duration of time in foster care and in a particular placement, as well as how child characteristics and placement characteristics affect those probabilities. He studied the foster care careers of a systematic sample of 1,196 children who first entered foster care between July 1, 1976, and May 31, 1984. He also analyzed additional samples from this period that were stratified by race, region, and reason for placement.

Goerge broke down his study by two units of analysis. The first looked at the reunification process during the first spell of foster care (the time between entry to care until the child returns home or reaches independence). He examined the issue of duration dependence during the first spell and the effect of covariates on the probability of reunification. Goerge hypothesized that there is negative duration dependence in exit rates from the first spell in foster care (i.e., he expected that the likelihood of a child leaving foster care decreases the longer a child is in care, all else being equal). The second type of analysis focused on the probability of reunification during each of the first three placements that a child might have during the first spell in foster care. Here Goerge hypothesized that the probability of reunification during a spell decreases with the number of placements a child experiences.

In the spell-level analysis, Goerge found that the number of placements, region of placement, placement type, child's age, and referral reason were all related to the probability of reunification. Specifically, an increased number of placements, initial placement in Cook County, and placement with a relative all decreased the odds of reunification. Similarly, children placed because of neglect fared better than children placed due to behavior problems or dependency. Children who were between 4 and 7 years of age at placement exhibited the fastest overall transition rate to reunification of any age group.

For the spell-level analysis, Goerge fit a parametric hazard-rate model to the data which implied a decreasing probability of reunification over time and allowed for the possibility that some children never exit foster care prior to their eighteenth birthday. He concluded that "there is large and significant negative duration dependence in the movement to the home of the parent" in the first spell of foster care, and that approximately 30 percent of children entering foster care during the study period will not exit foster care prior to emancipation (Goerge, 1990, pp. 435–436). He also concluded that a child's probability of returning home from their first placement fell below 50% after only 10 weeks in foster care.

In the placement-level analysis, Goerge modeled separately the transition from each of the first three placements a child might experience to the home of the parent. This analysis provided estimates of the effect of each additional day in a particular living arrangement on the probability of reunification, while controlling for the effect of each additional day in foster care. He concluded:

> For the first and second living arrangements, the probability of reunification decreases with each day in placement. For the third placement, the probability of reunification does not change with duration in care. Once a child has entered a third placement, the combined duration of the first and second placements may be a stronger determinant of the probability of reunification than duration of a third placement. These results show that, as a child experiences more placements, the probability of a rapid reunification decreases. (Goerge, 1990, pp. 436–440)

In addition, Goerge stratified his placement level analysis by several race or region samples. He found a number of interactions between race and region and duration dependence in transition rates. He concluded that all children experienced a strongly decreasing probability of reunification, with the exception of African-American children in Cook County who experienced a constant probability of reunification, had the most stable placements, and exhibited the highest probability of remaining in care.

Goerge also stratified his placement-level analysis by reason for placement (dependency, abuse, neglect, and child behavior). In general, dependent children exhibited a slower rate of reunification than all other children in the placement-level analysis, and all children showed a decreasing probability of return home as duration in the first placement increased. After the first placement, however, significant differences in duration dependence were noted between groups. For example, the analysis suggests that negative duration dependence does not exist during the second and third placements for children placed because of behavior problems, whereas it is quite strong in these latter placements for children placed because of parental abuse. Children from the four groups also exhibited different probabilities of remaining in any of the first three placements through to emancipation. Dependent children had a relatively high likelihood of staying in each of these placements, and children with behavior problems tended not to stay in any of them. On the other hand, although the model suggested that abused children were likely to stay in each of the first three placements, neglected children tended to stay only in the first two.

This is an appropriate point in the discussion to examine more closely the topic of *duration dependence*. It is important to distinguish between the phenomenon of a hazard rate for a particular event that decreases over time, from the inference that a hazard rate is decreasing *as a consequence of the passage of time in a particular state*. The latter is what is commonly meant by the term duration dependence. It is not necessarily the case, however, that a declining hazard rate implies that there is negative duration dependence in a hazard rate (Tuma & Hannan, 1984; Yamaguchi, 1991).

A common form of spurious duration dependence stems from unobserved heterogeneity in hazard rates within a population being studied. For example, consider a situation where (1) a population being observed over time can be stratified into two or more groups on some dimension; (2) the researcher does not have the ability to distinguish between the groups; and (3) the groups have different, but constant, hazard rates for a particular event. Figure 4.2 describes such a hypothetical situation wherein two groups each comprise one-half of the total population at risk at the beginning of the study period. Population 1 has a discrete-time hazard rate of .5 for each interval (i.e., one-half of the members of a population remaining in a particular state at the beginning of an interval will leave that state by the end of the interval), and Population 2 has a hazard rate of .1 that also remains invariant over time. Although these two rates remain constant, Figure 4.2 shows that the hazard rate for the overall population declines over time. At the beginning of the observation period (T_1), the hazard rate for the total population is .3, the mean of the rates for the two groups. As time passes, the group with the higher hazard rate represents a smaller and smaller proportion of the population, so that the mean hazard rate for the population declines over time, gradually approaching .1. Such apparent negative duration dependence is spurious in that it

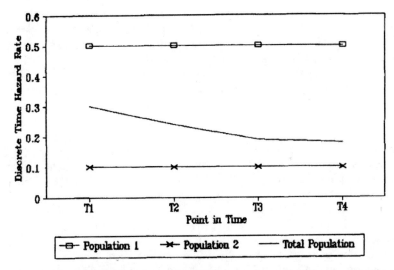

Figure 4.2. Illustration of spurious time dependence resulting from unobserved population heterogeneity.

derives from unobserved characteristics of the population, rather than a population member's duration in a given state.

Goerge attempted to control for the effects of such population heterogeneity on his models.[2] As he notes, the administrative data on which he builds his analysis is narrowly focused. It excludes, or has limited measures of, a number of factors that have been associated with foster care duration in the studies described (e.g., child school functioning, child behavior problems, child disabilities, family crises, family income and housing problems, parental cooperation with CPS personnel, and parental visiting). For instance, with the exception of race and region, Goerge's administrative data are devoid of information about a child's family of origin. Unmeasured factors that affect a family's ability to regain their children from the foster care system (e.g., poverty, the responsibilities of a single parent, or substance abuse) would need to be controlled for in Goerge's spell-level analysis of duration dependence. Similarly, unobserved characteristics of children and placements could be the actual cause of apparent placement-level duration dependence. Thus, because his primary concern was to examine duration dependence in transition rates of foster children to the home of their parent(s), Goerge had good reason for being concerned about controlling for unobserved population heterogeneity.

It is debatable, however, whether the methods he employed are adequate to the task in this particular case. An examination by Trussell and Richards (1985) of the properties of the procedure Goerge used to control for unobserved heterogeneity calls into question the utility of the parameter estimates of resulting statistical models.[3]

This is not to say that unobserved heterogeneity should be ignored, particularly when there is reason to believe that an important explanatory variable is missing from a particular model. In the case of Goerge's analysis, the most current methods available to control for such a possibility were employed. On the other hand, the issue of how to deal with this problem is far from settled, and all current approaches with significant merit require that one make assumptions about duration dependence in underlying hazard rates at the possible expense of accuracy in the estimation of all parameters of the resulting model. Thus, although Goerge has made an invaluable contribution to advancing the use of event-history methods in analyzing foster care stays and provided an important foundation for further study, his conclusions regarding duration dependence in foster care transition rates should be regarded with some caution.

McMurtry and Lie (1992) studied transition rates in foster care for a cohort of New Mexican foster children, using event-history analysis methods that specified time dependence in hazard rates. They reviewed case records for a sample of children (n = 775) who entered foster care in Maricopa County, New Mexico, between January 1, 1979, and December 31, 1984. The study's cutoff date for collection of data on these children was December 31, 1986. Their sample was restricted to children whose cases were open to child welfare services for at least 6 months (only 21 sample members were in foster care placement less than 6 months), which they estimated represented only about one-half of the children who spent time in foster care during the study period. Because of this limitation, their findings are of limited relevance to the subject of foster care duration. However, their use of event-history methods is unique in foster care research and deserves discussion.

Unlike most previous efforts that group different types of foster care exits together or focus on a single exit (e.g., family reunification), McMurtry and Lie directly modeled the "competing risks" of different foster care exits. In the context of foster care, the notion of competing risks suggests that children are "at risk" of a number of outcomes that should be distinguished from one another, rather than grouped together somewhat arbitrarily (e.g., considering family reunification and adoption as the same outcomes). The researchers estimated the differential effects of a number of child and family variables on four different exit types: (1) return home; (2) adoption; (3) "other success" (i.e., planned long-term foster care or exit to independent living); and (4) "failure" (permanently running away from placement, transfer to juvenile corrections, unplanned long-term foster care). They justified this approach in the following manner:

> foster care can be concluded in a number of ways, and each of the four exit categories is a unique destination state. To be maximally effective, analytic models for foster care must allow simultaneous examination of all possible exits and must produce estimates of the effect of predictor variables on the hazard rate for exiting into each destination state while holding constant effects associated with exits into other states. (pp. 44–45)

In contrast to Goerge, McMurtry and Lie were more interested in the effects of child, family, and foster care system characteristics on hazard rates than on duration dependence in hazard rates. Their analysis resulted in a model that estimated the effects of their explanatory variables on each outcome separately. For example, ethnicity only appeared to have a statistically significant effect on the rate of return home. African-American children were less likely than other children to go home and less likely to end up with an unfavorable outcome ("failure"). Increasing age at entry was associated with a lower hazard rate for adoption and a higher rate for both "other success" and "failure." Presence of a disability decreased the hazard rate for all outcomes but "other successes," where it had no significant effect. Children placed for reasons related to the child were less likely to go home or have "other success" than children placed because of reasons related to their parents. Children with siblings in foster care were less likely to be adopted than children without siblings in care. If a child's family paid part of the child's foster care costs, this also decreases the probability of adoption. Last, a child who experienced parental visitation (at least one visit) during the first 2 years in care was less likely than a child who was not visited to be adopted or to achieve another successful outcome. On the other hand, every child who returned home had been visited at least once while in care.

As mentioned, the narrow study population brings into question many of the findings we listed. In particular, hazard rate estimates for return to the home of a biological parent are of limited usefulness when based only on those children who return home after 6 months. Nearly all previous longitudinal research suggests that many, if not most, children who go home do so less than 6 months after entering foster care. Conversely, outcomes such as adoption, emancipation to independent living, or unplanned long-term foster care most often happen for children after more than 6 months in care. The findings of McMurtry and Lie regarding these outcomes may be of interest.

Perhaps a more significant difficulty in interpreting the results of the study by McMurtry and Lie stems from their assumptions regarding the dependence of the hazard rates they modeled on duration in foster care.

They assume that the probability of a child exiting foster care via any route will increase exponentially over time. This assumption—one that is both intuitively and empirically questionable—leads to serious questions about their conclusions.[4]

CONCLUSION

In summary, although much interest has been devoted to the paths of children through the foster care system over the past 30 years, the picture that emerges remains unclear. Only a few studies have examined foster care duration by using methods that are adequate to the task. These studies generally conclude that foster care is a relatively short-term experience for the vast majority of children who enter care. On the other hand, even fewer studies have employed methods that allow for multivariate analysis of factors associated with foster care stay (Benedict & White, 1991; Benedict et al., 1987; Goerge, 1990; McMurtry & Lie, 1992; Testa, 1985), and only one of these focused on the reunification process in particular (Goerge, 1990). Furthermore, the findings of these studies are not consistent with regard to the effects of child, family, and system variables on the exit process in foster care.

A reasonable question to ask at this point is why persons interested in child welfare policy and practice should care about the methodological limitations of existing research on foster care duration. From a policymaker's perspective, the need for sound and timely research should be clear. For example, over a decade after passage of Public Law 96–272, and in the midst of growing criticism of existing permanency planning mechanisms, we still do not have an adequate research base to evaluate the usefulness of current permanency planning time frames. In the absence of such research, we may soon find ourselves basing the next child welfare "revolution" on information that is little better than that which drove the last one.

The child welfare worker might still protest that such policy-relevant research is often of little use to those working on the front line. Although this criticism is sometimes valid, it does not appear to be so in this instance. Research that tells us what factors are related to outcomes for our clients (such as the length of time they spend in foster care) can often help us to examine our own practice and to advocate for our clients. For example, if outcomes appear to differ significantly by race, we may want to look into the cultural appropriateness of our practice. Similarly, if poverty and the lack of a second parent in the home are found to decrease the probability that a family will regain custody of a child placed in foster care, then social workers may want to place increased emphasis on advocating for concrete services to support such families. Last, if the research continues to show that the vast majority of families who regain custody of their children do so in the first few months after a child is placed, then social workers may want to reevaluate how they prioritize which cases to spend more or less of their limited time on.

Summary of Key Findings and Recommendations Regarding Length of Stay in
Foster Care

Finding	Recommendation
1a. Point-in-time analyses of foster care outcomes defined in terms of the duration of a particular condition (e.g., length of stay) are of questionable utility for two primary reasons: (1) measured of time in a particular state (e.g., in foster care) derived from these studies exhibit biases that cannot be assessed or corrected with point-in-time data; and (2) any interactions between population characteristics and length of time in a particular state are impossible to assess, even using multivariate methods.	1. Attempts to assess the outcomes of child welfare services by measuring the length of time it takes for certain outcomes to occur should rely on methods that are adequate to the task (e.g., event-history analysis).
1b. Up to the present day, child welfare researchers have primarily employed point-in-time analyses that result in potentially misleading information about the functioning of the child welfare system.	
2a. Existing longitudinal studies of foster care have been limited by the characteristics of the populations studied (e.g., only "long-term" stays, exclusion of the very young or adolescents, reliance on a single agency).	2. There is a need for long-term, large-sample studies of the pathways of children through the current foster care system. Such studies should assess a wide range of family, child, and system variables on a wide range of possible outcomes of foster care by using statistical methods that are appropriate to each particular research question.
2b. The statistical methods used in previous studies were usually inappropriate or limited in their ability to uniquely identify the effects of a particular factor while holding others constant.	
2c. Nearly all longitudinal studies regarding foster care duration are based on information gathered prior to the enactment of P.L. 96-272.	

NOTES

1. Although the phenomenon has not been reported regarding length of stay in foster care, it is also possible that a point-in-time analysis could provide an inaccurately *low* estimate of length of stay. This could happen if there were an inordinately large influx of children into the foster care system just prior to the study date.

2. Goerge controlled for unobserved heterogeneity by (1) including several covariates; and by (2) employing a nonparametric estimator developed by Heckman and Singer (1984) of the effect of unobserved heterogeneity on a hazard rate model. Heckman and Singer's approach requires that one assume a parametric form for the underlying hazard rate and includes a "mover-stayer" modification of the underlying parametric model (Blumen, Kogan, & McCarthy, 1955):

> This mover-stayer modification of the model controls for an unobserved characteristic of the child, which is that, while in care, one never knows whether he or she will exit care before the age of 18. The mover-stayer modification also results in an estimate of how many children will remain in foster care without experiencing reunification with their parents. (Goerge, 1990, p. 428)

Both of these controls for unobserved heterogeneity are useful in minimizing the possibility that observed duration dependence actually stems from population differences not accounted for in a statistical model.

3. Parametric hazard rate models assume that rates increase or decrease according to a particular underlying functional distribution (e.g., the exponential distribution, gamma distribution, Gompertz distribution, etc.). The researcher must choose from a number of possibilities, hoping to choose the parametric form that results in a model that best fits the data. Unfortunately, in an examination of the results of the properties of the Heckman-Singer procedure, using fertility data Trussell and Richards (1985) found that parameter estimates were quite sensitive to the particular functional form of the hazard rate chosen for a model, even between very similar distributions (e.g., those that implied monotonically decreasing duration dependence). In contrast, they found that this was less of a problem in models that neglected heterogeneity altogether. In short, in attempting to correct for unobserved heterogeneity, estimates of duration dependence and of the effect of explanatory variables on hazard rates can differ significantly depending on the assumption one makes about the underlying form of the duration dependence itself. Unfortunately, differentiating between possible functional forms for duration dependence is still by no means an exact science.

4. McMurtry and Lie (1992) employed a Gompertz model which implies that "the hazard rate varies exponentially over time, an approach that considers that the likelihood of some type of exit tends to increase gradually the longer a child is in care" (p. 45). There is nothing inherent in competing-risks hazard rate models that requires one to specify the parametric form of the underlying hazard function. Use of partially parametric approaches has been discussed extensively in the literature on event-history analysis (Allison, 1984; Holt, 1978; Prentice et al., 1978; Tuma & Hannan, 1984). Similarly, even if one is inclined to posit a specific functional form for the underlying hazard rates in a competing-risks model, it is reasonable to consider that each type of event (e.g., return home, adoption, runaway from placement) might have its own form of duration dependence.

In spite of these possibilities, and for reasons not explained in the report of their study (the focus of the discussion was entirely directed to effects of covariates),

McMurtry and Lie assume a positive duration dependence in the hazard rates of all of their outcomes. They give no theoretical justification for this assumption and provide no description of any goodness-of-fit analyses that might have been conducted to assess the validity of this approach. We have already mentioned the potential bias introduced into the parameters pertaining to the effects of covariates in a hazard rate regression model when the underlying hazard rate is misspecified. In this case there may be theoretical justification for assuming that such misspecification did take place. For example, it seems more reasonable to posit a nonmonotonic underlying hazard rate for adoption than the monotonic Gompertz model employed by McMurtry and Lie. One might expect the probability of adoption to increase gradually at first for the study population as members of entering cohorts are freed for adoption by the child welfare services system. After a time, however, as children become older and are therefore "less adoptable," the hazard rate would begin to decline. Furthermore, in spite of considerable empirical support for the notion that the probability of family re-unification *decreases* over time, McMurtry and Lie assume the opposite. This example illustrates the hazards of using parametric hazard rate models when one is primarily interested in the effects of covariates.

5

Reunification from Kinship and Nonkinship Foster Care

Since the pioneering work of Charles Birtwell more than a century ago foster care's aim has been to be a short-term service prior to restoring the child to the parent's care (Birtwell, 1886, cited in Kadushin, 1980). As shown in Chapter 1, approximately 200,000 children leave foster care each year. Although not all will return to the home of the parent, this chapter and other kindred studies described in the previous chapter show that the majority will return home.

From a practice standpoint, understanding the odds whether and when a child will go home is fundamental to child welfare services decision making. Risk assessment during preliminary contact with a child assumes understanding of two competing risks—the risk that the child will be harmed if he or she stays in the home and the risk that the child will be harmed if the child is removed. The solution to this comparison can only be achieved if social workers understand a substantial amount about the likely experience that a child will have in either setting. Some social workers work under the assumption that a child who is removed has a high likelihood of never returning home and never being adopted and a significant likelihood of being abused in foster care. Other social workers assume that foster care generally functions as intended—a short-term restorative program. Now, with the vast increase in the use of kinship foster care, social workers may have to understand that the answer to these questions may depend on the kind of foster home in which a child will reside.

In this chapter we report the results of an investigation of the child, family, and foster care system variables that are associated with the timing of family reunification. The study uses administrative data collected for California's Foster Care Information System to assess the impact of selected variables on the probability that a child will return home from foster care. California has the largest and one of the most ethnically diverse foster care populations in the United States. Trends in foster care in California, such as the growth of infant placements and kinship care, are similar to those found in other large states, such as Illinois and New York, where administrative data regarding foster care has been used to greatest advantage (Wulczyn & Goerge, 1992). Even between these states, however, differences are apparent. Furthermore, the administrative foster care database in California includes characteristics of children, families, and the child welfare system that are not available in these other large states. The findings of the study are presented in the context of other recent research on this subject. They suggest changes in child welfare policy and practice and directions for further research.

The analysis relies on administrative data pertaining to the foster care careers of all children who entered foster care in California for the first time between January 1988 and May 1991.[1] A random sample of 8,748 children (approximately 10%) was drawn from the larger group. Data from the sample were organized into a framework suitable to longitudinal analysis. Variables were created to indicate entries to and exits from foster care and from particular foster care placements for each child in the sample. This allowed for an analysis of the discharge outcomes for children who left foster care during the 3-year period or the final status of the children at the time of the study for those who remained in care. It also facilitates an examination of the timing of the reunification process.

The study examines the outcomes of foster care placement from a retrospective viewpoint. The data suffer from some significant limitations that deserve discussion. First, the relatively short time frame of the data currently limits its usefulness in examining foster care outcomes that take longer to occur (e.g., adoption, emancipation). On the other hand, this time frame does allow for the examination of events (e.g., initial placement, reunification) that take place within, and some time after, the permanency planning time line for California. Second, the administrative data that are the source of the data cover a relatively narrow range of child- and family-related factors. Third, some of the items recorded in the database are of questionable reliability and/or validity for various reasons.[2]

In spite of these limitations, the data provide a rich source of information regarding child, family, and system characteristics that are pertinent to the study of children's paths through foster care. In particular, knowledge of family characteristics such as family structure (i.e., single mother, single father, two parents) and AFDC eligibility of the child's family, provides a look at the effect of variables on reunification that were not present in previous large-sample studies using administrative data. The longitudinal format of the data facilitates the creation of important new information on the dynamics of foster care placement for a very large and diverse population. Nearly all of the items from the database that are used in the analysis are very reliable and valid because of either their simplicity (e.g., gender, age, region) or because their reporting is "money driven" in the sense that they are required for either the county or the provider to be reimbursed for services rendered (e.g., placement type and dates). With the exception of the items measuring preplacement services, removal reason, and health status, all of the variables used in this study are considered by state officials to reflect accurately the reality of a child's situation at any point in time in foster care. In order not to misconstrue the data, the variable "removal reason" is interpreted in this study as the primary reason for removal given by the social worker rather than an objective measure of the child's prior experience. Similarly, "health status" serves only to indicate those children who have easily identifiable and relatively severe physical, mental, and emotional health problems.

This study examines the outcome of the first "spell" in foster care. A foster care spell is the period defined by a child's entry into foster care at one end of the process the child's exit from care at the other. Although the first foster care spell for every child will eventually end for one reason or another, in this sample a great number of spells remain open in the sense that the child remains in care at the time of data analysis. It is interesting to note that, even over the relatively short span of three and a half years, over 10% of the children entering care experienced more than one spell in foster care, and some experienced as many as seven.

The following is a list of the explanatory variables that were used to create the event-history model developed during the study:

> Child's sex
> Child's ethnicity (Caucasian, African-American, Hispanic, ot'ier ethnicity)
> Child's age at entry into foster care converted to a catego'ical variable (preliminary analysis suggested that age, when meas'ured as a continuous variable, was not related to the outcomes of ir.terest in a log-linear fashion)
> - Medical, emotional, or behavioral conditions of the child as recorded by the child's social worker at intake
> - Whether or not the child's family was provided with placement prevention services prior to foster care placement
> - Whether or not the child's family was eligible for AFDC at the time of the child's placement (a proxy for poverty)
> - Whether a child was from a Los Angeles county, another urban or suburban county, or a rural county (a county with no population centers of over 50,000)

- What type of facility the child was initially placed into within the foster care system
- The recorded reason that the child was removed from home (e.g., physical abuse, sexual abuse, neglect).

The categories of the variables and their frequencies are presented in Table 5.1.

Event-History Analysis

A consideration of the problems involved in the analysis of the association between explanatory factors and the length of time between foster care entry and family reunification requires a divergence from the ordinary least-squares linear models traditionally employed in child welfare research (Goerge, 1992, provides a brief introduction to event-history analysis; for a more in-depth discussion, see Allison, 1984; Tuma & Hannan, 1984; and Yamaguchi, 1991). The group of statistical methods referred to alternatively as *survival analysis* in biostatistics, *failure time analysis* or *reliability analysis* in engineering, and *event-history analysis* in sociology, provides techniques for dealing with this type of question.

In order to assess simultaneously the effect of child, family, and foster care system variables on the reunification process, a regression model of the hazard rate for family reunification was created.[3]

Regression models of lifetime data often express hazard rates as a function of covariates and a function of time. Sometimes previous research or theoretical reasons lead an investigator to assume some parametric form for the relationship between duration in a particular state and the hazard rate for the transition out of that state. For example, as discussed in the previous chapter, Goerge (1990) tested the hypothesis that the probability that a child in foster care will be reunified decreases the longer a child is in care. A partially parametric model was employed for this study, however, because the study is primarily intended to examine the effects of explanatory factors on the family reunification process. Proportional-hazards models, such as the one employed in this study, assume that the hazard rates of two individuals with different characteristics are proportional over time (see Cox, 1972; Yamaguchi, 1991).[4]

Table 5.1 provides a breakdown of the sample by the child, family, and foster care system characteristics that are available for analysis. The sample is approximately evenly divided by gender, is reflective of the influx of young children into foster care in California over the last several years, and shows the racial diversity of the foster care population. Nearly 45% of the children were under 4 years old when they entered foster care,

Table 5.1. Child, Family, and Placement Characteristics of Foster Care Sample[1]

	Frequency	Percent
Gender		
Female	4,671	53.4
Male	4,074	46.6
(frequency missing = 3)[2]		
Race		
Caucasians	3,633	41.5
African Americans	2,720	31.1
Hispanics	2,122	24.3
Asian Americans	112	1.3
Other race/ethnicity	161	1.8
Age of child at entry into foster care		
Less than 1 year	2,166	24.8
1 through 3	1,732	19.8
4 through 6	1,305	14.9
7 through 12	2,173	24.8
13 or older	1,372	15.7
Child's health condition		
Health problems	394	4.5
No health problems	8,354	95.5
Initial foster care placement		
Foster home	4,763	54.4
Kinship home	2,811	31.2
Group home	623	7.1
Guardianship	271	3.1
Other	280	3.2
Home from which the child was removed		
Mother	6,923	79.1
Parents	1,223	14.0
Father	394	4.5
Other relative	208	2.4
Reason for placement in foster care		
Caretaker absence or incapacity	2,305	26.3
General neglect	1,689	19.3
Severe neglect	1,830	20.9
Physical abuse	1,388	15.9
Sexual abuse	918	10.5
Emotional abuse	121	1.4
Disability or handicap	137	1.6

continued

Table 5.1.   continued

	Frequency	Percent
Voluntary placement	275	3.1
Other reasons	85	1.0
Emergency Response (ER)	6,155	70.4
ER and Family Maintenance	840	9.6
None provided	1,753	20.0
AFDC eligibility of child's family		
Eligible	4,384	50.1
Not eligible	4,364	49.9
Placing county		
Los Angeles	3,495	40.0
Other urban/suburban	4,767	54.5
Rural	486	5.6

Total Sample   8,748 (approximately 10% of all children who entered foster care in California for the first time between January 1988 and May 1991).

[2] Gender of child was not recorded for three children who entered care shortly before the study date.

and just under 16% were in their teens. Fully 55% of the sample were of African-American or Hispanic heritage. Just under 5% of the children were recorded as having significant health problems. Approximately two-thirds of the children were placed as a result of reported neglect, and caretaker absence or incapacity. A much smaller number were placed because of physical abuse (15.9%) or sexual abuse (10.5%).

The children entering foster care appear to come from families living under relatively difficult social and economic conditions. Over four-fifths come from single-parent families, and about one-half come from AFDC-eligible families at the time of the child's placement.

Although four-fifths of the children in the sample come from families who received some type of service that was intended to prevent placement, only one-fifth of the families received more extensive in-home FM services. Over one-half of the children were placed initially in a foster home with unrelated caregivers, and about 31% were placed with kin. Seven percent were initially placed in group care of some form, and 3% with a guardian. Another 3% were placed in other facilities, most of these in county-run shelters. Forty percent of the sample were placed by the child welfare agency in Los Angeles county, between 5 and 6% by similar agencies in sparsely populated rural counties. The remainder were placed by child welfare agencies in counties other than Los Angeles with primarily urban and suburban populations.

Of children who entered care for the first time during the study period, slightly over one-half remained in their first spell in foster care as of May 1991. They continued to reside in foster care with a relative, a nonrelative foster parent, or in group home care. Of those who left care (44.5% of the sample), 79.1% were reunified with their natural families or sent home on a trial visit, 4.3% were placed with relatives, 3.8% were placed with guardians, 3.4% were adopted, and 1.3% were emancipated. The remainder (8.1%) left foster care due to a variety of reasons, including running away from placement, refusal of services, incarceration, placement in a state hospital, abduction, and death.

Although fewer than one-half of the children who entered care during the study period left care over the same period, this figure can be misleading, as some children had a much longer exposure to foster care than others and therefore a greater chance to exit care. For example, approximately 57% of a cohort of 648 children who entered care between January 1988 and May 1988 left foster care by the study date. In contrast to the overall sample, all members of this entry cohort had at least 3 years to exit care prior to the study date. Just under 40% of them had returned home prior to the study date, and another 17% had exited care via the other. Even with the longer time frame, however, the data indicate that two out of five children entering foster care in California will spend at least 3 years in care.

Before proceeding, a discussion of the censoring process used in this study is warranted. In the present study, observations are treated as censored on the date that the child in question leaves the foster care population for a reason other than reunification (e.g., adoption) or the date of the study for children who remain in care on that date. Those censored for the latter reason represent observations on which the duration in foster care is randomly limited by the fact that children entered care at different times in the study period and therefore have different probabilities of reaching the study date without experiencing reunification. They account for about 83% of the observations treated as censored in the study. This type of censoring does not present a particular problem for the methods employed in this study.

On the other hand, it is not ideal to treat the duration in foster care as censored at the time of exit for children who leave for reasons other than family reunification. Exit from foster care for a reason other than family reunification is not independent of exit via reunification. For example, some children in foster care (e.g., those whose parents are dead or will be incarcerated for a long time) will never be in a position to return home. Unfortunately, the administrative data on which this study is based cannot tell us which children fall into this category.[5] Furthermore, even if every child in foster care had some possibility of returning home, the various alternative exits function to some extent as competing risks for foster care exit. Thus, at any given point in time a child can exit via one of a number of mutually exclusive routes.

One method for dealing with a situation in which there is more than one exit is to construct a model of the competing risks (see McMurtry & Lie, 1992; Tsiatis, 1975; Yamaguchi, 1991). Such a model simultaneously specifies the effects of explanatory factors on the probability of each event. Unfortunately, a competing-risks approach was not possible given the limitations of the data available for this study. (Because the other eleven distinct exit types are difficult to group, a meaningful alternative risk category for exits could not be constructed. For a more in-depth discussion, see Courtney, 1992.)

What are the possible consequences of treating the multiple forms of exit other than reunification as censored? Conceptually this approach implies that the children who exited via these routes were treated as "at risk" of reunification prior to their date of exit. This does not take into account the fact that some of these children (e.g., those whose parents are deceased) were never in a position to go home, and that all of them were also at risk of exit via other routes. To the extent that the effects of the explanatory factors are related to these varying exits in different ways, the estimates of the coefficients of the regression parameters in a hazard-rate model would be subject to unidentifiable bias.

On the other hand, alternative exits do not account for a very large proportion of the censored observations in this study (about 17%), and about one-quarter of the overall exits, and they would be expected to result in less bias in estimates than would be the case if they represented a larger proportion.[6] Nevertheless, the estimates of regression parameters that follow, as well as the inferences drawn from them, should be interpreted with caution and regarded as preliminary assessments of the reunification process in California prior to the estimation of a multiexit model.

In the current sample, a child who experienced reunification after 155 weeks in care is counted as an open case because the reunification occurred after the limited time frame of the data. Therefore, the reunification process is undefined after approximately 3 years. However, as Figure 5.1 illustrates, the rate of reunification becomes relatively stable after about one and a half years of foster care. That is, reunifications after months are few and fairly constant. Thus, the current model may be a good approximation of the reunification process in general. Furthermore, unless the contributors to the reunification process are qualitatively different for those foster children who remain in care longer than 3 years,

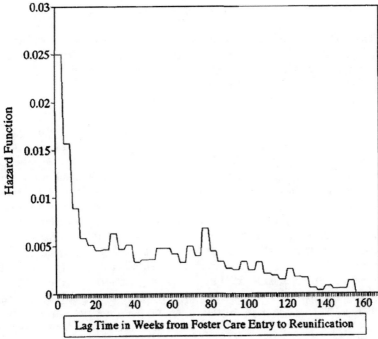

Figure 5.1. Hazard function estimates for transition from foster care placement to home of parent.

factors that affect the timeliness of reunification can also be interpreted as factors that affect the probability that a given foster child will ever be reunified with his or her family.

Overall, it appears that slightly less than one-half of the children entering foster care for the first time will be reunified with their parents within 3 years, the remainder either stay in foster care longer than 3 years or leave care for one of the other reasons mentioned. Furthermore, of those children who are reunified, nearly one-half go home within 6 months of entering care, and about 70% do so in 1 year or less.

In short, the probability of reunification is greatest immediately following placement, a finding that is consistent with previous research on length of stay in foster care (Fanshel & Shinn, 1978; Goerge, 1990; Jenkins, 1967; Lawder et al., 1986). The hazard rate declines rapidly for about 4 months and continues to decline at a somewhat slower rate thereafter with the exception of slight increases that appear to correspond to the 6-, 12-, and 18-month permanency planning hearings in front of juvenile court.

A PROPORTIONAL-HAZARDS MODEL

The first step in constructing a proportional-hazards model for the FR process was a test of the proportionality assumption for each of the covariates. For all variables except initial placement the ratio of hazard rates between strata was found to be constant over time. (For a technical discussion of testing the validity of the proportional-hazards assumption, see Yamaguchi, 1991.) Regarding initial placement, the experience of children placed with kin or guardians differed significantly from that of children in all other placements. In particular, preliminary proportional-hazards models indicated that hazard rates were essentially the same for children placed in group homes, foster homes, or other facilities on the one hand and kinship and guardianship placements on the other. For this reason, a dichotomous variable was created, representing kin placements versus all others. Figure 5.2 shows the estimated hazard functions for placement stratified by kin versus nonkin. It is clear that the hazard rate during the first several months of foster care for children placed initially with nonkin is much higher than that for kin placements. However, this difference in rates declines rapidly and is virtually eliminated after about 5 months. Thus, much of the difference in the proportion of each group remaining in care past a particular point stems from a large difference in the rate of transition home during the first 4 to 5 months and does not reflect a long-term difference in rates. It is also clear that the hazard rates in these two groups are not proportional over time.

As a result of this deviation from the proportional-hazards framework, the overall model was stratified into two separate models: one for children placed initially with kin, and one for all other children (Tables 5.2 and 5.3). Because all regression coefficients are allowed to vary in the two models, it is possible to examine indirectly the interaction of placement with the other variables in terms of their effect on reunification rates. In addition, indicator variables were created to model directly the effects of three two-way interactions (ethnicity by age category, ethnicity by region, and removal reason by age category) within strata. Interest in these interactions stems from their common use in previous research on foster care and its outcomes.

Tables 5.2 and 5.3 show the results of the proportional-hazards regression analysis for children not placed with kin and those placed with kin, respectively. The parameter estimates represent the change in the log odds of the hazard rate. They show the effects of child, family, and placement characteristics on the hazard rate for reunification, relative to the comparison category for each variable. Comparison categories were chosen to minimize the standard errors of estimated parameters and, where this was not a problem, to enhance the interpretation of findings. A

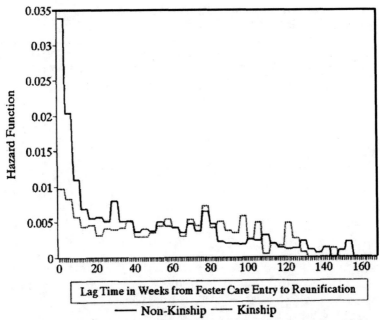

Figure 5.2.   Hazard function estimates for children placed initially with kin and for children placed with nonkin.

positive value indicates a higher hazard rate than the comparison category, and a negative value represents a relatively lower hazard rate. By taking e to the nth power where n is a parameter estimate, one obtains a risk ratio for two groups. For example, Table 5.2 indicates that the parameter in the additive log-odds hazard rate regression model for nonkin placements corresponding to "health problems" is –.585. This implies that, all else being equal, children with health problems have a *lower* hazard rate for reunification than children without such problems. The risk ratio for this variable is .557. This means that, on average, a child with health problems is just over one-half as likely to go home at any point as a child without such problems. The standard errors of the coefficients provide for rough comparisons between categories of the same variable in that the coefficients are approximately normally distributed (i.e., a difference of two standard errors is significant at $p < .05$). Table 5.2 shows the parameters of the model of family reunification for children placed initially with nonkin. All factors, with the exception of gender and pre-placement prevention services, are shown to be related to the hazard rate for family reunification.

Table 5.2. Stratified Proportional-Hazards Model for Family Reunification: Children Not Initially Placed With Kin

		Event and Censored Values			
	Total: 5,619	Event: 2,258	Censored: 3,361 (59.81%)		

	Testing Global Null Hypothesis: All Parameters = 0				
	Without Covariates	With Covariates	Model Chi-Square	df	*p*
−2 LOG L	36,969.406	36,585.989	383.417	49	<.001
Wald χ²	—	—	374.889	49	<.001

Variable	Parameter Estimate	Standard Error	Wald Chi-Square	PR > Chi-Square	Risk Ratio
Preplacement services					
Services					
No services	−0.124	0.070	3.129	0.077	0.883
Gender					
Male					
Female	−0.034	0.043	0.622	0.430	0.966
Home child was removed from					
Mother					
Father	−0.102	0.100	1.035	0.309	0.903
Parents	0.066	0.059	1.215	0T270	1.068
Other relative	−0.518	0.151	11.695	0.001	0.596**
Health					
No health problems					
Health problems	−0.585	0.116	25.266	0.001	0.557**
Poverty					
Not AFDC eligible					
AFDC eligible	−0.179	0.044	16.363	0.001	0.836**
Region					
Urban/suburban					
Los Angeles	−0.012	0.076	0.024	0.877	0.988
Rural	0.152	0.097	2.455	0.117	1.164
Removal reason					
Neglect					
Sexual abuse	0.658	0.283	5.386	0.020	1.930*
Physical abuse	0.263	0.140	3.526	0.060	1.301
Other reason	0.162	0.173	0.878	0.349	1.176
Age at entry to care					
Under 1 year					
1 to 3	0.121	0.109	1.247	0.264	1.129
4 to 6	0.285	0.117	5.862	0.016	1.330*
7 to 12	0.366	0.102	12.947	0.001	1.441**

13 and older	0.170	0.120	1.990	0.158	1.185
Ethnicity					
Caucasians					
African Americans	−0.531	0.124	18.320	0.001	0.588**
Hispanics	0.009	0.122	0.006	0.939	1.009
Other ethnicity	−0.344	0.284	1.463	0.226	0.709
Interaction Terms					
Ethnicity by age category					
African/1–3	0.439	0.170	6.656	0.009	1.552**
African/4–6	0.498	0.175	8.133	0.004	1.647**
African/7–12	0.330	0.155	4.517	0.034	1.392*
African/13+	0.317	0.189	2.823	0.093	1.374
Hispanic/1–3	0.230	0.167	1.896	0.168	1.258
Hispanic/4–6	0.036	0.172	0.045	0.831	1.037
Hispanic/7–12	−0.117	0.152	0.590	0.443	0.890
Hispanic/13+	0.018	0.171	0.011	0.917	1.018
Other/1–3	0.021	0.434	0.002	0.961	1.021
Other/4–6	0.304	0.442	0.476	0.490	1.356
Other/7–12	0.258	0.336	0.586	0.443	1.294
Other/13+	−0.093	0.387	0.058	0.810	0.911
Ethnicity by region					
African/LA	−0.089	0.121	0.545	0.460	0.914
African/Rural	0.100	0.337	0.088	0.766	1.105
Hispanic/LA	0.227	0.115	3.901	0.048	1.254*
Hispanic/Rural	0.081	0.227	0.125	0.724	1.083
Other/LA	0.684	0.288	5.639	0.018	1.982*
Other/Rural	−0.438	0.535	0.668	0.414	0.646
Removal reason by age category					
Sex abuse/1–3	−0.421	0.348	1.472	0.225	0.656
Sex abuse/4–6	−0.158	0.322	0.241	0.624	0.854
Sex abuse/7–12	−0.348	0.302	1.326	0.249	0.706
Sex abuse/13+	−0.681	0.319	4.465	0.033	0.506*
Physical abuse/1–3	0.113	0.189	0.361	0.548	1.120
Physical abuse/4–6	0.097	0.194	0.248	0.618	1.101
Physical abuse/7–12	0.089	0.174	0.262	0.609	1.093
Physical abuse/13+	0.014	0.193	0.005	0.941	1.014
Other/1–3	0.882	0.278	10.067	0.002	2.415**
Other/4–6	0.530	0.269	3.888	0.049	1.699*
Other/7–12	0.647	0.236	7.501	0.006	1.909**
Other/13+	0.707	0.235	9.074	0.003	2.028**

* Indicates $p < .01$
** Indicates $p < .05$

Table 5.3. Stratified Proportional-Hazards Model for Family Reunification: Children Initially Placed With Kin

	Event and Censored Values				
Total: 3,059		Event: 902	Censored: 2,157 (70.51%)		

	Testing Global Null Hypothesis: All Parameters = 0				
	Without Covariates	With Covariates	Model Chi-Square	df	*p*
−2 LOG L	13,596.572	13,368.845	227.727	49	<.001
Wald χ^2	—	—	727.817	49	<.001

Variable	Parameter Estimate	Standard Error	Wald Chi-Square	PR > Chi-Square	Risk Ratio
Preplacement services					
Services					
No services	−0.222	0.085	6.807	0.009	0.801**
Gender					
Male					
Female	−0.086	0.069	1.566	0.211	0.918
Home child was removed from					
Mother					
Father	−0.304	0.181	2.835	0.092	0.738
Parents	0.352	0.119	8.817	0.003	1.422**
Other relative	−0.786	0.417	3.559	0.059	0.456
Health					
No health problems					
Health problems	−0.348	0.237	2.164	0.141	0.706
Poverty					
Not AFDC eligible					
AFDC eligible	−0.366	0.071	25.911	0.001	0.694**
Region					
Urban/suburban					
Los Angeles	0.092	0.118	0.611	0.434	1.096
Rural	0.421	0.181	5.414	0.020	1.524*
Removal reason					
Neglect					
Sexual abuse	0.378	0.513	0.544	0.461	1.460
Physical abuse	0.047	0.269	0.031	0.860	1.049
Other reasons	−0.917	0.591	2.406	0.121	0.400
Age category					
Under 1 year					
1 to 3	0.083	0.184	0.204	0.651	1.087

4 to 6	0.207	0.192	1.166	0.280	1.230
7 to 12	−0.015	0.182	0.007	0.935	0.995
13 and older	0.110	0.244	0.201	0.653	1.116
Ethnicity					
Caucasian					
African-Americans	−0.606	0.222	7.470	0.006	0.546**
Hispanics	−0.771	0.254	9.221	0.002	0.463**
Other ethnicity	−0.628	0.616	1.042	0.308	0.534
Interaction Terms					
Ethnicity by age					
category					
African/1–3	0.110	0.255	0.186	0.666	1.116
African/4–6	0.278	0.264	1.110	0.292	1.321
African/7–12	0.134	0.256	0.275	0.600	1.144
African/13+	0.268	0.333	0.649	0.420	1.308
Hispanic/1–3	0.541	0.278	3.794	0.051	1.718
Hispanic/4–6	0.424	0.295	2.075	0.150	1.529
Hispanic/7–12	0.615	0.273	5.058	0.025	1.850*
Hispanic/13+	0.649	0.342	3.610	0.057	1.914
Other/1–3	−0.942	0.888	1.125	0.289	0.390
Other/4–6	−0.714	0.791	0.815	0.367	0.490
Other/7–12	0.527	0.647	0.665	0.415	1.695
Other/13+	0.301	0.726	0.172	0.679	1.351
Ethnicity by region					
African/LA	−0.044	0.174	0.066	0.798	0.956
African/Rural	0.249	0.551	0.205	0.651	1.283
Hispanic/LA	0.422	0.176	5.715	0.017	1.524*
Hispanic/Rural	−0.287	0.420	0.467	0.494	0.751
Other/LA	1.345	0.517	6.761	0.009	3.837**
Other/Rural	0.743	0.705	1.111	0.292	2.102
Removal reason by age					
category					
Sex abuse/1–3	0.272	0.574	0.225	0.635	1.313
Sex abuse/4–6	0.303	0.573	0.279	0.598	1.354
Sex abuse/7–12	0.146	0.542	0.073	0.787	1.157
Sex abuse/13+	−0.456	0.581	0.615	0.433	0.634
Physical abuse/1–3	0.362	0.320	1.284	0.257	1.437
Physical abuse/4–6	0.543	0.328	2.733	0.098	1.721
Physical abuse/7–12	0.402	0.320	1.576	0.209	1.494
Physical abuse/13+	0.223	0.383	0.338	0.561	1.250
Other/1–3	0.343	0.830	0.170	0.680	1.409
Other/4–6	−0.067	0.929	0.005	0.942	0.935
Other/7–12	0.829	0.747	1.235	0.266	2.293
Other/13+	−0.861	1.172	0.539	0.463	0.423

* Indicates $p < .01$.
** Indicates $p < .05$.

For nonkin placements, children removed from the home of a relative other than the parent go home to a parent at the slowest rate. Children removed from the homes of AFDC-eligible families also go home more slowly than the comparison group.

Several child characteristics are related to reunification rates for children placed with nonkin. As mentioned children with health problems or disabilities go home at a slower rate than children without these conditions. Interactions between explanatory variables complicate other relationships between child characteristics and reunification rates. At the main-effects level, sexual abuse is associated with a much higher transition rate home than the comparison group, neglect. Similarly, in general, children from 4 to 12 years of age at entry to foster care go home much faster than infants (the comparison group), while the rates for the 1 to 3 and 13 and older groups lie in between these extremes. However, removal reason and age interact with respect to the hazard rate for reunification. The strong effect of sexual abuse on hazard rates does not apply to older youths. On the other hand, being removed for "other reasons" (primarily voluntary agreement between a family and the child welfare agency) is shown to have a very significant impact on increasing the hazard rate relative to those children placed because of neglect for every age group except infants.

Age and ethnicity also interact with respect to FR rates. Although the model indicates that African-American children go home more slowly than Caucasian children (the comparison group) and Hispanics, the interaction terms suggest that this is primarily the case for infants and older youths, whereas transition rates for African-American children between these ages are not significantly influenced by ethnicity.

Last, the child's ethnicity and the region from which the child was placed interacted to help explain transitions home. Hispanic children and children of other ethnicity (primarily Asian Americans) went home faster if they were from Los Angeles.

Table 5.3 shows the parameters of the model of family reunification for children placed initially with kin. Gender, health conditions, and removal reason are not statistically significantly related to family reunification in the model.

Children from AFDC-eligible families generally experience a lower rate of transition home than nonpoor children. Children from two-parent families go home at a faster rate than children removed from single-parent homes or the home of a relative. Families who received preplacement prevention services have their children returned home from kinship homes faster than families who did not received such services.

Ethnicity interacts with both age and placement jurisdiction to affect the hazard rate for return home. African-American children generally go home at about one-half the rate of Caucasian children regardless of age group. Age appears to be an important contributor to the hazard rate for Latino children, but not for other ethnic groups. At the main-effects level, age is not related to reunification rates, and being of Latin-American heritage is associated with a slower rate than that for Caucasian children. However, much of the effect of Latin-American heritage on reunification rates seems to come from those Hispanics who enter care under 1 year old. Three of the four interacting terms for Hispanic children over 1 year old at entry approach or are statistically significant, at the $p < .05$ level. The coefficients of these interaction terms suggest that the transition rates for these older children are probably not much different from those of Caucasian children of similar ages, all else held constant.

Ethnicity also interacts with region for children placed with kin. Being of Hispanic or "other" ethnic heritage is associated with an increase in the hazard rate for reunification relative to other effects in the model when a child is from Los Angeles. Children from rural areas of California generally exhibit a higher transition rate from kinship homes to the home of their biological family than the rate for children from urban and suburban areas.

Discussion

The most striking results of the analysis of the time spent in foster care prior to family reunification for California's foster children is how large a proportion of entering children remain in care relative to other states. In previous studies, even recent ones in other large states, a majority of children have returned home within 1 year of entering care (Fanshel & Shinn, 1978; Goerge, 1990; Jenkins, 1967; Lawder et al., 1986). In contrast, for the study period, at the permanency planning deadline of 18 months, about 40% of entering children had returned home. Over 40% of all entering children in the first 6 months of 1988 remained in care for over 3 years.

Although the overall length of time in care seems to be higher in California than that exhibited in other states that have been studied, the rate of exits via reunification appears to decrease at a similar rate to that demonstrated in other studies. As mentioned, of those who return home in the first 3 years, around one-half do so within the first 6 months, and 70% do so within 1 year.

These broad contrasts and similarities in the outcomes for children in foster care in different states and even within states suggest that we still have much to learn about the dynamics of foster care careers. We need a better understanding of the differences in the foster care populations between and within states, as well as more information about how the foster care systems function differently between and within states.

Some have suggested that the rapid decline in reunification rates suggests a reconsideration of permanency planning timelines and that the decision to either return a child to his or her parents or to make other long-term plans should come sooner than mandated in current law (see Goerge, 1990; Wald, 1988). Although this idea may ultimately have merit, it is not clear that the observed rapidly declining transition rates for family reunification should be used as its sole justification. It is probably more prudent to invest increased energy and resources into understanding which factors contribute to increasing or decreasing a child's probability of going home and when. Without such information, the child welfare system may inadvertently and unjustifiably function to favor some children and families over others in its efforts to preserve families and protect children. For example, little is known about what factors influence the decision to place a child with kin as opposed to nonkin. Yet, this study suggests that such decisions may play a significant role in determining the likelihood that a child will return home rapidly.

Before moving on, a caveat should be raised regarding the longer length of stay before reunification in California. It may be that the tremendous growth in these much more stable and therefore long-term kinship placements has altered historic transition patterns that were more similar to those observed in other states. Similarly, this study covers a period in which most of the children entering foster care have been much younger than earlier entering cohorts in California and other states in which similar research has been conducted. The relatively longer stays of these young children may account for much of the difference observed between California and the other states. As the foster care system in California reestablishes an equilibrium under the new conditions, or as other states experience similar changes, the patterns may become more similar.

KINSHIP CARE: JUST ANOTHER PLACEMENT OPTION, OR SOMETHING COMPLETELY DIFFERENT?

The emphasis in permanency planning on finding the most familylike and least restrictive placement for foster children has helped to make kinship placement an important and growing element in the spectrum of placement resources available to child welfare workers. Court cases such as *Miller vs. Youakim* (1979) and similar legal mandates at the state level have contributed to the impetus to place children with kin by providing equitable financial support to kin caregivers. In spite of the rapid growth of kinship care as a placement option, little research has been brought to bear on the effects of this development on the permanency outcomes of foster care.

Although not made explicit in the stratified model, this study indicates that children placed with kin initially go home much more slowly than those placed with nonkin. Analysis of the comparative hazard functions for the two groups suggest as much. In addition, a preliminary regression model in which the interaction between time in a particular placement and the hazard rate for reunification was modeled directly suggested both a significant difference between hazard rates between the two groups and an interaction in which the difference decreased as a function of time. The finding of a slower transition home for children placed with kin is consistent with the findings of the studies done in Maryland (Benedict & White, 1991) and Illinois (Goerge, 1990).

It is reasonable to ask what these differences mean. Although the data used in this study cannot answer this question, the question is important enough to warrant some speculation. For example, it could simply be that there are unmeasured differences in families or children that actually cause the different transition rates. Anecdotal evidence indicates that the presence of kin willing and able to take a child increases the likelihood of removal. However, if this were the case, then one might expect that only those children in the most dangerous situations would be sent to nonkin placements. In this scenario, one might also expect that the children placed with kin would go home faster, as in general they would face less danger at home. This is not, however, the pattern observed in this study.

Analysis of the data, as well as our survey of providers in California (see Chapter 9), shows that kinship care is more likely to be provided to poor children of color by poor kin caregivers of color. Thus, an alternative hypothesis suggests that perhaps families who are already at some disadvantage in our society are more likely than Caucasian, middle-class families to take on the added burden of caring for the abused and neglected children of their kin. Although this study controlled for differences in race and gross differences in economic well-being, socioeconomic factors predominant in the unmeasured variables might explain the varying hazard rates between kin and nonkin placements.

On the other hand, it may be that the foster care system simply treats similar family/child situations differently when a kin placement is made. When a placement is made in a foster home, shelter, or group home, the imperative to reunify might be greater in the mind of the social worker or judge than if the child is placed with kin. This might result from a belief in the damage that might be more likely to happen to a child from a stay in a traditional foster care setting or from a shortage of available foster homes and institutional placements.

There is another scenario, one consistent with less scrutiny by social workers of kinship care, that might contribute to a slower reunification rate for children placed with kin. If kin are more likely to encourage parental visiting of the children in their care than are nonkin foster care providers, then the parents of children placed with kin may be less likely to feel a need to engage in efforts to regain custody of their children. They may see their children as continuing to reside "in the family."

It is not possible with these data to know if the difference in transition rates is good or bad for children and their families. It could be that children drift in kinship care, or it could be that family problems are simply given more time to be resolved. Indeed, existing evidence suggests that quick return home (such as that exhibited by many nonkin placements) is associated with a greater risk of repeated placement in foster care (Wulczyn, 1991). Thus, the delays in reunification associated with kinship care may be associated with safer and more stable returns when they occur.

More Kin and Nonkin Care Differences

The obvious similarities between the two strata in the model are that gender appears not to be related to the probability of reunification and that poverty is associated with a slower rate of return home in both strata. There are also similar region by ethnicity interactions in the two strata, with placements from Los Angeles exhibiting a more rapid transition home for Hispanics and children of Other ethnic or racial heritage.

The finding that poverty is related to a slower transition home, although not surprising, is nevertheless disturbing. Poverty should not be a reason for a child to remain separated from his or her parents, although some research suggests that it may be a good predictor (Lindsey, 1991; Pelton, 1989). Similarly, the child welfare system ideally ought to function in such a way that it provides the services and resources necessary to assist a family in regaining custody of its children when that can be appropriately done, regardless of the family's financial wherewithal. The child welfare system remains impoverished with respect to the resources needed to give families a fighting chance to remain intact.

The differences in the effects of explanatory factors between the two strata are manifold. The provision of preplacement preventive services is associated with a high hazard rate for kinship-placed children but not for nonkin placements. This could reflect the fact that the child protective services CPS system maintains better contact with those families who have already had contact with CPS prior to a child's placement than with those whose children are immediately placed with kin. It should also be mentioned that reporting differences between Los Angeles County and the remainder of the state limit the utility of this variable.

Family structure plays a different role in contributing to hazard rates between the two groups. The very small proportion of children placed in foster care out of the homes of a relative other than their parent fare similarly in any placement compared with the vast majority who came from the home of a single mother. Not surprisingly, these children return home at a slower rate (although the parameter estimate for the kinship care group is only significant at $p < .1$). If a child is already living away from his or her parent(s), it is understandable that return home would be unlikely.

On the other hand, coming from an intact, two-parent family significantly increases the rate of reunification over that for single-parent families for children placed with kin, but not for children placed with nonkin. This is difficult to explain. Perhaps kinship caregivers are less willing to engage in long-term care of children when there are two parents available to take the child back. Long-term care of the child of a single relative (and perhaps even direct support of the parent) may be more in keeping with the support patterns of extended families. In addition, this phenomenon may reflect the relatively greater ability of intact families to counter the inertia of the system after kinship placement has been made in getting their children back.

It is difficult to know without more qualitative information why health problems would slow down the reunification process for children placed with nonkin but not for children placed with kin. Are there qualitative differences not captured by the measures used in the study in the types or severity of health problems between the two groups? Do kinship care providers provide more support to parents of children with health problems, enabling them to regain their children faster than would otherwise be expected? These questions await the results of future research.

One of the most striking findings is the varying effect of removal reason on reunification rates for the two placement groups. A child's chances of returning home from kinship foster care seem to have no relationship to the reason of placement. On the other hand, for children (except teenagers) placed with nonkin, placement because of sexual abuse is associated with a much higher reunification rate than for placement because of neglect (the largest group).

The higher reunification rate for sexual abuse victims placed with nonkin relative to those suffering from neglect is contrary to the finding that children placed because of neglect in Illinois return home at a faster rate than those placed for other reasons (Goerge, 1990) but is generally consistent with the findings of Lawder, Poulin, and Andrews (1986) regarding the experiences of foster children in Pennsylvania. Adolescents who are sexually abused may not exhibit the faster rate of return home either because the problem has been ongoing for a much longer time before being disclosed and is therefore less amenable to treatment or because they prefer not to engage in efforts at reunification.

For nonkin placements, the interaction between placement for other reasons (primarily voluntary placements) and age is interesting. The effect may be absent in the model for kin placements because the number of kinship placements made for other reasons is very small. It is not surprising that voluntary placements are shorter in general than placements resulting from the court-ordered removal of a child from his or her home. Voluntary placements are often the result of an agreement between a family and the child welfare agency aimed at stabilizing a child's behavior. They can usually be easily terminated by the parent(s) at any time. On the other hand, voluntary placement of an infant may suggest more profound problems for the parent, resulting in a relatively lower probability of reunification. It remains perplexing, however, that removal reason was not related in any way to reunification for children who happened to be placed initially with relatives.

A similar difference in outcomes is evident when comparing reunification rates by age category between children placed with kin versus those placed with nonkin. For children placed with nonkin, those between the ages of 4 and 12 years old at entry go home the fastest, particularly when compared with the slow rate of reunification for infants. The discrepancy between transition rates for infants and older children is especially true for African-American children in foster care. This relationship between age at entry to foster care and the subsequent probability of reunification is generally consistent with the findings of the Illinois study, although they are difficult to explain. As mentioned, the proportion of young children entering foster care in California, particularly infants, has increased significantly since the mid-1980s. This trend has also been apparent in New York and Illinois (Wulczyn & Goerge, 1992). It coincides with the drug epidemic and may be largely a reflection of that epidemic. Perhaps the infants in the study population return home at a relatively slow rate because their parents are unable to participate in reunification efforts because of problems with substance abuse.

At any rate, the placement into foster care of large numbers of infants and very young children who exhibit a relatively low probability of return home should be a cause for great concern. Even with a leveling of the overall growth in foster care placements, the foster care population itself is likely to remain large as this multiyear cohort of children grows up in foster care. Increased efforts should be made to enhance early intervention programs aimed at the families of these children, so as to maximize their potential for reunification and to assess promptly the realistic chances of reunification. Adoption programs should also be bolstered, especially foster adoption, lest these youngest members of the foster care population have no permanent placement option other than long-term foster care.

In contrast to the relationship exhibited in the model for nonkin placement, the effect of age on reunification outcomes for children placed initially with kin is not very important, with one exception. The interaction between age and ethnicity for Hispanic foster children suggests that the lower estimated reunification rate for Hispanic children relative to Caucasians is primarily the result of a lower rate for Hispanic infants. Other than this, however, age appears to play little or no role in the timeliness of reunification for children placed with kin.

African-American children return home at a slower rate than Caucasian children when placed with kin, regardless of what region they are placed in. Of children placed with nonkin, African-American infants are reunified at a much slower rate than Caucasian children, and transition rates for African-American children of other ages do not differ much from those of Caucasians.

This is not true, however, for Hispanic children and children of other ethnic heritage (primarily Asian Americans). Hispanics and Caucasians return home at approximately the same rate when placed initially with nonkin, with the exception that Hispanics placed in Los Angeles return home slightly faster. Hispanic infants placed with kin return home more slowly than Caucasian children who are similarly placed. Perhaps Hispanic infants are particularly likely to be made a permanent part of the extended family. The interaction between Hispanic heritage and placement in Los Angeles holds true for kinship placements. Children of other ethnic heritage go home faster when placed in Los Angeles relative to other regions of the state, regardless of what type of placement they initially experience. Last, placement from a rural jurisdiction is generally associated with a faster return home for children placed with kin, although not for children placed with nonkin.

The findings regarding the effect of race on placement outcome are consistent with a number of studies that have demonstrated such effects (Goerge, 1990), although they contradict the findings of a few others (Benedict & White, 1991; Lawder et al., 1986). An interaction between race and region was found in this study as well as in Goerge's (1990) analysis of foster care in Illinois. Only future research can test whether this is a result of unmeasured child and family characteristics or variation in the way child welfare systems function for different racial groups in different regions.

It is imperative, however, to increase efforts to understand better the discrepancies in foster care outcomes experienced by children of different racial backgrounds. In addition to the results of this study and others regarding the effects of race on reunification rates, our analyses of data from California (presented in Chapter 7) show that race affects the odds of timely adoption. Research is needed to better understand these phenomena in order to provide appropriate services to families and children of color.

One general impression that the data give concerning the differences between initial placement with kin versus more traditional foster care placements is the leveling effect that kinship placement appears to have on the relationship between some child characteristics and reunification. In general, a child's age, health status, and reason for removal from the home—factors that have been shown to be related to foster care outcomes in previous studies—have a very limited impact on reunification rates for children placed with kin. Conversely, family characteristics that might indicate a family's relative ability to interact effectively with the child welfare system (e.g., poverty and family structure) appear to be more powerfully associated with the reunification process for children placed with kin.

It is hard to make sense of this disparity in the relationship of child and family variables to the reunification rate for children placed with kin. One direction for speculation, however, is consistent with the untested hypothesis mentioned that kinship placements are dealt with in a less pressing manner than other permanency planning placements. If this is true, then, child characteristics that might favorably affect the reunification process (e.g., a history of sexual abuse that is amenable to family counseling) might be paid less attention if a child is placed with kin. Similarly, if there is less of an impetus for the CWS to speed up the reunification process for kinship placements, then, the ability of a child's parent(s) to advocate independently on their own behalf might play a larger role than child characteristics in determining reunification rates.

SUMMARY

Kinship care has emerged as the placement of choice according to many in the child welfare services community. Yet, very little is known about how the availability of this placement resource has affected long-term outcomes for children placed with kin. This study suggests that initial foster care placement with kin is associated with a significantly slower rate of family reunification during the first several months of foster care than placement in other foster care settings. This initial difference in transition rates translates into a lower probability of reunification over a

3-year period for children placed with kin than for children placed elsewhere. Furthermore, a child's placement in kinship care interacts with other child and family characteristics to affect reunification rates in ways that are difficult to understand, given current knowledge and information.

Although this study cannot establish whether this pattern of effects is good or bad for children placed in foster care, it does raise a serious question. In the absence of measurable differences in the characteristics of children or families, why should children placed with kin fare differently than children placed elsewhere? Research is needed to explain the effects of kinship care on permanency planning and on the general well-being of children placed with kin. How does placement with kin affect the relationships between a child and his or her parents, a child and the kin caregiver(s), and the parents and the kin? What kind of services and support are provided to kin foster parents and how do they compare to those provided to other foster parents? Are the attitudes and expectations of the participants in the CWS (e.g., judges, social workers, kinship caregivers, and children) reflected in the outcomes of kinship care? These questions and others regarding the impact of kinship care on the foster care system and the lives of its clients await serious consideration.

Summary of Key Findings and Recommendations Regarding Reunification for Kinship and Nonkinship Care

Finding	Recommendation
1a. Over the time period of this study, by the permanency planning deadline of 18 months, only about 40 percent of entering children have returned home.	1. Research is needed to determine whether the recent trend towards a longer length of stay in foster care seen in California is typical of other states. It is essential that this research be able to help policy makers to differentiate between possible contributors to this trend (e.g., substance abuse by parents, the growth of kinship care, restraints on family preservation resources) since different causes may call forth different responses.
1b. Over 40 percent of all entering children in the first six months of 1988 remained in care for over three years.	
1c. It remains unclear whether these numbers suggest a much longer stay in foster care for children entering care in California than for children in other states, or evidence of a new trend in which the large number of infants and young children entering foster care nationwide tend to remain in care indefinitely.	
2a. This study, like those in other states, indicates that children placed with kin initially go home much slower than those placed with non-kin.	2. Research is needed to better understand the outcomes for children of kinship care placement and the interaction of the child welfare system with kinship care providers, particularly in terms of effects on permanency planning efforts. The results of this research may help give direction to efforts to redesign permanency planning mandates in keeping with the rapid growth of kinship care.
2b. Placement with kin seems to minimize the effect of other factors (e.g., removal reason, age, children's health problems, family structure) on reunification rates.	
2c. While the reasons for these differences are still unclear, the pattern of results suggests that once children are placed with kin, their progress through the system may receive less attention and support than if they had been placed with nonkin.	

3. Children from poor families (as measured by receipt of AFDC funding) returned home at a slower rate than children who came from familes that were not so poor. This was true regardless of whether or not the child was placed with kin, although the effect was greater for those children placed with kin.

3a. The child welfare system ideally ought to function such that it provides the services and resources necessary to assist a family in regaining custody of its children when that can be appropriately done, regardless of the family's financial wherewithal.

3b. Child welfare workers must have increased access to concrete services (e.g., housing, child care, respite care, employment assistance) to enable poor parents to make use of other family preservation services (e.g., counseling and parent training).

4. Infants and young children entering the foster care system are going home at a slower rate than all other age groups entering foster care, although this age difference in exit rates appears mainly to be true for children not placed with kin. This suggests the possibility of a foster care "baby boom" in which large cohorts of children spend their entire childhood in foster care.

4a. Increased efforts should be made to enhance early intervention programs aimed at the families of these children (in particular poor and single-parent families) so as to maximize the chance of preserving these families and to promptly assess the realistic chances of family reunification when a child is removed from the home.

4b. Public adoption programs should also be bolstered, especially foster adoption, lest these youngest members of the foster care population have no permanent placement option other than long-term foster care.

5a. Ethnicity and region of placement appear to interact with respect to the rate at which foster children return home.

5b. African-American children in particular tend to remain in foster care longer than other children.

5a. Discrepancies in outcomes for foster children should not be based on race. While this study indicates that outcomes do differ by race even after controlling for a number of other factors, more qualitative research is necessary to better understand the reasons for these differences.

5b. Attention should be directed at why some jurisdictions appear to exhibit more "race-neutral" outcomes than others.

6. Large-sample administrative data are best suited to exploratory analysis directed towards finding important trends and apparent relationships between explanatory and dependent variables where small sample sizes and/or cost would preclude such analysis using other methods. The use of such data in this study allowed for the examination of main and interaction effects of a number of important child, family, and foster care system variables on the rate of return home for children in foster care. The findings suggest a number of areas where these factors, and interactions between factors do appear to be related to this important outcome. The small number of factors studied in an area of such great complexity, however, tends to lead to more new questions than answers.

6a. Interpretation of the meaning of many relationships and trends uncovered through the analysis of administrative data requires more in-depth qualitative research than is possible using administrative data alone. Such research should be pursued.

6b. Many of the findings of this study and of those in the following two chapters provide important grist for the mills of child welfare researchers interested in furthering our knowledge of the foster care system. Comfirmation or disconfirmation of these findings should be pursued through appropriate studies.

NOTES

1.   It is possible that some of the children in the sample had experienced one or more spells in foster care prior to their entry to care after January, 1988, which would not be recorded in the database. Due to the procedure used to purge the state foster care database of cases that have been closed for more than three years, however, these episodes must have occurred prior to January, 1985, and ended prior to that date. Thus, for the purposes of this study, any foster care stay that occurs three years or more after the end of a previous stay is considered a "first" foster care episode for that child.

2.   It is unclear whether significant differences in the recorded usage of pre-placement preventive services between Los Angeles County and the remainder of California are due to different reporting practices or actual differences in service provision. Social workers are required to report only the primary reason that a child is removed from the home, whether or not there is more than one reason. Thus, a child who is known to be abused and neglected will be reported as one or the other, but not both. It is generally the case, however, that when there is good evidence that a child has been abused and neglected, the removal reason will be listed as abuse since this is a more justifiable reason for removal under existing legal mandates. Thus, it is not clear whether reports of abuse and reports of neglect indicate different types of events, or different intensities of events, or both. Social worker reports of the health problems of children are believed to underesti-

mate such problems, particularly since drug abuse has only recently been added to the list of recorded health problems. Similarly, reporting practices regarding the provision of other services to children and families (e.g., counseling, transportation, parenting training) and changes in the child's service plan are so inconsistent as to render them useless for analytic purposes.

3. In general, the continuous-time hazard function $h_{ij}(t)$ for the transition from state i to state j is defined as:

$$h_{ij}(t) = \lim_{\Delta t \to 0} \frac{PR\ (t \leq T < t + \Delta t \ | \ T \geq t)}{\Delta t}$$

If T is the time of the transition from an initial state i (e.g., placement in foster care) to another state of interest j (e.g., return to the home of the parent), the hazard function identifies the instantaneous transition rate at time t, given that the individual has remained in state i until t.

4. The proportionality assumption requires that if two individuals have respective sets of characteristics represented by covariate vectors X_1 and X_2, the ratio of their hazard functions, $h(t \,|X_1)/h(t \,|X_2)$, does not vary with time.

The most common expression of the proportional-hazards model expresses the hazard rate in terms of an unspecified function of time, $q(t)$, and a log-linear function of observed variables. This model can be written, $h(t) = q(t)e^{Bx}$, where B represents a vector of regression parameters corresponding to the vector of covariates. The fact that $q(t)$—the underlying hazard rate—is not specified is an attractive characteristic of the proportional-hazards model. This is useful when one is not primarily interested in duration dependence in hazard rates or where the hazard rate does not conform to easily-estimable forms. On the other hand, since $q(t)$ is not specified, maximum likelihood methods cannot be used to estimate the parameters of this model. However, as long as hazard rates conform to the restriction described above (i.e., they are proportional to each other over time), Cox's partial likelihood method provides for the estimation of regression parameters corresponding to explanatory variables (Cox, 1972). The partial-likelihood estimation process also allows for the inclusion of censored data. In the event that the hazard rates between two or more groups in a population are not proportional (i.e., there is an interaction between a covariate's effect on the hazard rate and time), the interaction between the covariate and time can be modeled directly, or the analysis can be stratified by those groups.

5. For example, some children came into foster care from the home of a relative. These children would be expected to have a low probability of reunification as undoubtedly some of them have no parents. Similarly, some children placed for reasons of caretaker absence or incapacity have been effectively abandoned. However, preliminary analysis of the data suggests that a significant proportion of children in these categories are reunified with their biological families. In the absence of information that would distinguish those children with no potential for reunification from those with some probability of returning home, all children in these categories were retained for the analysis.

6. One way to explore the possible impact of the nonindependence of a censoring process on the parameters of a regression model of hazard rates is to create alternative regression models that treat the observations in question in different extreme ways (see, e.g., Allison, 1984; Peterson, 1976). This method was employed with the data used in this study. While the magnitude of some regression parameters changed somewhat depending on the model, in no case was the direction of the effect of an explanatory variable that was significant in the final

model reversed. Furthermore, a logit analysis of the effect of the same explanatory factors on the odds that a child will be reunified by the permanency planning deadline (18 months in California), revealed similar relationships between the explanatory factors and this related dependent variable to those found in the proportional-hazards model. For a discussion of the logit model see Courtney (1992).

6

Factors Associated with Entrance to Group Care

For over a century there has been a debate about the appropriateness of group care for abused and neglected children (Lerman, 1982; Wolins & Piliavin, 1969). Controversy surrounding which types of children and youths should be cared for in these settings has never subsided, although the roles of children's institutions have changed over the years both in response to this debate and as a result of market forces.

Research has contributed to our knowledge of the characteristics of group care settings for children (Cohen, 1986; Dore, Young, & Pappenfort, 1984) and of the characteristics of the children themselves (Berrick, Courtney, & Barth, 1992; Fitzharris, 1985; Hulsey & Whdte, 1989; Wells & Whittington, 1993; Whittaker, Fine, & Grasso, 1989). A review of the literature, however, reveals no previous research that specifically addresses the question of what child, family, and service characteristics affect the odds of placement into group care. In California, the proportion of children in group care has not grown considerably over the past few years.[1] An appreciation of other developments in the dynamics of the foster care system in California helps to put in context changes that have occurred in the group home population. As described in Chapter 1, the foster care population in California has grown tremendously, is younger on the average, and increasingly exhibits significant medical, emotional, and behavioral problems.

The foster care system has not responded to these changes through proportional increases in traditional placement resources. On the contrary, different types of placements (e.g., foster family homes, kinship homes, group homes, specialized foster homes) have grown at widely varying rates (County Welfare Director's Association of California, 1990).

For example, placements in the home of a relative more than tripled between fiscal year 1984 and 1993 from approximately 10,000 to more than 35,000, far outstripping the overall increase in foster care. Similarly, placement in specialized foster care facilities more than doubled over this period. In contrast, placements into foster family care in general grew by 34%, and placements into group care grew by 51%.[2] Thus, the growth in the foster care population was accommodated more by a shift to kinship care and the response of private sector providers (group care and specialized foster care are provided almost exclusively by private providers in California) than by a growth in licensed foster family care.

It appears that the foster care system in California has been unable to create enough familylike placement resources to accommodate the large recent influx of young children and children with special needs. This has happened in spite of the rapid growth of specialized treatment foster care in the state. This relative dearth of familylike placement settings has likely contributed to the shifting age distribution of children in group care. The entrance of infants and very young children into the group care population, however, has added a new twist to the debate concerning the appropriate use of group care. Figures 6.1 and 6.2 illustrate the growth in both the number and percentage of infants and young children placed in group care in California during the enormous growth of out-of-home care in the late 1980s. The percentage of children in group home care under the age of 5 more than doubled between 1985 and 1990. During the same period, the percentage of group home children who were infants (under 1 year old) grew by more than 50%.

Between 1990 and early 1993, the rise of young children in out-of-home care grew more slowly, by 3% (2,004 children). Yet, the increase in young children identified as in a group home increased by 56% (837 children). The proportion of young children in group home care to all children in group home care increased from 20% in 1900 to 25% in 1993. Clearly, the abatement in placements of young children in out-of-home care did not reduce the practice of placement in group homes.

In addition, the escalating costs of foster care in general give rise to understandable interest on the part of researchers, practitioners, and policymakers about this relatively expensive type of care setting for abused and neglected children. For example, in California, group care settings cost for young children are approximately 10 times the cost of a conventional foster care placement and at least three times the cost of specialized foster care. This study uses administrative data to explore the relationships between selected child, family, and service characteristics and the odds that a child will enter group home care. Additionally, special attention is paid to the experience of infants in group care.

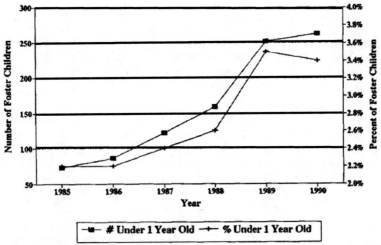

Figure 6.1. Number and percentage of infants in group home care in the state of California.

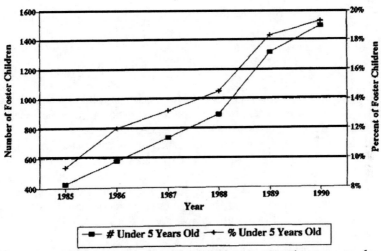

Figure 6.2. Number and percentage of children in group home care under 5 years old in the state of California.

SAMPLE AND METHOD

This analysis relies on the University of California at Berkeley Foster Care Database (UCB-FC Database) to examine the characteristics of children and families as they contribute to entry into group care.

The analysis is divided into two parts. The first part is a logit analysis that describes the effect of certain variables (gender, health condition, reason for removal from home, who the child was removed from, age at entry into foster care, preplacement prevention services, and AFDC eligibility) on the odds that a child's first foster care placement will be in a group home. This analysis relies on the entire 10% random sample from the UCB-FC Database ($n = 8,748$). The second part is a logit analysis describing the effect of the same variables on the odds that a child will be placed in a group home after his or her first placement. The sample consists of all children in the UCB-FC Database who entered care between January of 1988 and June of 1989 ($n = 3,627$). The members of this cohort were therefore exposed to the potential of entering group care for at least one and a half years in foster care prior to the time the data were entered into the database. Obviously, the relatively short time span of the current study (3 years) limits the accuracy of the second part of the analysis to the extent that only children and youths who entered group care 3 years or less after placement into foster care can be accounted for. However, the analysis does provide a good picture of the process of group care entry for this time frame. The validity of this type of analysis will improve as the UCB-FC Database is augmented over time.

FIRST PLACEMENT IN GROUP CARE

Before constructing a logit model of the odds of initial placement into group care, bivariate relationships between selected explanatory variables and group home placement were examined.

Table 6.1 illustrates these relationships. The bivariate analyses suggest the following conclusions. Approximately 7% of the children who entered foster care between 1988 and mid-1991 were initially placed in a group home. Gender, ethnicity, AFDC-eligibility status, and preplacement preventive services seem to play little or no part in increasing or decreasing the odds that a child is initially placed in group care. Children who are labeled by their social worker as emotionally disordered are more likely to be initially placed in group care than children with physical disorders or no health problems. Children placed voluntarily or removed from their homes for reasons of emotional abuse or physical disability are more likely to be placed first in a group home than children removed from their homes for other reasons. Youths (ages 13+) are more likely than other children to be initially placed in group care. Children removed from two-parent homes are least likely to enter group care first, and children who come from the homes of relatives (children who were living with relatives but were not in foster care with them) other than a father or mother are most likely to do so.

Logit models provide a useful method for examining the unique effect of each explanatory variable on a dichotomous dependent variable while taking into account interactions between variables. Examining variables for inclusion in a logit model for initial placement to group care revealed that gender, ethnicity, AFDC-eligibility status, preplacement preventive services, and the type of household from which the child was removed (e.g., single mother, parents) seem to play little or no part in increasing or decreasing the odds that a child is initially placed in group care, given the effect of more salient factors. On the other hand, child health problems, referral reason, and child's age at entry to foster care all significantly influence the likelihood that a child will be placed initially in a group home. These variables were entered into the final model.

Table 6.2 shows the parameter estimates for the final logit model of first placement into group care. The chi-square value and corresponding probability level associated with the model indicate that it fits the data from the sample well. This model illustrates the effects of several factors on the odds that a child will avoid initial placement in a group home. The table shows the log-odds parameter for each factor, the standard error of this parameter, the probability that this effect differs from 0, and the effect of this factor on the odds of group home placement. The intercept term refers to the predicted overall odds that a child will avoid group care on his or her first placement, all things being equal.

Of particular interest is the column showing the effect on the odds of group home placement, as this is the most easily interpreted measure of association between the explanatory variables and the item of interest. At the most basic level, any factor with a value in this column greater than 1 increases the odds that a child is not placed initially in a group home, or, conversely, decreases the odds that a child will first be placed in group care. Similarly, any factor with a value less than 1 increases the odds of initial placement in a group home. In general, older children and youths (ages 7 and over), children with health problems, and children who enter care for reasons other than abuse or neglect (particularly voluntary placements) are more likely to enter group care during their first placement. The model also suggests that referral reason interacts with both age and health problems in terms of the effects of these factors on the odds of group home placement. For the oldest youths, referral for physical or

Table 6.1. First Placement in Foster Care vs. Group Care

	Foster Care		Group Care				
	N	%	N	%	χ^2	Phi	P
Gender							
Female	4365	93	306	7	4.99	.024	.03
Male	3757	92	317	8			
Ethnicity							
African-American	2537	93	183	7	3.08	.019	.54
Asian-American	103	92	9	8			
Caucasian	3355	92	278	8			
Hispanic	1981	93	141	7			
Other Ethnicity	149	93	12	7			
Health							
Emotionally Disordered	73	67	36	33	112.7	.114	<.01
No Health Problem	7790	93	564	7			
Organic or Physical	262	92	23	8			
Removal Reason							
Caretaker Absent	2131	92	174	8	119.0	.117	<.01
Disability Handicap	116	85	21	15			
Emotional Abuse	106	88	15	12			
General Neglect	1608	95	81	5			
Other Reason	76	89	9	11			
Physical Abuse	1283	92	105	8			
Severe Neglect	1722	94	108	6			
Sexual Abuse	865	94	53	6			
Voluntary Placement	218	79	57	21			
Removed (Removed From)							
Father	365	93	29	7	22.28	.050	<.01
Mother	6431	93	492	7			
Other Relative	177	85	31	15			
Parents	1152	94	71	6			
Age							
Four through six	1255	96	50	4	216.25	.157	<.01
Less than one	2054	95	112	5			
One through three	1646	95	86	5			
Seven through twelve	2020	93	153	7			
Thirteen or older	1150	84	222	16			
Poverty (AFDC ELIG)							
AFDC Eligible	4082	93	302	7	.72	.009	.40
Not Eligible	4043	93	321	7			
Preplacement Services							
ER	5815	93	427	7	4.20	.022	.12
ER & FM	782	93	58	7			
None	1528	92	138	8			

Table 6.2. Parameters of the Logit Model for First Placement in a Group Home

Variable	Log Odds Coefficient	Standard Error	Approximate p-value[1]	Effect on Odds[2]
Intercept	1.923	.140	.001	6.841
Age				
<4	.919	.220	.001	2.506
4–6	.482	.206	.019	1.619
7–12	−.229	.140	.102	.795
13–+	−1.171	.123	.001	.310
Health Problems				
Health Problems	−.617	.125	.001	.540
No Health Problems	.617	—	—	1.852
Referral Reason				
Abuse	.573	.198	.004	1.773
Neglect	.566	.165	.001	1.762
Voluntary	−.642	.352	.068	.526
Other Reasons	.497	.217	.022	.608
Interactions: Age by Referral Reason				
<4 by Abuse	−.653	.247	.008	.521
<4 by Neglect	−.686	.228	.003	.504
7–12 by Neglect	.290	.158	.067	1.336
>13 by Abuse	.664	.156	.001	1.943
>13 by Voluntary	−.942	.288	.001	.390
Interactions: Health Problems by Referral Reason				
Problems by Abuse	.401	.184	.029	1.494
Problems by Neglect	.409	.149	.006	1.505
Problems by Other	−.399	.190	.036	.671

Note:
Goodness-of-fit statistics for the Model[3]
  Pearson chi-square = 5.98; df = 12; p = .917
  Likelihood ratio chi-square = 6.95; df = 12; p = .861
[1] Only those interaction parameters with $p < 0.1$ are shown.
[2] Odds that child will have first placement *other* than in a group home.
[3] Goodness-of-fit p-values closer to 1 show a stronger likelihood that the model accurately describes the data.

sexual abuse decreases the odds of group home placement even more than the overall effect of this factor. On the other hand, for this older group, voluntary placement increases the odds of group home placement over and above the already powerful affect of this factor. Placement for neglect has a particularly strong effect in decreasing the odds of group home placement for children between 7 and 12 years of age. Referral for abuse or neglect has a much different impact for younger children (under age 4) than for all others. Although referral for these reasons decreases the odds of group home placement for all other age groups, it has no such effect for young children. This interaction is largely responsible for the fact that slightly more very young children enter group care (about 5%) than do children in the 4 to 6 group (3.8%). Not surprisingly, older youths who are voluntarily placed in foster care and who have mental, emotional, or physical health problems are most likely to enter group care. In fact, they are more likely to initially enter group care than any other type of placement.

The interaction between referral reason and health problems is more straightforward. The effect of abuse and neglect on decreasing the odds of initial group care placement is even greater for children who suffer from health problems. On the other hand, the interaction between referral reason, other, and health problems increases the odds that children with these characteristics will enter group care over and above the main effects of these characteristics.

The odds model for group home placement is a multiplicative model. To find out the odds that a given foster child will enter a facility other than a group home, simply multiply the intercept term by each of the parameters for the characteristics of interest, keeping in mind any possible interactions. For example, Table 6.2 shows the predicted odds that a 13-year-old youth voluntarily placed in foster care suffering from health problems will be initially placed in a facility other than a group home. The model is:

Predicted Odds of Initial Placement
    = Intercept (6.8421) × 13 Years Old (.3098)
                      × Voluntary Placement (.5263)
                      × Health Problems (.5398)
                      × 13 Years Old and Voluntarily Placed
                      Interaction Term (.3897)
    = .2346 to 1.

Thus, this child has only a one in for chance of entering a foster care setting other than a group home.

One finding of particular concern that can be missed in analyzing the terms of the model is the surprisingly large number of very young children who are entering group care. Approximately 18% of the foster children who entered foster care in California during the study period and whose first placement was a group home were under 1 year of age when they entered care. Given the size of the sample, this suggests that over 1,000 infants were placed initially in an institutional setting within the foster care system of California over a three and a half year period starting in 1988.

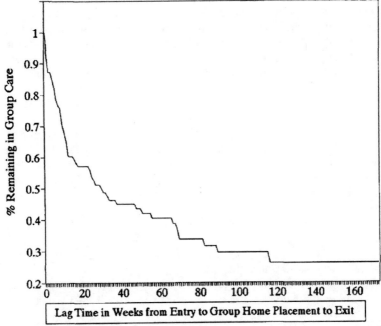

Figure 6.3. Infant placements in group care.

The large number of infants being placed in group care might not be a cause for alarm if these placements were relatively brief transitional stays. However, a survival analysis of the data pertaining to the infants who were initially placed in group care indicates that their stays were not brief. Figure 6.3 shows the Kaplan-Meier estimate of the survivor function for children initially placed in a group home (Lawless, 1982). This survival curve illustrates the estimated percentages of infants initially placed in group care who remain in those initial placements at various points after entering care. Although the data suggests that a large number of infants have relatively brief stays in care, approximately 40% remain in an initial group home placement over 1 year, and about one-quarter remain there for over 2 years.

LATER PLACEMENT IN GROUP CARE

Approximately 9% of the sample of children who entered care between January 1988 and June 1989 and who had been initially placed in a facility other than a group home, entered group care at some point during the study period. Again, bivariate relationships were examined to provide guidance in constructing a logit model. Table 6.3 illustrates these relationships. Gender, AFDC eligibility status, and preplacement preventive services are not related to subsequent group home placement. Ethnicity, referral reason, and whose home the child was removed from are weakly related to later group home placement at a bivariate level. Caucasian children and those in the other category appear slightly more likely to enter a group home. Physically and sexually abused foster children and those with disabilities are slightly more likely than others to enter group care. Children removed from the home of their single mother are slightly less likely to enter a group home after another placement. Age is strongly related to later group home placement with the probability of placement increasing with age at entry into foster care. Children with health problems (particularly those who are emotionally disordered) are much more likely than other children to have a stay in group care after their first placement. Children initially placed in either a foster home or a shelter are more likely to be placed in a group home later than are children initially placed with relatives or a guardian.

The bivariate relationships to placement in group care do not account for relationships between the explanatory variables. When the effects of all these factors are tested simultaneously, gender, removal reason, AFDC eligibility status, ethnicity, and preplacement preventive services seem to have little or no effect on eventual entry to group care. On the other hand, age at entry to foster care, presence or absence of health problems, and type of initial placement facility all remain significant contributors to subsequent entry to group care.

Table 6.4 shows the parameter estimates for the final logit model (that tests for simultaneous and interactive relationships) of placement into group care after initial placement in another facility. The chi-square value and corresponding probability level associated with the model indicate that it does not fit the data as well as the model for initial placement; there is, however, no compelling evidence to reject the general conclusions of the model because p does not approach significance. The limited variables clearly do not account for as much of the variation in later placements as they do for initial placements. Nonetheless, the model illustrates some important contributors to the likelihood of group home placement. Like Table 6.2, Table 6.4 shows the log-odds parameter for each factor, the standard error of this parameter, the probability that this effect differs from 0, and the effect of this factor on the odds of group home placement. Again, the intercept term refers to the predicted overall odds that a child will avoid group care during at least the first one and one-half years of placement, all things being equal.

Table 6.3. Later Placement in Foster Care vs. Group Care

	Foster Care		Group Care				
	N	%	N	%	χ^2	Phi	P
Gender							
Female	1786	91	172	9	.02	.003	.88
Male	1520	91	149	9			
Ethnicity							
African-American	1091	93	86	7	14.43	.063	.01
Asian-American	55	90	6	10			
Caucasian	1346	89	159	11			
Hispanic	765	93	61	7			
Other Ethnicity	49	84	9	16			
Health							
Emotionally Disordered	17	53	15	47	58.59	.127	<.01
No Health Problem	3199	92	295	8			
Organic or Physical	90	89	11	11			
Removal Reason							
Caretaker Absent	857	91	83	9	25.63	.084	<.01
Disability Handicap	14	82	3	18			
Emotional Abuse	51	93	4	7			
General Neglect	679	92	60	8			
Other Reason	32	91	3	9			
Physical Abuse	497	90	57	10			
Severe Neglect	766	94	50	6			
Sexual Abuse	322	86	54	14			
Voluntary Placement	88	93	7	7			
Removed (Removed From)							
Father	163	87	25	13	9.50	.051	.02
Mother	2686	92	239	8			
Other Relative	77	89	10	11			
Parents	380	89	47	11			
Age							
Less than one	854	97	27	3	206.30	.238	<.01
One through three	714	96	27	4			
Four Through six	540	94	33	6			
Seven through twelve	832	87	125	13			
Thirteen or older	366	77	109	23			
Poverty (AFDC ELIG)							
AFDC Eligible	1685	91	168	9	.22	−.008	.64
Not Eligible	1621	91	153	9			
Preplacement Services							
ER	2369	91	232	9	.14	.006	.93
ER & FM	426	92	39	8			
None	511	91	50	9			

continued

Table 6.3. Continued

	Foster Care		Group Care				
	N	%	N	%	χ^2	Phi	P
Facility							
Foster Home	1993	89	241	11	128.60	.188	<.01
Guardianship	116	97	4	3			
Kinship Home	1118	97	40	3			
Other	79	69	36	31			

Table 6.4. Parameters of the Logit Model for Placement in a Group Home After Placement in Another Type of Facility

Variable	Log Odds Coefficient	Standard Error	Approximate p-value	Effect on Odds[1]
Intercept	1.417	.210	.000	4.125
Age				
<	1.008	.120	.000	2.740
4–6	.399	.145	.006	1.490
7–12	−.448	.098	.000	.639
13–+	−.959	.106	.000	.383
Health Problems				
Emotionally Disordered	−.753	.193	.000	.471
Not Emotionally Disordered	.753	—	—	2.123
Facility				
Foster Home	−.051	.100	.613	.950
Relative/Guardian	1.109	.128	.000	3.031
Other Facility	−1.059	.155	.000	.347

Note:
Goodness-of-fit statistics for the Model[2]
    Pearson chi-square   = 7.17; df = 12; p = .846
    Likelihood ratio chi-square = 13.42; df = 12; p = .339
[1] Odds that child will avoid subsequent group home placement after initial placement in another setting.
[2] Goodness-of-fit p-values closer to 1 show a stronger likelihood that the model accurately describes the data.

In general, as a child's age at entry into foster care increases, the likelihood that he or she will enter group care after initial placement increases. Health problems also significantly increase the odds that a foster child will ultimately be placed in group care. A child or youth who is labeled emotionally disordered by his or her social worker is more likely than a child with physical problems or no health problems to enter group care. The initial placement also plays a strong role. Placement in a relative's home significantly decreases the odds of later group home placement compared to placement in a nonkin foster home. Initial placement in a small family home or county shelter has the greatest effect in increasing the odds of subsequent group home placement.

Like the model for initial group home placement, this model is multiplicative, allowing for easy estimation of the predicted odds of group home placement. (The predicted odds that a given foster child (intercept = 4.125) who is 13 years old (.383), is emotionally disordered (.471), and was initially placed in a county shelter (.347) will avoid subsequent placement in a group home for at least one and a half years (1.471 × .383 × .471 × .347) = .258 to 1. In other words, such a person would be nearly four times more likely than not to enter a group home during his or her first few years in foster care.

SUMMARY

The explication of the characteristics of welfare-supervised children and youth that seem to increase the odds of group home placement is instructive.

Older children are still much more likely than young children to enter group home care. Children and youths suffering from health problems, particularly emotional problems, are more likely to be placed in group care. Emotional disorders are especially likely to result in group home placement, even when initial placement was in another facility.

Referral reason is strongly associated with initial group home placement. Voluntary placement significantly increases the odds of initial group home placement, particularly for older entrants to foster care. Placement for abuse or neglect generally predicts the avoidance of group home placement but, oddly, this is not as true for children under 4 as for all other children. For all children, placement due to abuse or neglect partially mitigates the affect of health problems in increasing the odds of group home placement while placement for other reasons interacts with health problems to increase group home placement sharply. This may indicate that children whose health problems are secondary to their reason for placement (i.e., abuse or neglect) are less likely to experience group home placement, whereas children placed for other reasons (e.g., disability or handicap) have health problems that have a greater impact on the initial decisions to place children in a group home.

The logit models of entry into group care purposely exclude youths who enter group care through referral by county probation departments. This is important for two reasons. First, youths referred by probation to group home care may differ in significant ways from welfare-supervised group home children and youths. Court dependents are placed in group care and foster care in general because of parental abuse or neglect. Although probation youths also often suffer from exposure to the same experiences, they are not placed in group homes for these reasons. They are placed in care because of law violations. Furthermore, probation referrals to group home care are almost always over 12 years of age in contrast to the welfare-supervised group home population that includes increasing numbers of young children. Thus, the percentages of young children in group care actually refer to the percentages of welfare-supervised young children in group care. The percentages of young children in the overall group home population are about one-half as high as those found in the welfare-supervised sample.

Second, the issues involved in the debate surrounding the appropriateness of group home placements differ for probation and welfare group home placements. Although there has been some discussion of the use of specialized foster care for court wards (Chamberlain, 1990) and examples of this practice exist in California, the primary alternatives to group home placement for court wards are county probation camps and California Youth Authority institutions. Both of these settings are more restrictive than group homes and generally more expensive. On the other hand, discussion of alternatives to group home placement for dependents focuses primarily on less expensive and more familylike settings (i.e., specialized foster family care).

The most striking finding of the analysis of subsequent placement into group home care is the strong effect of initial placement. Nearly one-third of all children initially placed in county shelters will be placed in group homes within the following 2 to 3 years. The risk of group home placement for this group is nearly three times higher than it is for children and youths initially placed in conventional foster care and over nine times as great as that experienced by those initially placed with relatives (the group with the least risk of group home placement), regardless of a child's age or health problems.

Although the quality of the data is limited, these findings suggest areas of improvement in efforts to avoid unnecessary or inappropriate group home placements. If the mental and physical health needs of foster children can be met through the use of specialized familylike settings, it seems reasonable to expect that initial and subsequent group home placements can be decreased. Furthermore, it is not at all clear that the emotional and behavioral problems that are typical of children voluntarily placed in foster care can only be met in group care settings. Other research using the UCB-FC Database (see Chapter 5 on the reunification process) indicates that this group has a very good prognosis for reunification with their families. Specialized foster family care may be able to meet the needs of these children and return them home without resorting to expensive institutional placement.

The effects of initial placement setting on subsequent placement in group care are strong and provocative. The data cannot tell us for certain if children are initially placed in shelter care because they have emotional and behavioral problems that are predictive of the need for later group home care or if initial placement in shelter care increases the need for later group home placement. The strong and independent effect of shelter care placement over and above that of health problems and age, however, suggests that it may be wise to increase efforts to avoid shelter care placement whenever possible. The strong effect of initial kinship care placement in decreasing the odds of group care placement (at least in the short run) indicates that these families may be more willing than other foster parents to cope with the types of emotional and behavioral problems that often result in a child's placement in group care. Alternatively, the overall stability of kinship care relative to other placements regardless of child characteristics may account for the decreased likelihood of group home placement.

One of the most noteworthy findings of this study concerns the changing age distribution of the group home population. An increasing number of very young children are being placed in group homes, and their stays in group care are not brief. Over one-half of the infants placed initially in group homes are spending over 6 months in these facilities before going home or being placed elsewhere. Group home care does not offer a young child consistent parenting and should be used briefly and as a last resort. This is not the practice in California.

Simply put, group care is not the optimal environment for the care and development of very young children; the concept harkens back to the orphanages and institutions of the nineteenth century and does not speak well of our current priorities. In the past several years, however, the number of infants in group care in California has grown significantly. It is estimated that approximately 1,100 infants who entered foster care during the study period were initially placed in group homes. More broadly, over 2,000 foster children who were under 4 years old at entry to foster care were initially placed in group homes during the study period.

A thorough examination of alternatives to group home care for young children is needed. Pilot programs to divert children and youths from shelter care into specialized foster care or kinship care may reduce later group home placements. However, in spite of increased efforts to avoid group home placement for children and youths who could benefit from more familylike settings, it is unlikely that the ongoing debate about the appropriateness of group home care will be resolved through the elimination of these placement resources. There still appears to be a large number of foster children who will continue to need the structured setting of a group home.

Summary of Key Findings and Recommendations Regarding Entrance to Group
Care

Finding	Recommendation
1a. In general, older age at entry (ages seven and over), the presence of health problems, and placement for reasons other than abuse or neglect (particularly voluntary placements), increase the odds that a child will enter group care during their first placement.	1a. Some children entering foster care are best served by group settings. On the other hand, the potential of specialized foster care to help these often-troubled youth in dealing with their emotional difficulties has not been fully explored. Increased efforts should be made to make these more family-like settings available to youth entering foster care.
1b. Older youth who are voluntarily placed in foster care and who have mental, emotional, or physical health problems are more likely to initially enter group care than any other type of placement.	1b. Research is needed to assess the interaction between child (e.g., child's age and health problems) and child/family (removal reason) characteristics on initial entrance to group care.
1c. The interactions between referral reason, age, and health problems with respect to entry into group care are significant. They need to be better understood before clear practice and/or policy implications will become apparent.	
2a. In general, as a child's age at entry into foster care increases, the likelihood that he or she will enter group care after initial placement increases.	2a. Placement workers need to put increased emphasis on assessing the appropriate level of care for youth entering foster care.
2b. A child or youth who is labeled emotionally disordered by his or her social worker is more likely than a child with organic problems, physical problems, or no health problems, to enter group care after placement in another setting.	2b. Efforts need to be redoubled to develop resources to help care for emotionally-disturbed children and youth in family-like settings, including kinship care. In many cases the availability of such resources could eliminate the need to move a child from a family home to a group care setting.

2c. Initial placement also plays a strong role. Placement in a relative's home significantly decreases the odds of later group home placement compared to placement in a nonrelative foster home. Initial placement in a small family home or county shelter has the greatest effect in increasing the odds of subsequent group home placement.

2c. The strong and independent effect of shelter care placement in increasing the odds of future group care placement suggests that it may be wise to increase efforts to avoid shelter care placement whenever possible. More in-depth research is needed to clarify this relationship.

3a. Increasing numbers of infants and children under five are entering group care.

3b. Contrary to anecdotal reports, the stays of these youngsters in group care are not brief. Over half of the infants placed initially in group homes are spending in excess of six months in these facilities before going home or being placed elsewhere.

3a. Group care is not a developmentally-appropriate setting for infants and very young children, except for children with extreme health problems. A thorough examination of alternatives to group home care for young children is needed. Resources should be directed towards the creation of an adequate number of family-like placements for the large number of very young children entering the foster care system.

NOTES

1.   Unless otherwise cited, all statements regarding the foster care population in California are based on unpublished data from California's Foster Care Information System (FCIS).

2.   We had some difficulty distinguishing group home placements from treatment foster care placements in our data base when those placements are administered by a group home or residential care agency. The California Department of Social Services ran a comparison between the placement code on the FCIS data base that is the source for the data in our analysis and the Community Care Licensing (CCL) data base used for payment of licensed providers and found 78% agreement on facility type when the facility's license number matched.

7

Time to Adoption

Special-needs adoption is a cornerstone of the Adoption Assistance and Child Welfare Act. Under the provisions of the Act, families are to be provided with every reasonable effort for preservation for up to 2 years and, failing that, are to become eligible to exit foster care via adoption. The nations's success in freeing children for adoption and finding adoptive homes for children in foster care is certainly equivocal. The data indicating the increase in special-needs adoption are not especially telling. The National Committee for Adoption's (1989) 1982 and 1986 surveys suggest a slight decrease in the number of special-needs adoptions—from 14,005 in 1982 to 13,568 in 1986 (a 3% decline). The Voluntary Cooperative Information System (VCIS) reports that between 17,000 and 19,000 children were adopted from foster care in 1986 (with a larger number still awaiting an adoptive placement). Other evidence of a substantial increase in special-needs adoption is the steep increase in the federal cost of participation in the Adoption Assistance Program (AAP) that grew from less than $400,000 in FY 1981 to an estimated $144,000,000 in 1991 (U.S. Committee on Finance, 1990). Between 1987 and 1990, the average number of children receiving adoption assistance has nearly doubled from 69,799 to 132,040. California data indicate that 3,424 special-needs children were adopted in 1991–1992 as compared to 1,438 between 1980 and 1981 (a 138% increase).

Although the bulk of evidence indicates a significant growth in special-needs adoption, the hopes of child welfare specialists and adoption advocates that special-needs adoption would dramatically reduce the foster care census have not been met. The pathway from foster care to adoption is little understood, without such an understanding, constructive changes are certain to be overlooked, and mistakes likely to be made. We know something about the children who wait. Evidence is consistent that more of the children waiting for adoption are older and more likely to be African American than the children who were adopted (U.S. Committee on Finance, 1990: National Committee for Adoption, 1989; Massachusetts Department of Social Services, 1992). Research has generally not addressed the more dynamic aspects of that process or been able to determine which combinations of factors increase or reduce the likelihood of adoption.

Time limits and adoption subsidies were the fundamental foster care reforms intending to hasten the final disposition of a foster care career and result in a permanent case plan at the earliest point. When appropriate, adoption is the preferred choice for such permanent arrangements with long-term foster care reserved primarily for children whose characteristics (e.g., age, disabilities, behavior) render adoption unlikely. If adoption is to occur, that determination should be made within 18 months. In California, the time limits are 6 months less (i.e., 12 months is the expected time for the permanency planning decision, and 18 months is the outside time limit). In either case, adoptive placements can often be made well before 2 years, as evidence suggests that efforts to reunify a child with his or her parents will most often either succeed or fail in far less than 2 years (Goerge, 1990; see also Chapter 5).

Time limits for permanency planning decisions were initially developed with the primary concern of avoiding prolonged periods of uncertainty for children who enter foster care. Although recent years have witnessed a variety of strategies to prevent placement into foster care, 636,000 children were placed in foster care during federal FY 1991 (Tatara, in press). The initial hope was that almost every child who could not be permanently reunified with parents would be considered for adoption, another permanent family home, and that many would be adopted. As experience with permanency planning has accumulated, however, the low likelihood that adoption will occur has become clearer. On the whole, adoption provides an exit from foster care for less than 10% of the children who enter foster care (Barth & Berry, 1988b; Finch, Fanshel, & Grundy, 1986; McMurty & Lie, 1992). Many barriers to adoption exist, but one of them is certainly the aging of children prior to placement. As children get older, it is harder to find adoptive families for them and harder to keep them adopted (Barth & Berry, 1988b). For example, in 1989, fewer than 20% of all agency adoptions in California were of children older than 3 years old at the time of entry into foster care. Researchers consistently conclude that the older children are at the point of eligibility for adoption, the less likely they are to be adopted and stay adopted (Barth & Berry, 1988b; Finch, Fanshel, & Grundy, 1986; McMurty & Lie, 1999). In essence, adoption delayed is adoption denied.

Whereas many studies have considered the length of time that children stay in foster care (e.g., Benedict, White, & Stallings, 1987; Goerge, 1990; Jenkins, et al., 1983), few have considered the time to the specific outcome of adoption. Finch, Fanshel, and Grundy (1986) studied exits to adoption for a cohort of more than 20,000 foster children who were in foster care in 1974 over the subsequent 2 years. Among children with an adoption plan in 1974, just 13.9% were adopted in the subsequent 2 years. They clearly showed that the age of the child at entry into care and the length of time in care were strongly and negatively associated with the probability of exiting via adoption. Among the children who entered care before 1974, 25% were adopted within the 2-year study period. This indicates that adoption is the outcome for approximately 7% of all the children in their sample. In the cohort sample, Caucasian children had a greater probability of being adopted, and children placed because of neglect or abuse were less likely to be adopted than children placed for other reasons.

McMurty and Lie (1992) considered adoption as one of competing exits from foster care of children placed between the start of 1979 and the end of 1984. They ended data collection on the children as of the end of 1986. Less than 10% exited foster care via adoption. They did not confirm that African-American children were slower to make progress toward adoption but did report that every additional year of age at entry into foster care reduces the likely of an adoptive placement.

A number of strategies have been developed to facilitate the permanent plan of adoption. "Legal risk adoption," or "fost-adoption," has grown in use from its once controversial origins. Fost-adoption involves the placement of children into foster homes with the explicit intention of adoption if reunification of the child with the birth parent fails. Foster parents and adoptive parents have overlapped since the dawning of foster care in the United States. As foster care became more formalized and regulated by agencies, foster parents began to be considered a resource for crisis intervention and foster care workers began to avoid placing children in the homes of foster parents who wanted to adopt a child (Rathburn, 1944; Proch, 1982). This view was initially supported by the courts that sometimes demanded that the child be moved to another foster home in order to preserve this sanction against foster parents as adoptive parents.

The modern reemergence of fost-adopt placements is described by Hegarty (1973), Gill (1975), and Meezan and Shireman (1985). The justifications of this program were twofold: that the younger the child was placed in a permanent home, the more likely the child would be adopted and the more likely the child would experience fewer placement moves. Although numerous investigations have considered the characteristics of foster parents who adopt children and the dynamics of the fost-adopt program, none has explicitly compared the timeliness of adoption for children in the fost-adopt program compared to other children. Nor has significant attention been given to the characteristics of children who are adopted versus those of children who remain in foster care and which child characteristics are associated with the timeliness of transitions within the adoption process for children who are ultimately adopted. Reforms in practices and policies can be judged against their capacity to improve the timeliness of adoptions, especially for children who currently have the slowest transitions to adoption. To accomplish these ends, differentials in timing must be known.

In this chapter we examine the effect of family, child, and foster care characteristics on the likelihood that foster children will be adopted and of the timeliness of transitions that take place in the movement toward adoption. This involves three substudies. First, factors affecting the likelihood of being adopted are considered, using a stratified sample of all children entering foster care in California in 1988 and early 1989. The second issue explored is the effect of child characteristics on the odds that a child remains in foster care for a long time before an adoption agreement is signed between the adoptive parent(s) and an adoption agency. To the extent that a relatively quick move to a permanent placement is a goal of the CWS, this analysis indicates how well this goal is achieved for the children who are eventually adopted and what child characteristics impede this goal. The third analysis considers the time it takes for an adoption agreement to be legalized by the superior court. An adoption agreement is signed by an adoptive family and the placement agency at the time a child is placed for adoption. The court then gives its stamp of approval before the adoption is considered final. This is the moment when the child assumes rights of inheritance and the family assumes total responsibility for the child. Although nearly all relinquishment adoptions are ultimately legalized, the amount of time that it takes for this to occur varies considerably. An understanding of the factors associated with these delays might facilitate efforts to speed finalization.

We seek to determine contributors to a child's speedy adoption. The samples and analytic strategies used for this determination are each described in detail.

ODDS OF ADOPTION

All the children entering foster care in California between January 1988 and May 1989 were selected from a large data set that includes the current histories and placement histories of more than 80,000 children who entered care between January 1988 and June 1991 (the UCB-FC Database).

Whereas approximately 39% of the children entering foster care between January 1988 and June 1989 went home by May 1991, 2.9% were adopted. All children who entered foster care between January 1988 and May 1989 and who were adopted by May of 1991 (between 2.0 years and 3.5 years later, $n = 864$), are compared to a random sample of children who entered at the same time and did not return home or get adopted ($n = 1,754$). The initial analysis considers the characteristics and time to adoption of those children who were adopted and compares them to those who were not. The case information available from the FCIS data set is discussed in Chapter 5. To accomplish this end we have constructed a logit model with the dependent variable being the odds that a child who entered foster care during the specified one and a half year period was adopted by the time of data collection.

An attempt to describe the effects of various explanatory variables on a dichotomous dependent variable (i.e., whether or not a foster child is adopted or whether or not a foster child's adoption took place before or after a particular point) requires the use of different statistical methods from the ordinary least-squares (OLS) regression or analysis of variance models most often used in child welfare research. The preferred approach for the analysis of the effect of explanatory variables on a dichotomous dependent variable is the creation of a logit or logistic regression model using maximum-likelihood methods. A logit model, described in Chapter 6, is the approach employed for the analyses of the odds of adoption and of the timeliness of adoption agreements. The value of this approach to child welfare researchers is its ability to compute odds ratios that indicate the likelihood of the outcome—in this case, adoption—given case characteristics.

A consideration of the problems involved in the analysis of the association between explanatory factors and the length of time between adoption and adoption legalization requires strategies for analyzing events that have not yet occurred at the time the data are collected (Allison, 1984; Tuma & Hannan, 1984). In the present example, approximately 13.4% of the children in the study had not had their adoptions legalized at the time of the study. The event times for these children are censored in that we do not know their true value, only that they occurred after a particular point in time. Survival analysis, discussed in Chapter 4, provides methods for dealing with censored data. Although parametric and partially parametric regression methods have been developed for use with event-history data, the present analysis relies on nonparametric methods derived from Kaplan-Meier estimates.

Preliminary analysis of the UCB-FC data focused on the bivariate relationships between a number of explanatory variables and adoption. The first result of this analysis was the decision to reduce the sample to only those children who were 7 years or younger at entry into foster care. Children older than this represented less than eight percent of the adopted group (n = 66) and appear to be adopted for idiosyncratic reasons that are not well represented by the variables in the database. On the other hand, the remaining sample still contains a large number of older child adoptions and can be usefully examined with the variables at our disposal. The reduced sample had 798 foster children who were adopted and 1,131 foster children who were not reunified or adopted during the study period. Table 7.1 illustrates the bivariate relationships including the strength of the association between any particular factor and adoption. Child's age at entry into foster care, ethnicity, facility of initial placement, preplacement preventive services, and AFDC-eligibility status are all significantly related in varying degrees to whether or not a child is adopted out of foster care in his or her first years in care. The following characteristics appear, at first glance, to play the strongest roles in decreasing the odds that a child will be adopted:

Being over 1 year old at entry to foster care
Being initially placed in a facility other than a nonrelative foster home, particularly a kinship home
- Being African American or of "other ethnicity" (primarily Asian American or Native American)—grouped together because of their similar effects on the odds of adoption
- Coming from an AFDC-eligible family
- Coming from a family that received either services or no preplacement preventive services at all

Referral reason seems to have a relatively weak relationship to adoption, with children placed for reasons other than neglect (primarily physical or sexual abuse) faring slightly worse. On the other hand, gender, health problems, and whose home the child was removed from appear to have no effect on the odds that a child will be adopted.

A logit model was developed in order to examine simultaneously the effect on the odds of adoption of all five explanatory factors that exhibited both statistically and substantively significant effects (i.e., age, facility of initial placement, ethnicity, AFDC-eligibility status, and preplacement preventive services). Table 7.2 shows the results of the final model. Of particular interest is the final column that lists the effect of each parameter on the odds of adoption. (Because of the case-control sampling method, the intercept term is not directly interpretable.) All the main effects of the five variables, as well as four sets of interaction terms, contribute significantly to the model. Only interaction terms that were statistically significant at $p < .10$ are listed in the table.

Table 7.1. Adoption Status for Matched Sample

	Adopted		Still in Foster Care				
	N	%	N	%	χ^2	Phi	P
Age							
Less than 1	573	54	495	46	158.2	.29	.001
1 thru 3	159	30	367	70			
4 thru 6	66	20	269	80			
Gender							
Female	400	41	570	59	.01	.003	.91
Male	398	41.5	561	58.5			
Ethnicity							
African-American/							
Other	154	21	565	79	204.68	.33	.001
Caucasian	467	57	349	43			
Hispanic	177	45	217	55			
Facility							
Foster Home/Other	675	51	649	49	166.77	.29	.001
Group Home	26	33	53	67			
Kin or Guardian	97	18	429	82			
Removal Reason							
Abuse/Other	110	35	207	65	6.95	-.06	.008
Neglect	688	43	924	57			
Removed (From)							
Father/Other	23	31	51	69	5.55	.05	.06
Mother	676	41	966	59			
Parents	99	46	114	54			
Poverty							
AFDC-Eligible	382	35	700	65	37.35	-.14	.001
Not Eligible	416	49	431	51			
Preplacement							
ER	669	48	733	52	85.28	.21	.001
FM/None	129	24	398	76			
Health							
Health Problems	47	50	47	50	3.03	.04	.08
No Health Problems	751	41	1084	59			

The directions of the main effects on the odds of adoption of the explanatory variables are essentially the same as those found in the earlier bivariate analyses, although the logit model makes the relative effect of each level of a variable more easily interpretable. All effects with

Table 7.2. Estimated Effects of Foster Child Characteristics on the Odds that a Child Will Be Adopted

Variable	Log-Odds Coefficient	Standard Error	Approximate p-value	Effect on Odds
Intercept	−1.138	.141	.000	—
Age at Entry to Care				
Less than 1 year	.774	.169	.000	2.168
1 to 4 years	−.276	.195	.155	.759
4 to 7 years	−.498	.229	.030	.608
Initial Facility Type				
Group Home	.038	.260	.883	1.039
Kin or Guardian	−.694	.164	.000	.500
Foster Home/Other	.656	.146	.000	1.927
Ethnicity				
African-American/ Other −1.065	.166	.000	.345	
Caucasian	.595	.148	.000	1.813
Hispanic	.470	.180	.009	1.600
AFDC Eligibility				
AFDC Eligible	−.259	.058	.000	.772
Not Eligible	.259	—	—	1.296
Preplacement Preventive Services				
ER only	.184	.072	.010	1.202
FM or No Services	−.184	—	—	.832
Age by Facility Type				
Less than 1 year and Group Home	.535	.311	.085	1.707
Less than 1 year and Kin/Guardian	−.483	.193	.013	.617
1 to 4 years and Kin/Guardian	.403	.216	.063	1.496
Age by Preplace				
Less than 1 and ER	.216	.089	.015	1.241
4 to 7 and ER	−.270	.114	.018	.763

continued

a value greater than 1 multiplicatively increase the odds of adoption by that amount, and effects of less than 1 decrease the odds similarly. The main effects can be thought of as the effect on the odds of adoption played by any particular characteristic, all other things being equal. For example,

Table 7.2. Continued

Variable			Effect	
	Log-Odds Coefficient	Standard Error	Approximate p-value	on Odds
Facility Type by Ethnicity				
Group Home				
and Caucasian	−.515	.275	.061	.598
Kin/Guardian				
and Caucasian	.593	.177	.001	1.809
Kin/Guardian				
and Hispanic	−.588	.216	.006	.555
Ethnicity by AFDC				
Eligibility				
African-American				
and AFDC Eligible	−.187	.083	.024	.829

Note:

Goodness of Fit Statistics for the Model

Pearson chi-square   = 43.65; $df = 78$; $p = .999$

Likelihood ratio chi-square = 74.43; $df = 78$; $p = .594$

the last column of Table 7.2 indicates that, other things being equal, entering foster care under 1 year of age more than doubles a child's odds of being adopted but that being placed initially in a kinship home cuts the odds by one-half.

Of course, things are seldom equal, and the logit model also makes the interactions between the explanatory variables explicit in a way that is not apparent from bivariate analyses. All of the explanatory variables in the model interact with at least one other variable in terms of their effects on the odds of adoption. These interactions suggest the following conclusions.

Infants placed in group care are adopted at a slightly faster rate than this combination of factors would otherwise suggest. Conversely, placement of infants with relatives negates much of the advantage that these very young entrants to foster care have in terms of their potential for adoption. On the other hand, the slightly older group (ages 1 to 4 at entry) when placed initially with relatives fare better than either the infants or older children similarly placed.

The relationship between preplacement preventive services and later adoption is significant but relatively small and hard to interpret. Children who came from families who received only ER services were adopted at a higher rate than children whose families received either no services or FM services prior to a stay in foster care. Part of the problem in interpreting this finding stems from a lack of information regarding why certain families receive no services. Something about these families or children that is not accounted for by the other factors we examined decreases the odds that these children will be adopted. It may be that these are the most damaged or traumatized children entering foster care, which could explain their relatively quick removal from home with no services being provided. These children might also disproportionately exhibit developmental, behavioral, physical, or emotional problems that would lead to a decrease in their odds of adoption. The reason for the relatively lower likelihood of adoption among children whose families received FM services may be more straightforward. The families of these children might remain more involved with their child's foster care experience than other parents and could thereby either slow down or inhibit the process of finding an adoptive home for the child. Although much lip service is given to the notion that reasonable efforts, when they fail, provide an opportunity to document the need for an alternative permanent plan, such as adoption, we have no evidence that in-home services expedite later parental rights terminations.

The interaction between preplacement and age is also hard to explain. If the hypothesis that children from families who received ER services are somewhat less damaged than those who received no services is correct, then it might also be the case that very young entrants to foster care (e.g., under 1-year-old) who are also less-damaged are particularly likely to be adopted. Hence, the increase in odds for this group is 1.241. Conversely, the decrease in the odds of adoption for older children who received services suggests that increasing age may overcome any advantage derived from being less damaged or traumatized prior to foster care placement.

The effect of the interaction between ethnicity and initial placement type on the odds of adoption is striking. Being placed initially in a group home cuts the odds of adoption by one-half for Caucasian children but has little or no effect for all others. The effect of initial placement in relative care for Caucasian children is the opposite of that for Hispanic children. Although in general the effect of relative placement is to decrease significantly the odds of adoption, for Caucasian children the effect is quite small (a decrease of only about 10%). For Hispanic children the effect is much greater, decreasing the odds of adoption by nearly three-fourths.

Last, although being either poor (AFDC eligibility) or African American or of other ethnicity decreases the odds of a child's adoption, the combination of these two factors has an even greater effect, decreasing the overall odds by another 17%.

Examination of Table 7.2 allows for many comparisons between the relative effects of various factors on the predicted odds of adoption. For example, after averaging the effects of all other variables, the model predicts *that the odds of adoption for a child who enters foster care under 1 year of age are over three times that of a child who enters care between the age of 4 and 7*. Similarly, a Caucasian child's predicted odds of adoption are five times those of a child from the African-American or other ethnicity category. It is important to keep in mind when making these comparisons that any particular one-way comparison (e.g., one ethnic group compared to another) might obscure an important interaction with another factor.

ODDS OF TIMELY ADOPTION AND ADOPTION LEGALIZATION

The analysis of the likelihood of a timely adoption is based on a sample of 496 children drawn from 1,369 adoptions in the California Long-Range Adoption Study. The adoptive parents of 2,589 adoptive placements made between mid-1988 and mid-1989 were asked by their social workers about their interest in participating in a longitudinal study of adoptions. A total of 2,238 families (86%) agreed to participate. Questionnaires were mailed to all families (n = 2,058) with usable addresses, and 1,268 families (62%) returned questionnaires.

The sample of 496 children included those in the CLAS data set who were placed in foster care and whose adoptive families entered into an adoption agreement under the Relinquishment Adoption Program of California. (The other children in the sample were typically independent agency or intercountry adoptions.) *Relinquishment adoption* refers to the placement by a licensed adoption agency (public or private) of children who have been (1) voluntarily relinquished by their natural parent or parents to the adoption agency for adoptive placement; or (2) freed for adoption by the involuntary termination of parental rights by legal action. From this point on in the paper, *adoption* refers to the signing of an adoption agreement, while *legalization* refers to the court order approval of the adoption. Since the examination of the two aspects of adoption timeliness require different analytic tools, they are dealt with separately in the discussion of data analysis.

In the mailed CLAS questionnaire, parents were asked a multitude of questions about the child and the adoptive family. The instrument tapped child and parent information (health, problems, demographics); family constellation and support; the decision to adopt; knowledge of child's background; knowledge of birth family; the adoption process; the child's placement (including services and preparation); the child's school performance (if school-age); a child's Problem Behavior Inventory; foster parent adoptions; postplacement services; and satisfaction with the adoption. Questionnaire data was matched with state data files to provide background and demographic information on each of the adoptive families.

Odds of Timely Adoption

After an initial examination of the distribution of elapsed times between foster placement and adoption, the dependent variable of interest chosen for the first part of the analysis was a dichotomous variable representing those children who had been adopted within 2 years of entering foster care and those who remained in foster care for more than 2 years prior to adoption. Permanency planning asserts that children will be provided with a permanent adoptive home as the priority as quickly as possible after reunification is ruled out. Over one-third of the adoption agreements for the children in this study sample were signed less than 2 years after the child entered foster care, indicating that relinquishment adoptions can be done in a timely manner. However, the rest of the children remained in foster care for more than 2 years, with 15% waiting longer than 4 years before an adoption agreement was signed.

The first step in building a logit model for the odds of timely adoption was a preliminary examination of a range of the demographic, behavioral, and familial characteristics of the children in the sample. The question of interest was whether or not these characteristics had an impact on the probability that a child in the sample would still be in foster care 2 years after initial placement.

The bivariate relationship between a number of explanatory variables and the dependent variable E (dichotomized for children who remained in foster care more than 2 years prior to adoption and for children who were adopted sooner) were examined for potentially strong associations. Explanatory variables included the child's gender, ethnicity, and age; exposure to various types of abuse or neglect; fost-adopt status; behavioral problems; natural parents' education; adoptive parents' ethnicity and education; adoptive parents' income and employment status; whether the adoptive parent was single or related to the child; whether the adoptive family received an adoption subsidy; whether or not the child had medical problems; and in utero exposure to drugs or alcohol. The drug-exposure items asked parents for an indication of whether their child had been prenatally exposed to drugs or alcohol. Children were classified as substance exposed if parental responses to all three of the questions resulted in an indication of known prenatal substance exposure. A total of

190 (38.3%) children were classified as substance exposed. The remaining 306 (61.7%) children were classified as not substance exposed.

Most striking about this initial screening process was the fact that several characteristics that might be expected to influence the timeliness of adoption (i.e., gender, ethnicity, drug exposure, behavioral and medical problems) were not significantly associated with the dependent variable. The items found to be related to timely adoption were exposure to sexual abuse; exposure to physical abuse; exposure to neglect; a history of multiple foster care placements; severe behavioral problems; age at entry into foster care; and whether or not the social worker and foster family planned that the child would be adopted by the family at the time the child was placed in foster care.

Although these significant associations are noteworthy, entering them all into a logit model would result in a cross-classification table with 512 cells, which, given the size of the sample, would not result in very reliable maximum-likelihood estimates of the parameters of the model. Fortunately, it was possible to reduce the number of variables by a further process of examination. Entering the variables regarding abuse or neglect status and the variable indicating severe behavioral problems into a preliminary logit model of timely adoption showed that the effect of the behavioral characteristic was negligible when the effects of the other variables were taken into account. The behavioral item was then dropped from the analysis. Similarly, an examination of the effects of the abuse and neglect variables revealed that these characteristics both increased to a similar degree the odds that a child remained in foster care more than 2 years without adoption. To the extent that these items shared a similar empirical relationship to timely adoption and both represent the legal grounds for involuntary termination of parental rights, they were grouped into one variable.

The analysis was thereby restricted to the following four explanatory variables (A, B, C, and D) and one dependent variable (E). Their distributions are shown in Table 7.3.

Abuse and neglect (A). Abuse or neglect status represents whether or not a child was involuntarily removed from his or her parents because of abuse, neglect, or abandonment. $A = 1$ indicates that the child was removed for one of these reasons, and $A = 0$ indicates that he or she was not.

Placement history (B). History represents whether or not a child has a history of multiple homes. $B = 1$ indicates that a child has such a history, and $B = 0$ indicates that he or she does not.

Age (C). Age is a polytomous indicator of the age of the child when he or she was first placed in foster care. $C = 1$ indicates that the child

Table 7.3. Adoption Timeliness

	Remained in Car over 2 years		Adopted				
	N	%	N	%	χ^2	Phi	P
Abused/Neglected							
No	23	17	113	83	185.49	.61	.001
Yes	297	82.5	63	17.5			
Multiple Homes							
No	151	49	157	51	87.77	.42	.001
Yes	167	91	17	9.2			
Age at Entry to Foster Care							
Under 1 month	42	27	113	73	149.56	.55	.001
1 month–1 year	113	72	43	28			
Over 1 year	164	90	19	10			
Planned Adoption							
No	190	74	68	26	19.41	.20	.001
Yes	129	55	107	45			

was under 1 month old. $C = 2$ indicates that the child was more than 1 month but less than 1 year old. $C = 3$ indicates that the child was more than 1 year old. (Analysis of the effect of age on the probability of timely adoption indicated that the effect of age was essentially the same for all children over 3 years of age. This allowed us to create one category for this group.)

Fost-adopt (D). Represents whether or not the child's adoption by the foster family was planned at the time of the child's placement in the home. $D = 1$ indicates that the adoption was planned, and $D = 0$ indicates that it was not planned.

Stay in foster care past 2 years (E). An indictor of the timeliness of a child's move from foster care to adoption, given that the child was eventually adopted. $E = 1$ indicates that a child remained in foster care more than 2 years prior to adoption, and $E = 0$ indicates that the foster placement period was shorter than 1 year. The use of the three dichotomous variables and the one polytomous variable to predict E resulted in a cross-classification table with 48 cells—a more acceptable number given the sample size for the study.

Maximum-likelihood estimates for the parameters of the saturated logit model of E that includes A, B, C, and D, were computed (see Table 7.4).

Examination of the standardized values of the log-odds coefficients, although not an infallible method, suggested the elimination of terms from the saturated model in order to create a more parsimonious unsaturated model. (Note that the elimination of a term from the model implies that the parameter for that term is set to zero in the additive log-odds model of *E*, not that the variable has been eliminated from the model itself.) This "abbreviated stepwise procedure" (Goodman, 1978, p. 158) suggested that all of the four-way terms, all of the three-way terms, and the two-way terms *AD*, *BC*, *BD*, and *CD* could all be set to zero in the model without seriously undermining the fit of the model.

Thus, the final model included all main effects, the interaction between abuse status and placement history, and the interaction between abuse status and age. The small parameter estimate for the effect of level 2 of variable *C* (over 1 month but less than 1 year old) led us to simplify the model further by setting it to zero. This model is parsimonious while fitting the data well.

For purposes of illustrating the properties of the final model in more intuitively appealing terms, the log-odds parameter estimates were converted into equivalent parameters pertaining to the effect of the explanatory variables (*A*, *B*, *C*, and *D*) on the *odds* of a child being in foster care after 2 years (variable *E*) (see Table 7.5). The odds models is a *multiplicative* model as opposed to the log-odds model, which is additive.

Other things being equal, the expected odds of the adopted child remaining in foster care more than 2 years prior to adoption are 1.702 to 1. This corresponds to the effect of the general mean on the odds pertaining to *E*. A history of abuse, neglect, or abandonment increases the odds by a factor of 3. A history of multiple homes increases the odds multiplicatively by 2.3 times. An age of 1 year or older at entry into foster care more than triples the odds that a child will remain in care more than 2 years prior to adoption. On the other hand, the fact that an adoption is planned at the time of foster placement or that a child is under 1 month of age at placement both decrease the odds that a child will stay in foster care more than 2 years. Table 7.5 also illustrates the effects of interaction between variables *A*, *B*, and *C* with respect to the odds pertaining to the dependent variable. The interaction terms suggest that when more than one of the risk factors are found together, the overall effect is less than would be expected by simply multiplying each individual effect together. The child with the greatest risk of prolonged stay in foster care without adoption is the child entering foster care after age 1 (*C* = 3); with a history of abuse, neglect, or abandonment (*A* = 1); a history of multiple homes (*B* = 1); and who did not have an adoption planned at the time of their final foster care placement (*D* = 0). The predicted odds that a child described by these characteristics (which requires including the interaction terms of

Table 7.4. Estimation of Main and Interaction Effects in the Saturated Model Estimates of Parameters*

Parameter*		Log-Odds Coefficient	Z-Value
General Mean		.524	2.440
A		1.104	5.133
B		.839	3.901
C	1	−1.133	−3.411
	2	.081	.301
	3	1.052	3.418
D		−.373	−1.736
AB		−.438	−2.039
AC	1	.376	1.133
	2	.070	.263
	3	.447	−1.453
AD		.077	.358
BC	1	.178	.536
	2	−.129	−.479
	3	−.048	−.159
BD		.159	.742
CD	1	−.157	−.473
	2	−.012	−.047
	3	.169	.552
ABC		−.083	−.251
	1	.324	1.203
	2	−.240	−.781
ABD	3	−.241	−1.121
ACD	1	−.350	−1.056
	2	.135	.501
	3	.215	.701
BCD	1	.130	.392
	2	.031	.115
	3	−.161	−.524
ABCD	1	−.275	−.828
	2	.088	.329
	3	.186	.605

* Parameter estimates for all three levels of factors including variable C (age) are included to facilitate comparison of Z-values. Only one parameter estimate, representing the "1" level of the variable, is included for all other factors.

Table 7.5. Estimated Effects of Adopted Children's Characteristics on the Odds of Remaining in Foster Care More Than Two Years Before Adoption

Characteristic	Effect on Odds	
D (General Mean)	1.702	
A = 0	.333	
A = 1 (Abuse/Neglect)	3.007	
B = 0	.427	
B = 1 (Multiple Homes)	2.344	
C = 1 (Less than One Month Old)	.265	
C = 2 (One Month to One Year)	1.000	
C = 3 (Over One Year)	3.773	
D = 0	1.433	
D = 1 (Planned Adoption)	.698	
A equals B	.670	
A not equal to B	1.492	
A = 0 and C = 1	.541	Interaction Terms
A = 0 and C = 3	1.849	
A = 1 and C = 1	1.849	
A = 1 and C = 3	.541	

Note:
Goodness of Fit Statistics for the Model
Pearson chi-square = 13.87; $df = 17$; $p = .676$
Likelihood ratio chi-square = 16. 2; $df = 17$; $p = .508$

$A = 1 \times B = 1$ and $A = 1 \times C = 3$) will remain in foster care for more than 2 years prior to adoption are 23.51 to 1. Similar calculations can be made for adopted children exhibiting other characteristics.

Time to Legalization

In order to compute the survivor function for adopted children "at risk" of having their adoptions legalized, a variable was created that indicated the weeks between adoption and legalization for each child in the sample. The value of this variable for children whose adoption had not been finalized at the time of the study was the amount of time in weeks from adoption to the time of the study. Another variable was created to indicate whether or not the time value for each child was a "censored" value (i.e., the child's adoption had not yet been finalized at the time of the study) or an "uncensored" value. The censored observations are then dealt with differently in the Kaplan-Meier estimation process so as to avoid some biases that would otherwise be introduced by including such incomplete data.

Figure 7.1 shows the survivor function of the transition from "adopted" to "legalized" for the children in this study. It can be seen from the diagram that after a short initial period in which little activity occurs, adoptions are legalized at a fairly steady rate until approximately the first year after adoption, at which point the curve begins to level out gradually. After 89 weeks the survivor function is undefined, because there is no record of a child changing states after this point. The mean survival time computed from these data is biased because the last observation is censored. On the other hand, the Kaplan-Meier estimate of the survivor function does provide unbiased estimates of the percentage of children who experienced a transition at any particular point after adoption, an easily grasped graphic depiction of the process of adoption finalization over time, and a simple method to compare the survivor functions for different populations (e.g., children with differing characteristics).

Tests were conducted to assess the relationship between a number of categorical and continuous variables and the survivor function for children moving from adopted to finalized status. Qualitative explanatory variables included child's gender; child's ethnicity; medical, behavioral, and emotional problems of the child as recorded by the child's social worker; history of abuse or neglect; child's history of living in multiple homes; whether or not the child was drug exposed at birth; single adoptive parent; whether the adoptive parent was related to the child by blood or marriage; and ethnicity of the adoptive parents. Continuous explanatory variables include the age of the child in weeks at adoption; the adoptive family's annual income; the foster care rate received by the family prior to adoption; and the adoption subsidy received by the adoptive family.

None of the continuous variables had a statistically significant effect on the survivor function, and only three of the categorical variables (child's ethnicity, adoptive parents' ethnicity, and the fact that a child had an "adverse parental background") had an effect. Caucasian children made the transition to finalization more quickly than did children of color. Children who were adopted by white parents made the transition more quickly than children adopted by nonwhite parents. Last, the adoptions of children who had an adverse parental background according to their social workers were finalized more quickly than children without that characteristic.

Further analysis indicated that the effect of child's ethnicity interacts with adoptive parents' ethnicity on the survivor function. If a child was Caucasian or adopted by Caucasian parents, they would make the transition from adoption to finalization more quickly than if neither of these characteristics were present. However, Caucasian children adopted by Caucasian parents did not as a group make the transition as fast as would

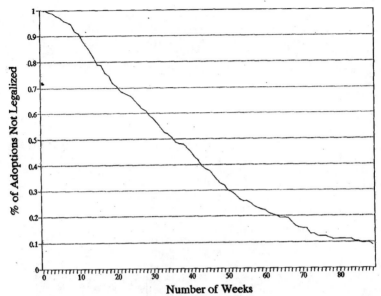

Figure 7.1. Survivor function for adopted children awaiting adoption legalizations.

be expected if the effect of these two factors were independent. Figure 7.2 indicates that children of color adopted by parents of color move to finalization at a slower rate than children with any other combination of characteristics. Two-way comparisons for homogeneity of survivor functions were done between the four groups representing different combinations of child and adoptive parent ethnicities. Of the six possible comparisons, the three that included the group consisting of children of color with adoptive parents of color resulted in test statistics indicating a rejection of the hypothesis of homogeneous survivor functions at the $p < .01$ level. More specifically, in all comparisons, the group consisting of children of color placed with adoptive parents of color had adoptions finalized at a slower rate than any other group. On the other hand, the remaining comparisons between the other three groups did not reject the hypothesis of homogeneous survivor functions between those groups. There are no interactions between adverse parental background and either child's ethnicity or adoptive parents' ethnicity.

In addition to these analyses, we examined the percentage of young children, ages 3 and younger, who were reunified or adopted within four years after initial placement. The overall percentage of young children

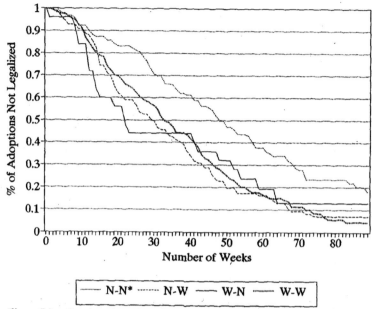

Figure 7.2. Survivor functions for adoption legalization.
Notes:
* N-N: Non-White Children with Non-White Adoptive Parents (n = 119)
N-W: Non-White Children with White Adoptive Parents (n = 97)
W-N: White Children with Non-White Adoptive Parents (n = 25)
W-W: White Children with White Adoptive Parents (n = 221)

who were reunified within 4 years was 46%, and 14% of the children were adopted (see Figure 7.3).

The adoption rates by ethnicity reconfirm our earlier findings—the rate at which African American children are adopted is half the rate at which Caucasian children are adopted and 24% lower than the rate at which Hispanic children are adopted. Perhaps most telling, an African American child is 5 times as likely to still be in foster care as to be adopted after four years, whereas Hispanic children are twice as likely to remain in foster care as to be adopted and Caucasian children are equally likely to still be in foster care as they are to be adopted. This is only partially attributable to the fact that more African American children enter kinship care (which yields lower adoption rates) than other children. Among children who enter nonkinship families, African American children still have an 89% lower adoption rate than Caucasian children but only 11% lower than Hispanic children. A young African American child entering

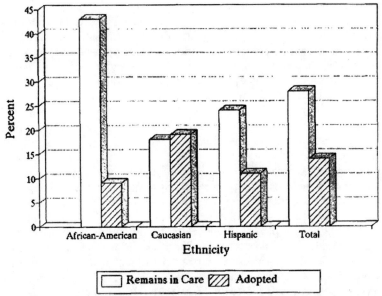

Figure 7.3. Status of children 3 years of age or younger at placement 4 years later.

nonkinship foster care is three times as likely to remain in foster care at four years as to be adopted whereas Hispanic children are 1.5 times as likely to remain in care as be adopted and Caucasian children remain in care and are adopted at roughly equivalent rates.

DISCUSSION

The analysis of the California foster care adoption data confirms some of what may be termed common knowledge in the field of adoption and simultaneously raises some important questions. Not surprisingly, the youngest children seem to have the greatest potential for adoption. Nevertheless, over 8% of the adopted foster children were over 3 years old when they entered care, and over 28% were over 1. There are clearly some families who are interested in adopting somewhat older children. If not adopted, these children face long and costly tenures in foster care. Better mechanisms are needed for identifying children for adoption who are not rapidly placed as infants and who are not likely to be reunified with their birth parent(s).

Unfortunately, although it is not particularly surprising, it is still disturbing that Caucasian children are much more likely to be adopted than African-American children with similar characteristics. Somewhat surprising is the fact that Hispanic children seem to be nearly as likely to be adopted as Caucasian children. Although it is important to increase efforts to find adoptive homes for all adoptable children in foster care, it is crucial that we redouble efforts to find homes for African-American children who are awaiting adoption. It also seems reasonable to emphasize finding adoptive homes for children from poor families. These children, regardless of race, are less likely at present to end up in such a home.

Given the increasing number of young children entering group care, it is disturbing to see that initial placement in group care is associated with a threat to a child's potential for adoption (particularly for Caucasians). The data suggest that increased efforts to avoid institutional placements of young children by placing them in foster care will contribute to an increased likelihood of adoption for these children. The argument is sometimes made that a group home placement facilitates improvements in a child's level of functioning so that they can join an adoptive family. If this process occurs, it apparently takes longer than we were able to measure here. Indeed, any delays in adoptive arrangements would appear to decrease chances of adoption.

On the other hand, initial placement with a relative is associated with a much greater decrease in the odds of adoption for non-Caucasians. This is especially true for Hispanics. The current analysis, however, suggests that differential reunification and adoption rates for different ethnic groups are not simply a reflection of differences in the utilization of kin as a permanent placement. These findings, along with others regarding the ambivalent attitudes of kinship caregivers to adoption (Thornton, 1991) and those that demonstrate a slower reunification rate for children placed with relatives call for a closer look at the effect of the growth of kinship care on the permanency planning process.

The logit model of timely adoption agreements shows that children who are older, who come from unstable backgrounds, or who experience abuse or neglect prior to foster care placement are much less likely than children without these characteristics to be adopted in a timely manner. This suggests that the existing permanency planning time standard for adoption may be unreasonable for such children. At the same time, the fact that these children were all adopted indicates that efforts should continue to be made to find adoptive homes for these supposedly hard-to-place children. Similarly, the evidence that the presence of a plan for foster parent adoption at the time of foster care placement increases the odds of a timely adoption provides support for the continuing development of fost-adoption programs.

The event-history analysis described provides more new questions than answers. It is not altogether clear what is meant by social workers when they say that a child suffers from an "adverse parental background," but it is clear that this characteristic is associated with a more rapid move to adoption legalization. It may be that the natural parents of these children are less likely to be involved at all with their children and thus pose less of an obstacle to quick legal action in completing the adoption process. Further research is necessary to help to clarify this phenomenon.

The other finding of the analysis is more troubling. Given that many of the children in the child welfare services system needing permanent homes are children of color (in California most such children are children of color), it is disturbing that adoptions by parents of color are taking considerably longer than adoptions by Caucasian parents. For example, there is a 13-week difference between the amount of time it takes for 50% of adoptive parents of color to have their adoptions legalized (45 weeks), compared to the amount of time it takes for a similar proportion of Caucasian adoptive parents to have theirs legalized (32 weeks). That difference increases to 22 weeks when one considers the time it takes for 75% of the adoptions to be legalized. Nearly one-half of all adoptive families of color must wait over 1 year to have their adoptions legalized. At a minimum, this suggests that a continued effort be made by child welfare personnel to ascertain the types of support needed for families of color to speed up their adoptions toward legalization (Giles & Kroll, 1991).

The findings that Caucasian parents are typically involved in speedier adoptions regardless of the race of the child is provocative. Whereas this supports the argument that services need to be better tailored for parents of color, it also suggests that Caucasian families can and do provide timely exits from foster care for children of color. This resource deserves more attention as we face growing numbers of young children of color in foster care limbo.

Summary of Key Findings and Recommendations Regarding Time to Adoption

Finding	Recommendation
1. Entering foster care before the age of 1 doubles the odds of being adopted within the first 3.5 years of care.	1. Older child adoptions are still the exception. Recruitment efforts must be redoubled for older children.
2. African-American children are five times less likely to be adopted in the first three and one-half years of care than Caucasian children.	2. African-American children must be provided with more adoption opportunities. Additional recruitment efforts are needed as are more flexible policies that support adoption of African-American children in less idealized homes (especially, homes that do not contain two African-American parents).
3. Overall, children who enter kinship care are one-half as likely to be adopted during the first 3.5 years of care as other children. This effect is far greater for Hispanic children and considerably less for Caucasian children.	3. Kinship foster care should not be seen as a substitute for adoption but must also, under the law, be understood as an option for adoption. The possibility that this law is particularly counter to Hispanic culture deserves exploration.
4. Children entering group home care as their initial placement—especially Caucasian children—are less likely to be adopted within the first 3.5 years of placement.	4. Young children should not be placed in group home care unless absolutely necessary, because placement in familylike settings expedites the permanent placement of adoption.
5. Adoptions by parents of color are taking longer than adoptions by Caucasian parents to be legalized.	5. Additional financial and social service support is needed to ensure that parents of color are well prepared and not financially penalized for pursuing the legalization of their adoptions.

III

Child and Placement Characteristics

8

Specialized Foster Care: A Home for Children With Special Needs

The child welfare system has evolved and changed in part through developments in the research community and also because practitioners have recognized the complex needs of children and families. In previous chapters we have noted increases in the foster care caseload, along with changes in the types of placements in use (i.e., a shift toward greater use of kinship foster care), length of stay in foster care, and the age at which children enter the system.

As the census of children in care has increased, the type of the children served in out-of-home care has changed as well. Although we have just an inkling of evidence about the mental health status of the children in foster care (e.g., Klee & Halfon, 1987; McIntyre & Kessler, 1986), some evidence suggests that certain groups of children coming to care are especially challenging to serve (Fein, Maluccio, & Kluger, 1990; Kamerman & Kahn, 1990). Either due to medical problems that compromise their health or particular behavioral problems that make them unlikely to be served in foster family homes, a new type of service provider has been drawn into the field to care for these especially needy children.

Specialized foster care is an emerging concept that shows promise as an alternative service-delivery model for special-needs children. This new approach in foster care has developed swiftly across the country (Hawkins, Meadowcroft, Trout, & Luster, 1985); in California the introduction of specialized foster care (SFC) has changed the foster care landscape dramatically. In 1984, there were 71 SFC agencies in California, today, that number has doubled to almost 150 agencies across the state. These agencies are licensed to certify and support specialized foster care homes. In 1992 there were approximately 4,354 SFC homes in the state serving about 5,997 children (personal communication, Woolman, 1993).

Specialized foster care is one alternative along a continuum of care. Although specialized foster care is called many things by various professionals (e.g., treatment foster care, therapeutic foster care, professional foster care), for our purposes it will be broadly defined as "specialized," because it aims to address the individual needs of challenging children with particularly complex medical needs and children with elevated behavioral problems. As an alternative to group care, SFC provides a homelike environment for the child. In California, SFC homes can be certified to serve up to six children. However the majority of providers prefer to place three or fewer children in a home. Some of the features that distinguish SFC homes from conventional foster homes across the country are the additional training and support provided to the SFC family, the involvement of the foster parents in case planning, the involvement of the birth parents, and individualized programming for children (Meadowcroft & Trout, 1990; Nutter, Hudson, & Galaway, 1990; Terpstra, 1990; Webb, 1988). Other features include respite care, small caseloads for program staff, and 24-hour on-call availability of social work support (Friedman, 1988; Hudson & Galaway, 1989). Among the more controversial aspects of specialized foster care is the higher board rate offered to these parents. When used as an alternative to group care, specialized foster care can provide a significant cost savings to the state. Nevertheless, as the field grows, professional fostering may begin to usurp the role of conventional foster care. When professional foster care starts to tip the scales in prevalence, age-old concerns arise about the motives that bring families to the foster care profession.

The growth of specialized foster care is partially a result of a crisis in foster family care that must be addressed. A recent study by the General Accounting Office (GAO, 1989) showed that, although the demand for foster care has continued to increase, most states and counties report that the number of available foster homes is sharply declining. This has been explained primarily by the entrance of women into the labor force and higher rates of single parenthood (Kahn & Kamerman, 1990); families that used to provide foster care are now unable or unwilling to offer this service.

We have very little information about the characteristics of the providers still in the field. Lindholm and Touliatos (1978) conducted an extensive study describing the characteristics of foster parents in the United States and Canada. Foster parents in their study were characterized as lower middle-class with a mean education of 12 years and an average annual income of approximately $12,000. Fein, Maluccio and Kluger (1990) also found an average income of $15,000 among long-term foster parents, although the educational background of their foster parents was somewhat higher. Approximately one-third of foster parents were women managing the stresses of poverty and single parenthood (one-fourth of foster parents had incomes below the poverty line). The other two-thirds of foster parents were married, well-rooted in their neighborhoods, and active in a religious community. Studies of kinship foster parents (Meyer & Link, 1990; Thornton, 1987; 1991) also report an older population in which ethnic minorities are heavily represented.

Other than these basic demographic figures, we know that foster parents are a diminishing resource. The GAO's report sheds some light on the reasons for foster parents' flight from the profession. First, foster parents do not experience their work as a profession. Because social workers do not include them as a team member in serving the child, they perceive the social service agency as disrespectful. Second, many foster parents feel that their personal insight and knowledge regarding the child are not valued as they are rarely consulted by the social worker or the juvenile courts for information about the child's progress in care. At the same time, social service workers often neglect providing essential information to the foster parent about the child (Gershenson, Rosewater, & Massinga, 1990). Third, foster parents feel ill-supported in the critical responsibility that they face. Few foster parents ever receive preservice or in-service training that might help to prepare them to serve these challenging youths. As a result, they often feel worn down. Their job is that of a parent, only the population that they serve is far more difficult than the average child. The fact that most foster parents receive little or no respite from the everyday burdens of their job contributes to their exodus from the field.

A factor that also encourages their frustration is the board rate. Foster parents have always received extremely low stipends for the care they provide to children. Although the income is supposed to cover the child's expenses, foster parents often complain that the stipend is insufficient to meet the child's many needs. But there is an historical reason for this minimal pay. Foster parenting has been viewed traditionally as the community's altruistic response to child protection. In anthropological literature, child lending and foster care are referred to as "redistribution" (Korbin, 1991). That is, societies throughout the world have developed social systems with shared responsibility for children. Abused or neglected youths can be "redistributed" to other members of the social network either temporarily or permanently for protection. Several authors (Carson, 1981; Hays & Mindel, 1973; Martin & Martin, 1978; Stack, 1974) have documented the practice of informal foster parenting within the African-American community in the United States. Young (1980) has also pointed to the informal adoption system prevalent within the

Hawaiian community. To pay parents well, and thereby "professionalize" foster care, might diminish the charitable aspect of the work and increase that facet of the job that resembles a businesslike transaction.

Into the heart of this debate falls the profession of specialized foster care. Here, the role of the foster parent has been reconceptualized toward a more professional, better trained, better paid, and more therapeutically oriented business. As the foster care landscape shifts, it is natural to ask: Who are the professional foster parents that provide general care and supervision, moral guidance, direction, and homelike care to these children every day? We have little descriptive information about this new breed of specialized foster parents and about the services that they receive from their parent SFC agency. Hawkins and Breiling (1989) suggest that these programs are only slightly more "intensified versions of regular foster care." But what this means in terms of actual services provided is unclear. In order to begin this exploration, we designed our study as a starting point for the field. Questions put to foster parents included (1) demographic characteristics; (2) reasons for fostering; and (3) the training and services they received from their parent agency. Many of the questions we asked SFC agency administrators centered on the staffing of their agency, including the wages, educational background, length of employment, and ethnicity of employees.

To understand the characteristics of SFC agencies better a cross-sectional mailed survey was distributed to all SFC agencies in the state of California ($n = 103$ as of spring, 1990). This survey included information regarding agency services, training, and SFC staff. Of the agencies surveyed, seven indicated that their primary service centered on adoption rather than foster care, reducing our population to 96 agencies. By these, 48 surveys (a 50% return rate) were completed.

We also conducted a survey of SFC homes across the state. Each agency director received a number of surveys proportional to the number of foster homes they certified. Agency directors were asked to distribute these surveys to a random sample of their foster homes. In total, we asked that 569 foster homes be sampled. However, each agency had ultimate control over the distribution of surveys. Using this method, we received 123 (22%) returned surveys. One should bear in mind that we only received a 50% response rate from the SFC agency survey. In only one case did we receive surveys from foster homes when their parent agency did not complete a survey. This would suggest that perhaps one-half of all of the foster homes we had anticipated surveying never received a questionnaire in the mail. If we can assume that when a SFC agency did not return a survey the foster home survey was never mailed, then our sampling frame is much reduced, and our return rate on foster homes increases to 45%. Unfortunately, there are some unavoidable drawbacks to this sampling method. However, we were unable to contact specialized foster parents in any other way.

We designed the surveys after careful review of the literature (see, for example Cohen, 1986; Fanshel, Finch, & Grundy; 1989a; Fitzharris, 1985; Hulsey & White, 1989; Lawder, Poulin, & Andrews, 1986). Surveys were also reviewed by four prominent residential treatment providers, the president and five board members of the California Association of Foster Parents to confirm the face validity of the measures. Based on their comments, the final surveys were developed and distributed.

WHO IS THE PROFESSIONAL FOSTER PARENT?

About 70% of the SFC parents in this sample were dual parents providing foster care services. Foster parents had lived in their neighborhoods on average for about eight and a half years. Seventy-three percent of the sample owned their own homes, with 24% renting, and only 3% receiving subsidized housing. Their homes were quite large, often with three or four bedrooms, and their income was substantial. The mean household income for our sample of foster parents was approximately $44,000 per year, (median = $38,000). The median income in California in 1990 was $42,700 (Children Now, 1991), so our sample is roughly comparable to the state figures. Ten percent of the sample made $20,000 or less, and only two families' annual incomes fell below $10,000. On the other hand, six families had annual incomes of $100,000 or more. A large proportion of these families' incomes came from work and wages (78%), and only about 10% came from foster care funds. The next largest category of income came from investments. About 60% of foster mothers were employed outside of the home. Among the foster mothers who worked, most were employed full-time. Foster fathers generally worked full-time, with 20% of foster fathers working between 42 and 60 hours per week.

As Figure 8.1 shows, the majority of parents had completed some college. Specialized foster parents were in their mid-40s (foster mothers were, on the average 42.6 years old and foster fathers 44.4 years old). The youngest foster mother in our sample was 20 years old, and the oldest foster father was 80.

Unlike the majority of foster children across the country, most of these foster parents were Caucasian. Over 70% of foster mothers and foster fathers in this sample were Caucasian, 11% of foster mothers were African American, and 6% were Hispanic. The following list provides a description of the characteristics of SFC foster parents compared to children.

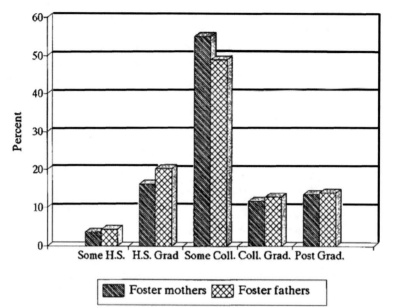

Figure 8.1. Educational level of foster parents.

All foster parents to all children	1.0–1.0
Caucasian foster parents to Caucasian children	1.5–1.0
African American foster parents to African American children	1.0–1.2
Latino foster parents to Latino children	1.0–1.8
Other foster parents to other children	1.0–2.0

WHY BE A SPECIALIZED FOSTER PARENT?

What brings these families to the profession? Parents (61%) stated an overwhelming sense of love and commitment to children. Some of their comments are captured below:

- We wanted to help. Our family has a lot to offer. The desire to do some good and try to make a difference in children's lives.
- We wanted to be part of a solution.
- We wanted to give something back to society.
- My husband is in the Marines. I was lonely at the time and wanted to share my house and life with someone.

- As our older children left home, the house felt empty.
  We lost our daughter. We had two sons and thought it would be nice to take in a girl.

Love of children is also cited as the primary motivation for conventional foster parents (Carbino, 1980). Why, then, did these parents choose to work in specialized foster care rather than foster family care? About one-half of the sample (43%) stated that the additional support provided by their parent agency was pivotal to their decision. One parent summed up the comments of others by stating: "My agency provides more social worker and staff services; closer location; 24 hour-availability; knowledge of local services; close support group; local training, and more money." Although support and training were listed as the most important determinants in the foster care decision (respondents receive about 20 hours of formal training per year), pay was also listed by 23% of the sample. The average monthly rate for each child in care was $610 per month (ranging from $250 to $800 per month). As the average family had three foster children living in the home, parents received approximately $1,800 per month for their service with the SFC agency. (These data would suggest that SFC payments may have accounted for up to 50% of total household income.)

LENGTH OF STAY IN THE FIELD

Because of their love of children and their commitment to their communities, families came to specialized foster care, but what would eventually make them quit? Generally, these parents expected to remain foster parents for the next 8 years. Describing their reasons for eventually leaving the system, their responses fell into a few general categories. Many (40%) expected to leave foster care only after reaching retirement age; at that point they expected to be "too tired, too old, or failing in [their] health." Other responses found among the minority of foster parents (13%) were similar to the following:

- It's too much stress put on my family and myself.
- We're tired of dealing with the "system." We're getting legal custody/guardianship of our babies and then we're getting out.
- It's frustrating when the courts don't listen or want what's in the best interests of the child.

The sample of parents had provided foster care services for approximately 4.8 years. One particularly involved foster parent had been serving children for over 41 years; seventeen foster parents (14%) had been in foster care for 10 years or more. One foster care provider had served over 300 children in her lifetime. On average, however, most foster parents had served approximately 17 children during their tenure in the field. Most specialized foster parents had only worked with their SFC agency for a short time. On average, parents had been with their parent agency for only about one year.

SATISFACTION WITH THE EXPERIENCE

Although some parents expressed frustration with the system, many were satisfied with the experience. Almost one-half of our sample (47%) suggested that they were "very satisfied" with their experience as a foster parent. Another 48% indicated that they were "satisfied.' Only 5% of the sample indicated any dissatisfaction with their experience at all. About 56% of parents said that they were "very satisfied" with the services and support they had been provided by their SFC agency, and 38% were "satisfied." Again, only about 6% of the sample indicated any dissatisfaction with their parent agency.

We thought this cheerful attitude might be influenced by their length of stay in the field; the fresher the foster parent, the happier they would be with the system. However, analysis of variance tests showed that there was no relationship between the length of time as a foster parent and their satisfaction with their foster parent experience. Yet, for reasons that are unclear at this time, parents who had been working in foster care longer showed greater dissatisfaction with the support they received from their SFC agency ($F = 4.26$, $p < .05$). In spite of this finding, we should reiterate that almost 100% of the sample were satisfied in some way with their agency. Therefore, what is being presented is a matter of degree—this is not a group of foster parents who are likely to exit the field due to serious frustrations with their SFC agency.

Part of foster parents' dedication to the field can also be seen in the rate at which these families adopt children in their care. Eighteen percent of the sample suggested that they had previously adopted a foster child, and another 38% indicated that they planned to adopt a foster child in the future.

A LOOK AT SPECIALIZED FOSTER CARE AGENCIES

Social Work Staff

Almost two-thirds of all social workers had a MSW in social work. Another 28% had an MA or MS in the behavioral sciences. Additionally, one-quarter of the social work staff also had LCSW (Licensed Clinical Social Worker) or MFCC (Marriage, Family, Child Counselor) credentials. Almost one-half of the SFC agencies (49%) reported that their social work staff had been employed for more than 2 years. The average social worker received an annual salary of about $30,000.

The caseload per social worker ranged from about 10 to 16 children, depending on the number of sibling groups in service. There were fewer social workers of color to serve this diverse group of children. The following list provides a description of the ethnic breakdown of social workers as related to the ethnicity of children.

All social workers to all children	1.0–2.0
Caucasian social workers to Caucasian children	2.0–1.0
African-American social workers to African-American children	1.0–6.0
Latino social workers to Latino children	1.0–3.0
Other social workers to other children	2.5

On average, these social workers have six telephone contacts and four in person contacts with the foster home per month. Each foster home receives about 8.5 hours of social worker support, 2 of which are spent by social workers specifically with the foster child.

Services to Foster Parents

Foster parents were asked to indicate the types of services they receive from their parent SFC agency. A list of predetermined services were provided in the survey, although parents were also asked to describe other services, as appropriate. The following list outlines the types of supports foster parents indicated receiving:

Support group for foster parents	67.5%
Training for work with special foster care populations	54.6%
Respite care/babysitting	38.3%
Childcare during working hours	5.8%
Other	25.8%

On average, SFC agencies provided two of these special services to parents. Most of the foster parents also received some training from their

SFC agency. Generally, foster parents had received about 22 hours of formal training from their parent agency in the previous year. Other parents received training from local community colleges. About 68% of foster parents received this additional training, which added on average another 24 hours.

In addition to these general kinds of services, foster parents have direct contact with a social worker from their SFC agency. Foster parents were asked several questions regarding the professionalism of their placement workers. On a scale from 0 to 28, with higher numbers indicating greater professionalism, foster parents rated their social workers as a 23.5. (When tested for reliability, the alpha coefficient for this scale was .95.) Similarly, foster parents were asked about their relationship with their social workers. On a scale from $0 - 63$ (higher numbers indicating a closer relationship), foster parents indicated that they felt very positively toward their agency workers ($M = 55.9$; alpha $= .98$).

These social workers are also responsible for the placement of children. We asked foster parents to describe whether or not the placements they received were generally appropriate or inappropriate for their homes. The majority of parents felt that the social workers with whom they had interacted had made "very appropriate" (60%) or "fairly appropriate" (24%) placements to their homes. Foster parents also felt that the information they received about each incoming child was generally "very good" (34%) or "good" (31%).

Although foster parents receive a good deal of training, the children they serve have many needs that must be addressed by other service providers. When asked about the availability and adequacy of health care services for their foster children, foster parents gave modestly positive responses. About one-half of the foster parents said that the availability of health care services was either "very good" or "good." Sixty-four percent said that the quality of these services was either "very good" or "good." Foster parents were somewhat less satisfied with the mental health services available to their children. Over one-half of parents felt positively about the availability of mental health services, and about an equal number of parents felt positively about the quality of services. Only 5% of the sample felt that the quality of mental health services was "very poor."

The Future of Specialized Foster Care in the Social Context

Although specialized foster care is one of the fastest growing segments of the foster care profession, most SFC agency administrators report challenges in locating and recruiting qualified foster parents and social work staff. Conversations with several California SFC administrators reveals that the majority of all SFC parent applicants are screened out; the standards for selection are very high. In this study, one third (33%) of administrators reported that there were "few" or "very few" qualified foster parents currently available. Many (56%) reported that currently there were "some" qualified foster parents. Their outlook for 5 years from now was less optimistic (although the differences were not statistically significant). Fifty percent of the sample was concerned that there will be "few" or "very few" qualified foster parents by 1996.

In spite of these difficulties, however, agency administrators are hopeful about the future of specialized foster care. When asked how they expected SFC agencies to differ in the year 2000, many shared the following thoughts:

> More social workers with lower caseloads and increased resources
> More family-oriented services
> - Higher standards of practice in place; accountability and evaluation measures at all levels
> - Simple bureaucracy and more emphasis on early intervention and care

Forty percent of respondents foresaw increased supportive services for families, and another 36% imagined that the care children received would be more therapeutic in nature. But many of the changes they suggested hinged on a few key factors. About one-third of the sample suggested that foster parents needed more support and recognition for their work if they were to bring the profession to a new level of sophistication. One-third of respondents also said that the way to ensure such positive changes would be through increased funding for services and for payment to foster parents. When asked what factors would make the job of being a foster parent more desirable, a full 62% of specialized foster care administrators said that increased pay was central to accomplishing this goal.

DISCUSSION

Specialized Foster Parents

Although the literature expresses much concern regarding foster parents, including low morale, poor qualifications, and general dissatisfaction with the field, our study indicated that specialized foster parents do not resemble this picture. The foster parent population represented in our sample might be characterized as stable, middle-class, and well educated. A further contributor to these parents' high socioeconomic status was their level of education. This contrasts with past studies of foster family parents (e.g., Carbino, 1980; Gruber, 1978) that generally show an average educational level of high school completion. The SFC parents in our study were in their 40s; these figures do not indicate the "greying" population that many experts believe is characteristic of conventional foster parents. In addition, the parents represented in this sample were a somewhat homogenous group, with a majority of Caucasians. This contrasts sharply with the composition of the specialized foster care population in California, where approximately 52% of children are Caucasian, 25% are African-American, 19% are Hispanic, and the remaining children are either Asian, Pacific Islander, Native American, or of other ethnicity. The unequal distribution of ethnic foster parents to children suggests that children of color will be less likely to be placed in a home with parents of the same race or ethnicity than in homes with Caucasian foster parents. Caucasian children, however, are probably served mostly by Caucasian parents.

The ethnicity of foster parents may also suggest a number of things with regard to the recruitment and selection of specialized foster care providers. The overrepresentation of Caucasian foster parents may be indicative of a larger problem SFC agency administrators face in locating, training, and maintaining well-prepared foster parents of color. It should be noted, however, that although the 11% figure for African-American foster parents is well below their representation among the foster child population, the African-American foster parent population closely mirrors the overall African-American population in the state. The very low percentage of Hispanic foster families, however, shows a serious under-representation of this ethnic group as service providers.

Reasons for Fostering

The foster parents in this sample showed a deep devotion to the children in their care. Their sentiments indicate a high degree of altruism; a commitment to care that is so strong that children are actually taken in and raised by these families. But as Titmuss (1971) has suggested, foster care is one of many "gift relationships" where the motive of altruism may be as powerful as one's self-interest. About 16% of the sample noted that their reasons for becoming a foster parent were related to their personal loneliness and their need to "fill" their home or their lives. Although these comments were less common, they pointed to the reciprocal nature of foster care. Parents' primary motivation for fostering was child centered, but in helping they also expected some personal reward and satisfaction. Money also plays a role in these families' decisions to become specialized foster parents. However, this study did not measure the hierarchy of parents' attitudes toward money and fostering.

Length of Stay in the Field

When specialized foster parents in this sample join the field, they appear to stay for a long time. Their length of stay in the field appears far longer than that indicated by the 60% per year turnover rate reported of conventional foster parents by the GAO (1989). Because this sample represents only those foster parents who have remained in the field, we have no idea whether or not the actual turnover rate is much higher.Yet, their level of dedication to children and to their work was quite pronounced.

Satisfaction

The SFC parents in the sample were pleased with their experience. This result is, of course, in sharp contrast to the literature that suggests a dejected and frustrated foster parent population. Their overall sense of satisfaction may be attributed, in part, to their relationship to their SFC agency as many parents received additional services. Their enthusiasm for the work is likely a combination of factors. Part of it may result from their regular interaction with their SFC agency through the child's social worker. This individual is the regular contact person between the child, the foster parent, the biological parent, and the SFC agency; their contact appeared to be frequent and gratifying.

Services

Some of the specialized foster parents' positive opinions regarding their SFC agency may be related to the types of services they and the children receive from the placing agency. Results from the worker satis-faction scales indicate a very high degree of enthusiasm for the social workers affiliated with the SFC agencies. These ratings probably play a role in foster parents' overall sense of loyalty to their agency and to the profession.

Future Issues

Although SFC parents command rather high payments in comparison to conventional foster parents, many suggested that further increases in payment would be helpful. This is not surprising, as many of the children placed in these homes have extraordinary medical needs and behavioral problems. For these parents, as with conventional foster parents, there is a tension between their commitment to these children and the financial cost of caring.

Becoming a foster parent is a statement of altruism and commitment to one's community. The practice may occur on an individual level, but it belies a recognition that child protection is a civic responsibility. Many families would probably consider fostering, but they are often disinclined to reduce their standard of living. As wages continue to fall behind inflation in many sectors of the economy, families will work harder simply to maintain the status quo.

If demographic forces such as the movement of women into the labor market and the increase in single parenthood reduces the pool of traditional foster parents, then new foster parents need to be encouraged to join the field. Part of the way that good business executives lure the most qualified workers to their organization is by offering quality training and a salary that indicates status, professionalism, and value. Foster care appears to be moving in this direction, too. Does this shift toward greater professionalism suggest that the motives that bring adults to the field will shift as well? That the concern for children will diminish as income rises? That the adults who are drawn to this field will be more profit oriented than child centered?

These questions are long-standing. As far back as the late 1800s, a spirited debate has accompanied the payment of foster parents. Charles Loring Brace, a leader in early foster care once noted that paid fostering altered "an act, which is at once one of humanity and prudence, into one purely of business" (1876, p. 254). To guard against the pure mercenary who might attempt to become a foster parent, reimbursement of costs was always kept at a minimum. Zelizer (1985) also suggests that early foster parent agencies were encouraged to reject foster parents who did not personally provide more for the child than their rate would pay for. In practice, this ethic continues today in conventional foster care. In spite of foster parents' complaints that their payment does not cover the cost of care, there is much resistance to increasing their regular board rate. Careful screening should diminish much of the concern regarding ill-motivated foster parents. Furthermore, as foster parents receive intensive training and regular in-home visits from agency social workers, abuses that might otherwise occur in foster care will be prevented. Evidence to support the notion that specialized foster care may be an effective treatment modality for children is growing (Chamberlain, 1990; Chamberlain & Reid, 1991). This, coupled with the fact that this form of care offers an additional alternative to children with special needs, suggests a continued and perhaps increasing reliance on specialized foster care across the country.

Summary of Key Findings and Recommendations Regarding Specialized Foster
Care

Finding	*Recommendation*
1. Agency administrators report a fair degree of training for their foster parents, in addition to regular social worker support.	1a. Many children served in specialized foster care have special medical and emotional needs. Training that addresses the unique needs of these children better prepares parents for the difficulties they will inevitably face. 1b. Training may also mitigate against early burnout, increasing the likelihood that these foster parents will remain in the field. 1c. Foster parenting is a difficult job, and advice and support are often welcome. In-home social worker support is critical in ensuring that foster parents feel as though they are an important member of a treatment team and that their work matters to the agency and to the child.
2. In addition to social worker support, specialized foster parents value access to additional services in the community.	2. Efforts to increase access to health, mental health, and child care services for these families may have a significant effect on specialized foster parents' attitudes, in addition to the likely positive effects on the child.
3. Although many specialized foster parents report general satisfaction with the field and with their experience, the dissatisfaction expressed by some parents suggests needed attention in some areas.	3a. Communication between the child welfare agency and specialized foster parents should be encouraged whenever possible. The concept of a new form of "professional" foster parent can only work if these providers are truly considered part of the treatment team. 3b. In-service training for juvenile court personnel may also be important to enhance their role as part of the "team" of providers serving the child. Court personnel may need information about the role that specialized foster parents play in the treatment approach so that they will be open to SFC parents' concerns regarding the child.
4. Specialized foster parent agencies report that higher rates of pay help in their recruitment efforts.	4. Although specialized foster parents are paid more on average than conventional foster parents, agency administrators report that funding is critical to quality foster parent recruitment.

9

Kinship Care: Rights and Responsibilities, Services and Standards

with Barbara Needell

In recent years, the child welfare system has shifted toward the greater use of kin as a placement resource for children. In large metropolitan communities especially, kin are heavily relied on to serve the growing numbers of dependent children.

The Child Welfare League of America recently reported that "over 31 percent of all children in legal custody had been placed with extended family members" (1992, p. 6). In some states and cities, the use of kinship foster parents actually overshadows the use of foster family care. In 1990, kinship foster care accounted for 48% of all placements in New York (Meyer & Link, 1990), and in California, two-thirds of the growth in the foster care caseload from 1984 to 1989 could be accounted for by the dramatic rise in kinship foster care (see Figure 9.1).

THE EVOLUTION OF KIN PLACEMENT

Rising numbers of kin placements have been ushered in by way of the courts. Until the 1980s, kin were not commonly given the full responsibilities and reimbursements of foster parents. Yet in 1979, the U.S. Supreme Court ruled in *Miller vs. Youakim* that relatives could not be

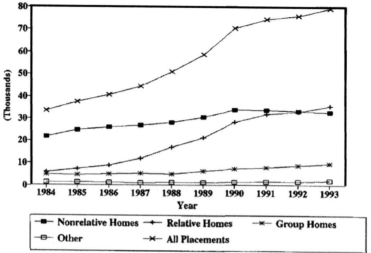

Figure 9.1. Children in foster care by type of placement at end of calendar year.

excluded from the definition of foster parents eligible for federal foster care benefits. Child welfare practices have changed rapidly with the entrance of kin into the formal foster care system, but child welfare nomenclature has not caught up as quickly. In this chapter we use three terms: (1) "kinship caregivers" who provide informal care for kin outside of the foster care system; (2) "kinship foster parents," who provide care for children and are formally recognized by the child welfare system as foster parents; and (3) "foster care," which is provided by nonkin. We believe that this tripartite nomenclature is preferable to distinguishing between kinship care and foster care (Takas, 1992), because the differences between parents inside and outside the formal structure of the CWS may be as great as those between kinship and nonkinship foster parents. At least the differences and similarities deserve discussion, and that discussion will be facilitated by more precise terms. This chapter will only contrast kinship foster care and foster care. As kinship caregivers are hidden from the CWS we know even less about these families.

An increased number of children in foster care have brought escalating costs to child welfare departments and a reconsideration of the prudence of kinship placements. In 1989, the *New York Times* suggested that kinship foster care was largely related to the crisis in foster care costs, noting that kinship placements accounted for 19,000 of the city's placements—a number exceeding the total placement rate 2 years previously (Daley, 1989). The growth in kinship placements may be related to the overall reduction in the foster parent work force, but part of the growth in kinship arrangements is also reflected in society's commitment to the extended family as a profound source of strength and stability for children. Social workers in many states are now being encouraged to search actively for kin before considering other care arrangements. When kin are unavailable or unwilling to care for a child, other placement options are explored.

With the growth of kinship foster care placements, a number of issues arise that merit examination. Advocates of kinship foster care placements note the potential for increased visitation with birth parents and the maintenance of family bonds that may not be achieved with strangers. The placement experience is also noted as qualitatively different when children are placed with known relatives. Yet, others are more skeptical of kin, questioning their ability to protect children fully and doubting the quality of their care. Some authors report a tendency for child welfare workers to remove children from an entire kin network assuming that parental failure must be a function of the network's failure as well (Gray & Nybell, 1990). Meyer and Link (1990) explored this issue, however, and were satisfied that a strong majority of kin placements in their study provided a safer environment for children than continued living arrangements in the birth home. The authors also noted that in many cases, the abusive or neglectful parent was the only dysfunctional family member in the kin network.

There is also a growing tension regarding the rights of kin to receive standard foster parent services, versus kinship foster parents' responsibilities to provide a high standard of quality care for these children. Quality of kinship care is extraordinarily difficult to assess. Whether or not kin should be held to the same standards of quality is certainly a question, although it is also uncertain what steps social workers take in ensuring quality of care. Some studies point to the lack of supervision many kinship foster homes receive from county social workers. A review of the kinship system in Maryland indicated that fully one-third of caregivers in their sample had not had *any* contact with their county caseworker in the previous year (Dubowitz, 1990). Another study of kinship foster care in New York City revealed certain inadequacies in the services kin providers received from their caseworkers. For example, little evidence was found for caseworker compliance with supervision requirements of kinship foster homes; when supervision was provided, it generally was poorly documented (Farber, 1990). Similarly, although visitation between the child and the birth parent occurred somewhat more regularly than visitation between parents and children placed in foster family care, few steps were taken to monitor visitation or to provide supervised visitation when court-ordered (Meyer & Link, 1990). The associated services designed to support foster parents may be irregularly provided to kinship foster parents. Conclusions about diminished or different quality of care by kinship providers are speculative. Because the phenomenon of formalized kinship care is relatively new, few studies test the issue.

Much of the increased attention to kinship foster care may be generated in part by the fact that these providers represent a different group of caregivers than those regularly found in formalized foster care. Thornton (1987; 1991) describes an older population and one heavily represented by single women of color who are struggling themselves with limited incomes. Their age may also contribute to a number of problems that may be less prevalent among foster family providers. For example, one study found maternal foster grandmothers reporting high levels of depression and poor health (Kelley, 1992). These grandmothers also expressed some concerns about their abilities to continue parenting young children. Some studies also point to the challenge these providers face as they voluntarily take on a new set of roles with little preparation or planning (Kennedy & Keeney, 1987; Shore & Hayslip, 1992; Thornton, 1987). Indeed, kinship foster parents have traditionally been differentiated from foster family providers by their route to foster care. That is, although foster family providers generally prepare for their new role as substitute parents, kinship caregivers more often drift into older parenthood as a response to a set of pressing circumstances.

The difficulty in caring for these children is probably exacerbated by the fact that many of the youngsters have a variety of health and mental health problems that exceed rates in the general population. In addition to the toll young children may take on a grandparent's health, there is a financial cost. One study found over one-third of grandparents were financially pressed after taking kin into their homes. Well over one-half of the sample suggested that their income was not sufficient to meet the needs of their expanding families (Minkler, 1993).

Financial troubles may be aggravated by the lack of uniformity in payments to kinship foster parents. If kin are located to care for a child, kin providers may qualify to receive AFDC-FC (Foster Care funds). With the *Miller vs. Youakim* (1979) decision, kin were recognized as eligible for federal foster care funds under certain conditions. If a child is removed from the custody of his or her parents through a decision by the courts and if the child comes from a birth parent's home that is AFDC eligible, the family may receive foster care funds. In California (the site of this study), the rate of payment for AFDC-FC is graduated with the age of the child. Foster care providers and kin providers of children under 4 receive a payment of $345 per month per child. When children are ages 5 to 8, providers receive a payment of $375. Payment rates increase to a maximum base rate of $484 per month for youths over 15.

If kin do not qualify for foster care payments, they may receive AFDC-FG (Aid to Families with Dependent Children-Family Group) payments. AFDC payments are lower per child than foster care payments. For example, the AFDC rate for one child is $317 per month. The AFDC rate for two children is $522, an increase of $205 per child. Rates are not graduated by the age of the child and only increase marginally with multiple children in the home—a situation that is particularly problematic as foster children often arrive in sibling groups.

The difference between AFDC and foster care funds appears to be a significant matter. One recent study of grandmothers providing foster care suggested that many resent the stigma attached to welfare and would prefer regular foster care payments. The author noted many grandmothers' anger as they pointed to the inequity of paying "strangers" (i.e., foster parents) more than kin (Minkler, 1993). The contradictory message that results from agency preference for kinship foster care placements but lower pay for them has caused a certain degree of discussion in the professional literature (Johnson, 1990; Takas, 1992) which is as yet unresolved. For birth parents who receive AFDC, there may also be some resentment that the state will provide more to relatives to care for children than it will pay poor parents to raise their own children.

For children who reside with relatives, their experience of foster care is different not only qualitatively, but their path out of the CWS is also unique. Among kin placements, reunification with birth parents is much slower (Goerge & Wulczyn, 1992). As noted in Chapter 5, after 1 year, fewer than 25% of children formally placed with kin in California were returned home, yet about 40% of all other children had been reunified with their families by that time.

However, although children placed with kin are less likely to be reunified, they also return to foster care at a much lower rate than children placed with nonrelatives. Using the UCB-FC database, we examined recidivism, or re-entry to foster care, for an exit cohort of children who were reunified with their birth parents during the last half of 1989. After 3 years, 13% of children whose most recent placement was in a kinship home had re-entered care, compared to 22% of children who had been in foster care, and 25% of children who had been in group care (Figure 9.2).

The effects of kinship placement on adoption have also been examined. Although adoption is considered a positive goal for children who otherwise cannot be reunified with their birth family, adoption appears more problematic among kin. Evidence in Chapter 7 indicated that children initially placed with kin and *not* reunified are far less likely to be adopted

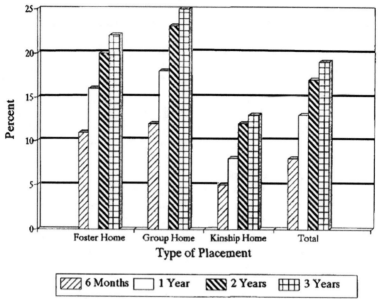

Figure 9.2. Children re-entering foster care following reunification with birth families.

Note: rates at 3 years may underestimate actual recidivism due to late reporting.

than children placed in other settings. Some suggest that kin are reluctant to adopt as the procedures for terminating parental rights may be too painful and because kinship caregivers already experience the child as a family member (Carson, 1981; Rowe, Cain, Hundleby, & Keane, 1984; Thornton, 1991). Others, however, believe that kin might adopt if they were fully informed of their rights to adoption subsidies (Meyer & Link, 1990). Yet, Thornton's sample of families (1991) largely knew about adoption subsidies and continued to reject the notion. Instead, they planned to keep the child in the home until the child was "able to take care of himself," that is, essentially, on a permanent basis.

STUDY FORMAT

Much of the controversy surrounding kinship foster care stems from its rapid growth and the paucity of information about the placement type compared to our knowledge of other forms of foster care. Although a few small-scale studies have begun to answer some of the questions regarding kinship placements, much of the field continues to operate on the level of anecdote and assumption. Our study was conducted to assist the policy and practice discussion with much-needed information about kinship care as it compares to foster family care and to consider practice alternatives that may not be currently in use.

The explosion in the census of children residing in kinship foster care has not been met with a significant increase in research. Policymakers and practitioners are left unguided. We endeavored to address some information gaps with a survey of kinship foster parents and nonkinship foster parents

The sample for this study was drawn from the UCB-FC Database (see Chapters 5 and 6). For our purposes, a 50% random sample ($n = 4,234$) was selected from the larger sample. One-half of the selected children were purposively drawn from foster homes, and the other half resided with kin. A two-page mailed survey was distributed to the sample with a selection of demographic questions. Respondents were also asked to participate in a second, larger survey either by telephone or mail, at their preference. Respondents were informed that they would receive a small stipend for their time if they participated in the second survey. The reasons behind the two-tiered approach to the survey were several. The approach was designed to obtain as much basic demographic information about these different foster care providers as possible at the lowest cost. Due to the limited free time and literacy skills anticipated among providers, we also wanted to give parents the option to complete the study by telephone.

The response rate to the minisurvey was 28% ($n = 1,178$). Sixty percent of respondents were foster care providers, and the remaining 40% were kin foster parents. The final sample size of respondents completing both surveys included 246 kin providers (113 completed a telephone interview and 133 completed the survey by mail) and 354 foster care providers (186 by telephone and 168 by mail). Table 9.1 provides detail regarding the response rate among foster parents and kin.

Although the total sample size ($n = 600$) was much smaller than the original sample drawn from the larger data set, the information gleaned from these caregivers provided a depth of information that is not otherwise available. Data from the minisurvey was essentially the same for the larger sample ($n = 1,178$) as the smaller sample ($n = 600$); therefore, all the data reported here is confined to the smaller sample. Comparison of our respondents to children in care across the state with the limited information we have from the UCB-FC Database indicates that the groups of children served in these homes was not appreciably different with regard to gender. Our sample of children was somewhat older with a mean age

Table 9.1. Sample Construction

Original Sample Size for "mini-survey"	4,234
% Kin	2,157 (51%)
Returned Mini-surveys	1,178 (28%)
Mailed Full Surveys	579 (64%)[1]
Attempted Phone Surveys	321 (36%)
Final Sample Size	
Kin	246
Foster Care Providers	354
Total	600 (14%)

· A number of parents (*n* = 92) asked not to be re-contacted and were therefore excluded from further surveys. Another 186 parents noted that they no longer provided foster care. They too were excluded from further surveys.

of 7.9 for kin and 7.7 for foster children. The average age of children in placement at the time of this study was 5.3 for kin and 5.9 for foster children. There were also minor variations in children's ethnicity. We had fewer Caucasian children in our foster care sample compared to the state data, while our sample also contained somewhat more African-American and Hispanic kin than the state population of kin children in care. Because the UCB-FC Database does not include information about the care providers, we have no way to determine the representativeness of our sample of providers to all providers in the state. One may speculate that those who took the time to complete the survey were more satisfied with their experience as foster parents and perhaps had more time available to participate in the study.

Surveys were designed based on the studies discussed in Chapters 8 and 10. Other studies of kinship foster parents were also consulted (Bell Associates, 1992; Thornton, 1987). The survey included a series of demographic questions, regarding providers' perceptions of the field of foster care and about the types of services they received from their local child welfare agency. Respondents were also asked to rate their social workers on a "Worker Quality Scale" and an adapted version of the "Child Protection Worker Scale" developed by Fryer, Bross, Krugman, Denson, and Baird (1990). The scales include several questions with Likert scale response categories. Scoring for the questions resulted in a scale ranging from 20 to 140, with higher scores indicating greater satisfaction with the worker. (The internal consistency reliability coefficient for this scale was high (alpha = .97).) The survey also included questions about the dynamics between the foster parents, child, and birth parent, along with questions about plans and expectations for the child's future.

DEMOGRAPHIC CHARACTERISTICS OF CAREGIVERS

Kinship foster parents and foster care providers were different in many respects. Although a female parent was present in all but six of the families in our final study sample, 52% of the kinship caregivers were single parents, compared to 24% of the foster parents ($\chi^2 = 46.70$, $df = 1$, $p < .001$). Female kinship foster parents were more likely to be employed outside of the home than foster parents (48% vs. 37%; $\chi^2 = 7.10$, $df = 1$, $p < .01$), and those who were employed worked more hours per week, averaging 31 hours as compared to 27 hours for foster parents ($t = 2.01$, $df = 228.45$, $p < .05$). Of those homes with male providers present ($n = 106$ relative caregivers, $n = 259$ foster parents), 67% in kinship homes were employed compard to 87% in foster homes ($\chi^2 = 19.41$, $df = 1$, $p < .001$). All males who were working averaged a 40-hour workweek.

Kinship foster parents were somewhat older than foster parents. The average female kinship caregiver was 48 years old, whereas the average female foster parent's age was 46 years ($t = 2.15$, $df = 579$, $p < .05$). More telling about the difference in their ages, 29% of the female kinship foster parents were 55 or older, which was true of only 19% of female foster parents ($\chi^2 = 7.3$, $df = 1$, $p < .01$). For males the average kinship foster parent age was 50 years, and the average foster parent age was 47 years ($t = 2.32$, $df = 376$, $p < .05$). Most respondents had some college or trade school education, but more kinship than foster parents did not have a high school diploma (26% vs. 10% for female; $\chi^2 = 25.30$, $df = 1$, $p < .001$ and 20% vs. 9% for males; $\chi^2 = 9.36$, $df = 1$, $p < .01$). Kinship foster parents were less likely to own their own home than foster parents (53% vs. 85%; $\chi^2 = 70.50$, $df = 1$, $p < .001$) and were more likely to have moved at least once in the past 3 years (23% vs. 17%; $\chi^2 = 4.04$, $df = 1$, $p < .05$).

Kinship foster parents reported more often than foster parents that they were not in good health. Twenty percent of female and 25% of male kinship foster parents were in fair or poor health, which was true of only 7% of female and 6% of male foster parents (female: $\chi^2 = 20.39$, $df = 1$, $p < .001$; male: $\chi^2 = 26.64$, $df = 1$, $p < .001$). (See Tables 9.2 and 9.3 for a detailed description of providers' demographic characteristics.)

There were ethnic differences between kinship and foster parent groups. (Because women are generally the primary caregivers for children, most data will be reported for female kin and foster parents.) African-Americans were the largest group of kinship foster parents (43%), whereas the majority of foster parents were Caucasians (63%) (see Figure 9.3). One-third (34%) of kinship providers were Caucasians, 17% were Hispanics and 6% of other ethnicity. Twenty-two percent of foster parents were African-Americans, 9% Hispanics, and 4% of other ethnicity ($\chi^2 = 49.9$, $df = 3$, $p < .001$).

Table 9.2. Similarities and Differences in Kinship Caregiver and Foster Parent Characteristics

Variable	Kinship N	Kinship (%)	Foster (%)	Foster N
Number of adults in the home***				
1	123	(51.7)	(24.1)	83
2 or more	115	(48.3)	(75.9)	261
Ethnicity-Female***				
African-American	101	(43.0)	(21.8)	74
Caucasian	80	(34.0)	(62.8)	213
Latina	40	(17.0)	(9.1)	31
Other	14	(6.0)	(3.7)	21
Ethnicity-Male***				
African-American	28	(26.7)	(14.0)	36
Caucasian	57	(54.3)	(69.3)	178
Latino	17	(16.2)	(12.1)	31
Other	3	(2.9)	(4.7)	12
Formal Education-Female***				
Less than high school gradute	62.	(26.2)	(10.2)	35
High school graduate	49	(20.7)	(23.2)	79
Some college or trade school	116	(48.9)	(45.7)	156
College graduate or more	10	(4.2)	(20.8)	71
Formal Education-Male***				
Less than high school graduate	21	(19.8)	(8.5)	22
High school graduate	29	(27.4)	(24.6)	64
Some college or trade school	43	(40.6)	(40.0)	104
College graduate or more	13	(12.3)	(26.9)	70
Female provider employed outside the home***	110	(48.0)	(36.8)	124
Male provider employed outside the home***	71	(67.0)	(86.9)	225
Housing status***				
Own	129	(53.1)	(84.7)	294
Rent	94	(38.7)	(13.5)	47
Subsidized	20	(8.2)	(1.7)	6
Number of housing moves in the last three years*				
0	184	(76.7)	(83.4)	281
1 or more	56	(23.4)	(16.4)	55
Use own money for foster children**	240	(87.1)	(83.4)	286
Health-Female***				
Excellent	75	(31.3)	(45.7)	156
Good	118	(49.0)	(46.9)	160
Fair	43	(17.8)	(7.0)	24
Poor	5	(2.1)	(.3)	1
Health-Male***				
Excellent	37	(33.9)	(52.5)	139
Good	45	(41.3)	(41.5)	110
Fair	22	(20.2)	(4.9)	13
Poor	5	(4.6)	(1.1)	3

*p < .05; **p < .01; ***p < .001

Table 9.3. Similarities and Differences in Kinship Caregiver and Foster Parent Characteristics

Variable		Kinship			Foster	
	N	mean	(SD)	N	mean	(SD)
Number of foster children	238	2.538	(1.63)	330	2.773	(1.63)
Months providing foster care***	242	49.09	(42.04)	348	99.72	(97.54)
Amount of own money spent on child	160	$134	(111.61)	214	$118	(98.36)
Age of female provider*	241	47.98	(11.67)	340	46.02	(10.15)
Age of male provider*	113	50.13	(13.65)	265	47.13	(10.48)
If working female*, number of hours per week	110	31.25	(15.24)	124	27.24	(15.17)
If working male, number of hours per week	71	40.96	(12.45)	225	40.40	(11.41)
Total household income (includes foster care payments)	199	$32,424	(21091)	294	$51,320	(25562)

*$p < .05$; ***$p < .001$.

The two groups differed sharply in income. The average annual gross income, including foster care payments, was $32,424 for kinship foster parents and $51,320 for foster parents ($t = 8.63$, $df = 491$, $p < .001$). (These data were missing from 20% of kinship providers and 12% of foster parents.) Disregarding money received specifically for foster children (either AFDC-FG or AFDC-FC) kinship foster parents' annual income was $21,854, while foster parents' income was $36,402.[1]

Caucasian foster parents had higher overall incomes than any other group. African-American and other kinship providers were not as well-off. Caucasian kinship foster parents reported an average gross annual income (including foster care funds) of $40,156, but this amount was $29,386 for African-Americans, $25,467 for Hispanics, and $35,464 for other kinship providers ($F = 5.05$, $p < .01$). Caucasian foster parents had an annual income of $56,052, compared with $42,960 for African Americans, $38,105 for Hispanics, and $48,938 for other foster parents ($F = 6.39$, $p < .001$). In addition, sources of income differed by ethnicity within both kinship and foster parent groups (see Table 9.4).

Where their income came from also helps to clarify the differences between providers. Sixty-three percent of kinship homes reported some income from wages or salary, compared to 80% of foster parents ($\chi^2 = 19.52$, $df = 1$, $p < .001$). Twenty-five percent of kinship providers were

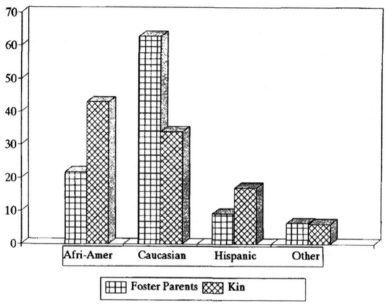

Figure 9.3. Ethnicity of female providers.

receiving some Social Security benefits compared to 17% of foster parents ($\chi^2 = 4.84$, $df = 1$, $p < .05$), and more kinship providers than foster parents had some income from SSI or disability funds (17% vs. 9%; $\chi^2 = 8.81$, $df = 1$, $p < .01$). One-third of kinship providers were receiving welfare (AFDC-FG), which was true of only 6% of foster parents ($\chi^2 = 66.02$, $df = 1$, $p < .001$). Twenty-two percent of kinship foster parents and 38% of foster parents had investment income ($\chi^2 = 15.77$, $df = 1$, $p < .001$). Many parents had a very difficult time describing where their income came from. That is, some were receiving foster care funds and others AFDC-FG, but they could not articulate the difference. From the data we discerned that some caregivers were not getting paid to care for the children in their homes. As a low estimate, we found that 10% of kinship foster parents were not receiving any funds from state foster care, whereas only one foster parent reported not receiving any foster care funds (this parent was in a fost-adopt program, but the adoption had not yet been finalized [$\chi^2 = 30.05$, $df = 1$, $p < .001$]).

Kinship foster parents were newcomers to the field of foster care compared to foster parents. They had been providing care for one-half as long as foster parents on average (4.2 years vs. 8.3 years; ($t = 8.60$, $df = 505.25$, $p < .001$). Foster parents' length of stay in the field may partly

Table 9.4. Sources of Household Income by Ethnicity of Female Provider[1]

Source of Income	Ethnicity	% Kinship Caregivers	% Foster Parents
Wages or Salary	African-American	55	65
	Caucasian	75	84
	other[2]	65	78
		$\chi^2 = 7.73^*$	$\chi^2 = 11.31^*$
AFDC	African-American	41	7
	Caucasian	19	5
	other	36	8
		$\chi^2 = 10.78^{**}$	$\chi^2 = .64$
Social Security	African-American	21	30
	Caucasian	28	13
	other	17	22
		$\chi^2 = 2.38$	$\chi^2 = 11.70^{**}$
SSI/Disability	African-American	23	16
	Caucasian	11	6
	other	18	14
		$\chi^2 = 3.82$	$\chi^2 = 8.14^*$
Foster Care Funds	African-American	88	100
	Caucasian	90	99
	other	92	100
		$\chi^2 = .44$	$\chi^2 = .53$
Investments	African-American	13	33
	Caucasian	37	41
	other	16	36
		$\chi^2 = 15.63^{***}$	$\chi^2 = 1.38$

$^*p < .05;$, $^{**}p < .01;$ $^{***}p < .001$
Notes:
[1] Source was counted if respondent indicated that it accounted for any amount of household income.
[2] Latino, Asian, mixed and other groups have been combined into "other" category.

explain their preparation to leave foster care altogether. Almost one-half (49%) of the foster parents expected to stop accepting foster children within the next 5 years.

There was no difference in the average number (approximately 3) of foster children currently in the home. Twenty-nine percent of kinship providers and 38% of foster parents also had at least one birth or step-child living at home ($\chi^2 = 4.87$, $df = 1$, $p < .05$). Only 2% of kinship parents and 21% of foster parents had at least one adopted child in the home ($\chi^2 = 43.88$, $df = 1$, $p < .001$), and 7% of kinship foster parents and 4% of foster parents had at least one nonfoster relative child living with them.

As noted, families in our study were caring for an average of three kin or foster children. The range was from one to seven, and of those families with more than one kin or foster child (168 kinship homes and 239 foster homes), at least two of the children were siblings in 95% of the kinship homes and 52% of the foster homes ($\chi^2 = 87.93$, $df = 1$, $p < .001$). Kin often care for large sibling groups. In 19% of the kinship homes with more than one child, four or more siblings were placed together. This was true of 7% of the foster homes ($\chi^2 = 7.66$, $df = 2$, $p < .05$).

Ethnicity played a role in some of the differences found within both kinship and foster parent groups. Sixty-eight percent of African-American kinship providers were single parents, compared with 33% of Caucasian kinship foster parents ($\chi^2 = 21.68$, $df = 2$, $p < .001$). For foster parents, 49% of African-Americans and 17% of Caucasians were single parents ($\chi^2 = 29.82$, $df = 2$, $p < .001$). African-American female foster parents were older than other parents, on average 51 years compared to 44 years for Caucasians and 46 years for Hispanics or other foster parents ($F = 10.42$, $p < .001$). (There were no significant differences by race with regard to the age of the female provider in the kinship group.) In both kinship and foster parent groups, fewer Hispanic caregivers had completed high school. Fifty-six percent of Hispanic kinship providers, compared with 77% African-American, 80% Caucasian, and 71% other, had a high school diploma ($\chi^2 = 8.3$ $df = 3$, $p < .05$). In the foster parent group, 77% of Hispanics had completed high school compared with 87% of African Americans, 93% of Caucasians, and 91% of other ethnicity ($\chi^2 = 9.3$ $df = 3$, $p < .05$). The rate of high school completion did not differ by ethnicity among male providers.

THE PATH TOWARD PLACEMENT

Fifty-seven percent of kin children and 31% of foster children had been living with their birth parents immediately prior to placement, and 22% of kin and 34% of foster children had been in another foster home. A small percentage of children had resided in emergency shelter homes, residential treatment, or with other family members. Fewer kinship children than foster children had previously lived in these kinds of arrangements ($\chi^2 = 43.30$, $df = 5$, $p < .001$). Of those children who were in school, at least one-half of the children in both kinship and foster homes had changed schools with this placement.

Kinship foster parents became involved with the social services agencies and courts regarding their selected child in a number of ways. Almost one-half (47%) said that the agency contacted them and asked if they would take the child. However, nearly one-third (31%) called child protective services themselves to report abuse or neglect and offered to take the child. Another 17% already had the child living with them when formal placement was made. The reasons providers gave for children coming to care centered primarily on issues of neglect. Among the one-third of families who knew why the child had been placed, 62% stated that at least one of the factors related to the child's placement was due to the parents' drug use. Forty-eight percent noted parental neglect, and 18% said that the child had been abandoned by his or her parents.[2] In telephone interviews, kinship foster parents repeatedly affirmed that they loved these children and that they were determined to keep them from entering foster care.

We asked all respondents whether or not they thought the child had been in danger when he or she was living with birth parents. Fully one-fourth of the foster parents did not know enough about their foster child's history to comment on this. Those who did respond were more likely than kinship foster parents to think that the child had been in grave danger (62% vs. 52%) and less likely to think the child had been in no danger (8% vs. 14%). (About one-third of all providers thought that the child had been in a little or some danger in the birth home, $\chi^2 = 7.23$, $df = 2$, $p < .05$.)

There were some ethnic variations in the data about the child's entry into placement. In African-American kinship homes, one-third (35%) of the children had changed schools with this placement, compared to two-thirds (65%) of the children in Caucasian kinship homes and 47% of Hispanic and other kinship homes. African-American foster parents were less likely than all other ethnic groups to know if the child placed with them had been in danger in the birth home, and more African-American foster parents felt that the birth parents viewed the placement positively. Visitation with birth parents, when it did occur, was more likely to be arranged directly by African-American kinship caretakers and foster parents than Caucasians, Hispanics, or others.

CHARACTERISTICS

Visitation with Birth Parents

Regular contact with birth parents was maintained to a much greater degree with kin. Eighty-one percent of kinship foster parents compared to 58% of foster parents had some contact with the birth parents ($\chi^2 = 34.21$, $df = 1$, $p < .001$). Regarding visitation between children and their birth parents, more than half (56%) of children in kinship homes saw their birth parents at least once a month, which was true for less than one-third (32%) of foster children. Beyond these somewhat limited visits, some children saw their birth parents quite regularly. Nearly one-fifth (19%) of kin children saw their birth parents more than four times a month; virtually no (3%) foster children did ($\chi^2 = 55.99$, $df = 5$, $p < .001$).

When visitation did occur between birth parents and children, it was informal and familylike for kin. More than three-fourths (79%) of kinship foster parents arranged visits directly with the birth parent. In contrast, more than one-half (54%) of foster parents had visits arranged by the courts or social service agency ($\chi^2 = 40.26$, $df = 1$, $p < .001$). Only 11% of kinship providers indicated that they had little or no control over visitation, yet over one-third (38%) of foster parents felt this way ($\chi^2 = 60.38$, $df = 2$, $p < .001$). Although many providers saw a warm relationship between the child and the birth parent, more kinship than foster parents felt that the child had a "close" relationship with their birth parent (61% vs. 40%; $\chi^2 = 17.37$, $df = 1$, $p < .001$). Many providers also asserted that birth parents viewed the placement positively. Slightly more kinship providers than foster parents reported that the birth parents were at least somewhat please with the placement (84% vs. 78%), however this difference was not statistically significant.

Services

Services provided by placement agencies were much more likely to be offered to foster parents than kinship foster parents. More foster parents received respite care (23% vs. 6%; $\chi^2 = 31.26$, $df = 1$, $p < .001$), support groups (62% vs. 15%, $\chi^2 = 129.03$, $df = 1$, $p < .001$), training (76% vs. 13%; $\chi^2 = 224.17$, $df = 1$, $p < .001$), and specialized training (for example, training to care for drug-exposed infants) (59% vs. 5%; $\chi^2 = 179.32$, $df = 1$, $p < .001$). Fewer than 10% of either kinship providers or foster parents received child care services or other services from their placement agencies. Within a range of zero to six possible types of services, the mean number provided for kinship foster parents was .53 and 2.30 for foster parents ($t = -18.04$, $df = 583$, $p < .001$). The average number of services varied by ethnicity for foster parents, with Caucasian foster parents receiving more (2.43) services than African-American, Hispanic, or other foster parents (2.08) ($F = 3.28$, $p < .05$). Among kin, there were no significant differences in services received by race. Although most providers had received no formal training in the past year, this was especially true for kinship foster parents. Almost the entire sample (91%) of kinship providers had not received any training. In contrast, about one-third of foster parents had received training of some kind in the past year ($\chi^2 = 197.9$, $df = 1$, $p < .001$). Many providers, both kinship and foster, felt that additional services

Table 9.5. Additional Services Requested by Providers

Type of Service	% Kinship Caregivers (n = 246)	% Foster Parents (n = 354)	Chi square, df, p value
Training			
Specialized	46	50	2.94, 2 ***
Training[1]	42	54	20.77, 2 ***
Respite Care	48	71	31.22, 2 ***
Child Care	47	64	17.48, 2 ***

*** p < .001
Note:
[1] For example, training for caring for drug exposed infants.

would be helpful. Both groups of parents suggested a need for more training, respite care, and child care (see Table 9.5).

Many providers experienced a scarcity of services; they also appeared to have rather minimal contact with social workers. Kinship foster parents had less contact with agency social workers than did foster parents, and children in kinship care were seen by social workers less often than children in foster care. Twenty-seven percent of kinship providers and 19% of foster parents had no contact with a social worker in the month before the study. The average number of contacts that month was 1.4 for kinship caregivers and 2.0 for foster parents ($t = -4.37$, $df = 554$, $p < .001$). Among the children, 46% of kin and 35% of foster children had not been seen by their social worker in the past month; the average number of hours per month a child in kinship care spent with a social worker was .65; for foster children it was .88 ($t = -2.76$, $df = 537$, $p < .01$). African-American kinship foster parents were less likely to have had contact with a social worker in the month prior to the study than other ethnic groups ($\chi^2 = 7.59$, $df = 2$, $p < .05$). African-American foster parents reported fewer hours of contact between social workers and the children in their care ($F = 5.41$, $p < .01$).

In spite of the paucity of services offered to all caregivers in the sample and the minimal level of contact with social workers, most providers in this study were quite satisfied with their social workers. Although kinship foster parents received fewer services and spent less time with social workers, they had a more positive view of their social workers than did foster parents. To measure providers' attitudes, we constructed a scale consisting of 14 items. With a possible range from 20 to 140, kinship caregivers gave their workers a mean score of 115, compared to a mean score of 108 for foster parents' workers ($t = 2.78$, $df = 483.61$, $p < .01$). When asked to describe the characteristics of the "best" worker they had ever had, the most frequent response from foster parents and from kin (37%)

was that their worker listened, was supportive, and cared about their individual needs. Others noted their worker's interest in the child, impressed by the fact that the worker appeared to be a real child advocate (24%). Yet, many providers felt that their relationships with their social workers could be improved. Thirty-eight percent of kinship providers and 51% of foster parents wanted more contact with their social worker, 45% of kinship foster parents and 63% of foster parents thought that better communication would be helpful, and 44% of kinship parents and 63% of foster parents wanted more respect from their social workers. Few comments stood out among providers regarding the characteristics of their "worst" worker. Responses were evenly distributed among both groups in several areas. About one-quarter of providers (24%) remarked that their worker was not responsive, not available when needed, or readily accessible. Another one-quarter (23.9%) felt that the worker was not professional in his or her manner, and another 22.5% felt that the social worker was not informative about the child's situation.

Significantly, more foster children than kin children were receiving mental health services at the time of the study (48% vs. 29%; $\chi^2 = 22.53$, $df = 1$, $p < .001$), yet kinship providers were more likely than foster parents to be satisfied with the availability of health and mental health services for their children. Sixty-three percent of kinship foster parents vs. 45% of foster parents thought the availability of health care services was good or very good; 17% vs. 35% thought it was poor or very poor ($\chi^2 = 26.39$, $df = 2$, $p < .001$). Regarding the availability of mental health services, 60% of kinship foster parents vs. 43% of foster parents thought availability was good or very good; 26% vs. 34% thought it was poor or very poor ($\chi^2 = 12.92$, $df = 2$, $p < .01$). When the question was worded differently, respondents did not have such a positive view of mental health services. Over one-half of all providers suggested that more family counseling, children's counseling, or counseling with the birth family would be helpful.

Kin not only received fewer services but also they received less money to care for children. California allows for federally eligible kin to be paid at the same rate as foster parents. Nevertheless, there were differences in the payments that providers received for children placed in their care. Although the modal monthly payment for both kinship providers and foster parents was $345, the average was $367 for kin children and $480 for foster children ($t = -8.34$, $df = 543$, $p < .001$) in spite of the fact that the mean age of children in both groups was very similar. Part of the difference in monthly payments can be explained by the fact that many more foster parents than kinship foster parents received a Specialized Care Increment for special needs children (28% vs. 10%, $\chi^2 = 30.86$, $df = 1$, $p < .001$).

For all selected children, payments were only slightly correlated with the total number of medical problems reported for the child ($r = .26$, $p < .001$), the level of behavioral problems ($r = .20$, $p < .001$), and the probability that the child was enrolled in special education classes ($r = .21$, $p < .001$). No matter what payment rate they received, the majority of providers reported that they could not care for their children with this money alone. Over four-fifths of both kinship caregivers and foster parents used their own money, above and beyond payments, for the children in their care ($134 per month per child for kin children and $118 per month per child for foster children).

When we asked respondents what would be most helpful to them in providing care for children, higher foster care payments was chosen most often (35% kinship and 28% foster parents). Thirteen percent of foster parents chose respite care, and 13% of kinship providers chose counseling for their children. Eight percent of kinship foster parents and 11% of foster parents wanted other services or special funding, such as clothing allowances, transportation funds, and better medical assistance.

Expectations of the Children's Futures

Kinship foster parents were more likely than foster parents to think that the selected child would remain in foster care until emancipation (58% vs. 38%, $\chi^2 = 21.66$, $df = 1$, $p < .001$). Of those children who would probably stay in placement, kinship foster parents expected to keep almost all of them (93%) in their homes until the child became of age; 80% of foster parents expected to keep those children who would remain in foster care ($\chi^2 = 10.80$, $df = 2$, $p < .01$). Indeed, when asked about their own expectations for remaining in the field of foster care, kinship foster parents described their exit from the field as contingent on the child's circumstances. Whereas about 10% of foster parents described their exit from foster care within the next 5 to 10 years based on reasons such as their age, health, stress, or frustration with the system, kinship foster parents only spoke of their leaving the field when kin left their home. Fifty-two percent of kinship foster parents and 28% of foster parents expected that the children would be reunified with their birth parents; kinship providers were less likely than foster parents to expect that the child would be adopted (37% vs. 58%; $\chi^2 = 16.87$, $df = 2$, $p < .001$).

Over one-half of the respondents told us they were not likely to adopt the selected child. When asked about the reasons they were not planning to adopt, the reason most kinship foster parents chose for not considering adoption was: "We are already family" (65%). Thirty percent of kinship providers also indicated that they "could not afford it." For foster parents, 29% chose "I am too old," 20% suggested "I do not wish to become a permanent parent to this child,' and 11% could not afford the cost of changing from foster care to adoption. Yet, some of these families were planning on keeping children beyond foster placement. Fourteen percent of kinship foster parents and 22% of foster parents who would not consider adoption were planning to assume legal guardianship.

DISCUSSION

Our study confirms other research in the field regarding the characteristics of kinship foster parents and clarifies differences between them and other foster parents. On demographic variables, kinship foster parents are older, less well-off financially, and have more health problems than foster family providers. Kinship providers are also largely represented by women of color, many of whom are single parents.

Children in both groups present a number of difficulties for their providers (see Chapter 11); therefore, one might expect an array of similar services to be offered to their caregivers. Yet, kinship providers consistently receive fewer services from their local child welfare agency, including regular services, such as visitation, and external services, such as respite care, babysitting, and counseling. In addition to fewer services, kinship foster parents typically receive lower payments for the children in their care. Although many of the kin children were described as having more special medical needs than foster children, additional funding (in the form of the specialized care increment) was generally more available to foster parents than to kin.

Several recent state reports have underscored the need for the development of policies that facilitate out-of-home placement with relatives, including expanded financial and agency support (County Welfare Director's Association, 1990; California Child Welfare Strategic Planning Commission, 1991). Nationally, the National Association of Black Social Workers (1991) has called for the reduction or elimination of barriers to kinship placements, along with training for child welfare professionals on the use of kinship foster care. Support is growing for the notion that the use of kinship foster parents can allow children to remain with people who know them and their family background, traditions, and culture. Placement with kin may also cause less trauma than placing children with strangers (Chipungu, 1991).

Although reunification rates are slower for kin, and adoption is less likely for these children, it is hard to judge these outcomes harshly at this point. In principle, long-term foster care does not meet the best interests of children as well as adoption and runs counter to the original goals of the permanency planning movement. Further examination of the issue, however, points to the importance of kin in raising children to adulthood in stable, familylike settings. Our sample of kin providers were less likely than foster parents to suggest that they would adopt the child in their care, but they were more likely to indicate that they would continue caring for the child until the child came of age. They also reported that they were "already family" to the child, suggesting that kinship foster care has many of the same characteristics of adoption and in some respects, provides the "family continuity" the child welfare system seeks. These findings, however, do not guarantee the functional equivalence of kinship foster care and adoption; research is particularly lacking on children's and birth parents' attitudes regarding these differences.

Kinship foster care is a very stable placement for children. We have previously indicated the evidence that children placed in kinship foster care are less likely to be reunified. They are also less likely to experience any other placements during their tenure in foster care. As reported in our sample of children who entered foster care in 1988 in California, over one-half of the 58% of children placed in foster family homes experienced at least one subsequent placement during the following 3.5 years. In contrast, only 23% of children placed initially with kin experienced another placement. This difference is particularly significant in that children placed with kin had a longer average time in foster care than children placed in foster care.

Recent family preservation initiatives point to the importance of providing services to families in trouble. Kinship foster care can be viewed as a form of extended family preservation; original ties to the family are maintained, but under the close supervision and support of the social services agency. If one assumes that kinship foster parents, who themselves are older, in more fragile health, and less financially stable, will be able to care for these very difficult children with fewer financial and concrete supports than foster parents, then our expectations are unrealistic. Until kinship providers are offered the same services, training, and reimbursement as foster parents, a fair assessment of quality cannot be conducted. Indeed, it is incumbent on *social services agencies* (not the kinship foster parents alone) to ensure quality of care for children.

A recent review of state policies on kinship care (Kusserow, 1992) also points to the lack of knowledge regarding this form of foster care. Quality of care needs assessment through more research on the topic, but quality can only be ensured if social service agencies play an active role in working with kinship foster parents. Children placed with kin under the supervision of the CWS demand quality care; standards that ensure safety and protection for children must be equivalent regardless of a child's placement arrangement. But standards cannot be guaranteed without the supportive services provided by social workers. Indeed, over one-third of the kinship providers represented in this study would have welcomed more contact with their social worker.

SUMMARY

As a variety of social service agencies work toward maintaining family ties and safeguarding against placement, kinship care is a unique response to the growing need for out-of-home placement. Indeed, some children cannot and should not remain with their birth parents in spite of the provision of family-based services. Kinship care may provide the protection children require while allowing them to remain with family. We have presented some evidence that parental contact is facilitated by kinship foster care, although future research needs to clarify how the birth parent–kinship foster parent relationship impacts reunification.

In light of the potential that kinship placements offer to the child welfare community, new initiatives should be explored to support the kinship home fully and to develop a range of alternative approaches that create an appropriate balance between underserving and overly intruding in kinship arrangements. These would allow children to live in extended, permanent families. For children who will never go home, long-term kinship foster care or guardianship may be acceptable alternatives to adoption. This too awaits research to confirm that the permanence and stability of these practices are roughly equivalent to adoption.

Although our research focuses primarily on kinship care, data from our study suggest striking inequalities in social worker support and service provision related to the ethnicity of foster parents. African-American foster parents reported fewer hours of social worker contact with their children than did other ethnic groups, and Caucasian foster parents were provided with more services by their agencies than were other ethnic groups. Our study also suggests that children of color, especially Hispanic children, are less likely to be placed in ethnically similar homes than are Caucasian children. For children who must be placed outside of their families, these differences require critical examination and explanation.

Much of the increase in the foster care caseload is associated with substance abuse, particularly the crack-cocaine epidemic. Some practitioners continue to consider family, especially the parents of crack-cocaine addicts, to be somehow responsible for their offsprings' neglectful or abusive behavior. They reason that these grandparents failed in their first attempt at parenting and are therefore unfit to raise another generation of children. "Blaming the victim" (or her mother) is a tired and futile way to avoid facing the real issues of institutionalized poverty, racism, and unequal opportunity as they relate to the hopelessness and despair bound up with crack addiction. Researchers who have taken the time to look closely at kinship foster parents provide us with glimpses of great courage and strength (see Minkler, 1993). These families are heroic allies in a terrible war against children, and they deserve far more respect and support from the CWS and from the community.

Summary of Key Findings and Recommendations Regarding Kinship Foster
Care

Finding	Recommendation
1. Consistently with other emerging studies in the field of kinship care, kinship foster parents in this study received fewer services from their child welfare agency that foster family parents.	1a. All children under the supervision of the courts should be ensured quality care. In order to hold kinship foster parents to the same standards of care as foster family parents, all parents must be provided with the same level of services, monitoring and supervision.
	1b. Although kinship foster parents may be reluctant to participate in conventional foster parent "training," agencies should design innovative programs, where support groups or discussion groups are offered. These groups would cover the same materials as those presented in a training, although the methods for presenting the material might differ somewhat. The children served in kinship care had a number of emotional and behavioral problems that exceed rates in the general population; it is likely that these children are indeed difficult to care for. Greater support and information about how to manage children's challenging behavior might make the experience more pleasurable for kinship foster parents, but it would also help to ensure greater quality of care in these settings.
2. Because of financial status and their advanced age, kinship foster parents may be in somewhat more fragile health than foster family parents.	2. Social workers providing services to children in kinship foster care should try to assist kinship foster parents in accessing needed health services whenever possible.
3. Many kinship foster parents are reluctant to adopt the children in their care, as they already view their relationship as one of "family."	3. Policies on payment under guardianship (similar to an adoption assistance subsidy) might encourage kinship foster parents to choose legal guardianship over foster care, thereby giving children a greater sense of permanence.

| 4. Although the children served in kinship foster care bear certain similarities to children served in foster family care, certain inequities exist in the payment structure for some kinship foster parents. | 4a. Social workers should make every effort to identify whether kinship foster parents are eligible for foster care payments.

4b. Policies should be reviewed to asses the prudence of variable board rates for these children given that the standards for their care in both settings are the same. |

NOTES

1. These data, like data from SFC parents regarding income, should be read with some caution. Many of these providers had difficulties describing what portion of their income came from foster care funds.

2. Frequencies will sum to greater than 100, as this was coded as a multiple-response question.

10

Group Care for Children

As noted in previous chapters, group care continues to be used as a placement resource for children of all ages. At times, large numbers of children were served in group care, a service corresponding to popular beliefs in the convenience and appropriateness of this form of supervision for children (Kadushin, 1980). At other times, however, popular and professional concerns about the importance of childrearing in the most homelike environment have shifted the emphasis on care for dependent children to foster family care and away from group care (Ashby, 1984; Lerman, 1982; Wolins & Piliavin, 1969). Although that debate continues to provoke controversy, many see group care as an appropriate alternative for children who might not otherwise be served in foster family homes. Seen as one residential alternative along a continuum, the group home offers one more option for hard-to-place children. Wells (1993) sees group care as an essential placement option for seriously emotionally disturbed children but also notes that it should be used sparingly, because it is "a radical and costly intervention" (p. 165). For many adolescents, group care may be the placement of choice, when, under the supervision of their county probation department, they might otherwise be served in far more restrictive environments.

This chapter provides descriptive information about group care settings in California. Group care is variously referred to as group care, group home care, or residential treatment. Residential treatment represents the far end of the continuum in group care in terms of restrictiveness, intensity of services, and cost. Although the nomenclature and the intensity of services vary, the feature all share is a group residence for dependent children and youth. Children discussed in this chapter are served in group care settings under the auspices of the CWS. The group

221

homes can range in size from six beds to facilities where hundreds of children are housed (groups of 12 or more must be divided into distinctive living arrangements, although these "cottages" may be located on a single "campus"). Group homes may be managed as single units, or one agency may have administrative authority over numerous group homes. Children are supervised 24 hours a day, usually by staff who are not residents of the home. With higher staffing ratios than foster family care and a wider variety of services available to children and families, it is expected that more challenging children can be served in these settings.

Group care is often considered a last attempt to serve children who are unlikely to remain in a stable placement elsewhere. For many adolescents, group care may be an appropriate transition to independent living after emancipation. Group care may also serve as a time-limited placement for severely emotionally disturbed children. The basic assumption—and growing evidence (Small, Kennedy, & Bender, 1991)—suggests that children in group care are more disturbed, more aggressive, and far more difficult to serve than children in foster family care. Some agencies provide around-the-clock awake staff to supervise these children out of concern for their acting-out behavior at all hours of the day or night; others provide general supervision and a reduced staffing ratio. Group homes may not be the ideal placement for all children, but they are inevitable for some children who cannot be served in other forms of out-of-home care.

Popular acceptance of group homes has shifted again over the past 20 years. Dore and associates' (1984) study of group care, nationwide, found a major shift, not in the total number of beds available to serve children, but in the size of the facilities. The greatest growth occurred among the smallest facilities (housing seven to 12 children)—a growth of over 800%. Similarly, the most dramatic decreases were seen among facilities serving over 500 children at a time. The total number of these facilities was reduced by almost 50% over the 20-year period. Although the size of institutional facilities has shifted, smaller group homes are still used in great numbers. In the 1960s, Pappenfort and Kilpatrick (1969) found that children were often placed in group care settings under less-than-ideal circumstances. Because of administrative problems or the lack of placement alternatives, many children were inappropriately placed in group homes. Shortly after that study, however, Maluccio (1974) found that the decision to place children in institutional care often occurred after other alternatives in the community had first been exhausted. Today, we know very little about the decision-making process that occurs when children are placed in group care settings. According to Wells (1991), placement criteria are vague and vary considerably across agencies.

We know even less about the quality of care children receive in group homes. Cohen's study (1986) of group homes in Los Angeles, California, was not encouraging. Although his study included a small sample size and the generalizability of the results cannot be fully determined, his findings are interesting. Cohen observed that children received basic supervision and care, yet the majority of group home administrators themselves rated the overall quality of group homes as either "fair" or "poor." Furthermore, Cohen found that the cost of care was not associated with quality or with the difficulty of the children served. In fact, he found a surprising reversal. Children who appeared to be more disturbed were placed in settings with fewer children where reimbursement rates were low. It is unclear from his study whether or not higher-cost facilities were better able to screen out difficult children. However, the results may suggest that social workers may refer inappropriate placements to lower-cost facilities.

In FY 1991–1992, California spent over $800 million on out-of-home care (including group care, specialized foster care, foster family care, and kinship care) serving more than 80,000 children. Of the total out-of-home care budget, about 63% of total costs are allocated to group care settings (personal communication, Ray Bacon, 1993), but only about 14% of all children in out-of-home care are served in group care. The County Welfare Directors' Association (1990) estimates that the average cost of care in group homes increased by almost 45% from 1985 to 1989. Costs in other states have increased dramatically as well (Barth, Albert, Lawrence, Courtney, 1993). Yet, in spite of the high costs, policymakers and administrators know very little about group care; they are largely unaware of the staffing in these facilities, the turnover rate, and the ethnicity of social workers and childcare staff.

Ethnicity matters when it comes to services for children in out-of-home care. Children of color are overrepresented in out-of-home care across the country (Barth, Berrick & Courtney, 1990; Pelton, 1989; Watahara & Lobdell, 1990). For example, although African-American children represent only 9% of the child population in California, they represent about 40% of the out-of-home care population. In group care, we generally find that 50% of children are Caucasian, 30% are African-American, 17% are Hispanic, and 3% are of other ethnicity (County Welfare Directors' Association, 1990). The extent to which agency administrators can recruit and hire people of color to work directly with children, the greater the likelihood that other issues of culture and ethnicity may be considered in serving these vulnerable children.

A SURVEY OF GROUP CARE PROVIDERS

The form of study was a cross-sectional mailed survey. A list of all licensed group care agencies (agencies that supervise, organize, and administer several group homes, and independent, individual group homes) in the state of California, including the addresses, telephone numbers, and the name of the agency administrators was provided by the California Department of Social Services.

A letter describing the study and an 18-page questionnaire were mailed to the administrator in each agency ($n = 630$). Approximately 5% of the agencies surveyed were no longer in business, lowering our sample size to 598. In all, 196 surveys (33%) were returned, following a postcard and a reminder telephone call.

The group care facilities participating in this survey represented a range of service providers. Analyses of returned surveys indicated that the sample was representative of the range of group homes across the state. Following state guidelines regarding rate-classification levels (i.e., allowable costs per child), the distribution of this sample mirrored the state population very closely. Analyses of those agencies responding to the survey and those who chose not to respond revealed no differences along the dimensions of agency size or cost per child. Although the response rate was lower than we hoped, these analyses suggest that the sample was representative of the overall state population of group care agencies.

The survey design built on previous studies in the out-of-home care field. The survey was also reviewed by four residential treatment providers who are prominent in the two statewide group care associations. Their comments regarding the content and wording of questions provided additional face validity to the questionnaire.

Questions in the survey centered on six areas: (1) the size of the agency, number of beds, childcare workers, social workers, and administrators; (2) costs per child; (3) the types of services provided within the agency; (4) the types of services available to children outside of the agency and the adequacy of those services; (5) staffing matters, such as turnover, pay, educational status, age, ethnicity, and language spoken by staff; and (6) administrators' general comments about the future of group care. Administrators were also asked to share the survey with the head social worker in the agency for responses regarding the characteristics of children served in the agency.

There are relatively few studies of group care that include a review of agency size, services provided, staffing patterns, turnover rates, ethnicity of workers, and educational status of workers. Some studies have been designed to draw a portrait of the typical child in group care (Fitzharris, 1985; Hulsey & White, 1989; Wells & Whittington, 1993), but few studies have combined agency-level data with child-centered information. We designed our study to answer some of the questions regarding staff characteristics and agency characteristics while looking to the future of group care.

Agency Size

Approximately 31% of group homes provided care for no more than six children at a time, and on average, group care agencies generally cared for 50 children or fewer ($M = 25.74$, s.d. $= 38.84$). One group care agency provided care for up to 410 children (although as mentioned, groups of these children are housed in separate "cottages"). The median number of children per group home agency was 17.

Costs per Child

The price tag for serving these children was high. Among the agencies surveyed, the monthly rate of reimbursement ranged from $725 per month, per child, to a high of $4,423 per month, per child. This translates into an annual cost of approximately $8,700 to over $53,000. The mean rate of reimbursement was $2,877 per month (s.d. $= 591.9$).

Group Home Services

Although group homes must provide care and supervision for children, many also provide additional services to the child or the family. As might be expected, the more services the agency offers, the higher the reimbursement rate per child. (The number of services provided to children was modestly correlated with reimbursement rates ($r = .24$, $p < .001$).) The types of services provided varied only slightly by agency. Of 16 possible services (predetermined by the survey), the mean number of services provided to children and families (beyond general care and supervision) was about seven ($M = 7.07$, s.d. $= 2.9$). Most common among the services provided to children and families were: transportation for children (89%); group psychotherapy (83%); individual psychotherapy (80%); family therapy (72%); and independent living skills (70%). Other services provided included diagnostic services and assessment (64%); substance abuse treatment (36%); nonpublic schools (33%); job training (33%); special health services (22%); programs for pregnant teens (9%); and childcare (5%).

In addition to this rich variety of services, time with their agency social worker is also a service that children receive from their agency. On average, providers reported that social workers carry a caseload of about 12 children and that they spend about one hour per week with each child.

Over one-half of the sample suggested that their children exhibit a "great need" for mental health and health services; yet, the availability and quality of these services outside of their agency boundaries is somewhat limited. Table 10.1 shows agency administrators' responses to ques-

Table 10.1. Availability of Services

	Mental Health Care Services		Health Care Services	
	Availability (%)	Quality (%)	Availability (%)	Quality (%)
Very good or Good	16	32	42	66
Fair	25	34	27	25
Poor or very Poor	59	34	31	9

tions regarding the availability and quality of mental health and health care services.

Staffing. The average child care worker is fairly young. The following list provides a description of the age breakdown of childcare workers. As shown, the majority of workers are in their 20s (although there are a few child care workers younger than that).

Less than 20 years	2.7%
21–30 years	52.8%
31–40 years	31.7%
More than 40 years	12.7%

In addition to their youth, childcare staff are well educated. About 40% of workers are college graduates, and another 30% have some college background. But turnover is high. Agency administrators reported that about one-quarter of their childcare workers had been on staff for less than 6 months; and another quarter had been employed for more than 6 months but less than a year. This turnover rate suggests that a full 50% of all childcare workers leave their group home on a yearly basis. Part of the turnover may be explained by the rather low salary scales of these workers. The average hourly rate of pay for child care workers is $7.47 per hour (s.d. = 1.2), although some workers make less than the minimum wage ($4.25) and some make far more ($17.00).

In this study we found a relationship between salary rates and turnover ($F = 8.16, p < .01$). The strongest predictors of turnover, however, were the size of the agency and the ratio of children to workers. The larger the agency, the greater proportion of workers who left within the first 6

Table 10.2. Factors Predicting Child Care Workers' Turnover within six months

Predicted by	$R = .63$, $R^2 = .39$, $F = 31.98^*$ Beta	t	Sig t
Agency size	.62	8.69	.001
Staff Ratio	.41	5.88	.001
Reimbursement Rate	.15	2.35	.02

[1] Stepwise multiple regression with individual workers as the unit of analysis. Specified model: Step 1: agency size, including total number of children per agency; Step 2: Child care worker staff to children; Step 3: Reimbursement rate per child.
$^*p < .001$.

months of employment. Similarly, the lower the worker to child ratio, the more workers were inclined to leave rapidly. Table 10.2 provides a description of the variables predicting staff turnover in a regression model.

The strongest predictor of group care workers' salaries was the rate of reimbursement agencies received per child ($R = .52$, $F = 8.11$, $p < .001$). Not surprisingly, resource-rich agencies pay their workers better.

Social Worker Staff. In contrast to the group care staff, social work staff were older, better educated, more stable in their employment with the agency, and they commanded higher pay. A surprising 15% of social workers possessed a Ph.D. About one-quarter had an LCSW (Licensed Clinical Social Worker) license, and another 22% had an MFCC (Marriage, Family, Child Counselor) license. Social workers were also more likely to have been employed in the agency for more than 2 years. Figure 10.1 compares the stability of employment between childcare workers and social workers.

The hourly rate of pay for nonlicensed social workers ranged from $5.00 per hour to $50.00 per hour (the average was $15.00 per hour (s.d. = 5.3). There were no differences in the salaries of social workers in larger agencies compared to smaller agencies. And unlike the findings for childcare workers, social worker pay was not predicted by the rate of reimbursement. In fact, although length of employment was related to social worker salaries, no other variables could predict their salaries.

Ethnicity of Staff. We examined the ratio of childcare workers to children and found that agencies match fewer Hispanic childcare workers to Hispanic children (1:3), whereas the ratio of Caucasian childcare workers to children is 1:1.2. Overall, however, we do see a high ratio of workers to children (almost 1:1). This ratio must be understood as referring to the total number of staff, rather than an average working ratio of line staff to

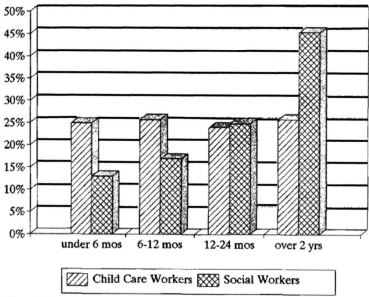

Figure 10.1. Stability of employment.

children at a given time. Thus, it does not necessarily indicate that individual children are always supervised one-to-one, but, rather, it may indicate staffing patterns that require 8-hour shifts per worker.

The ethnicity of social workers and children was also reviewed. Caucasians generally dominated social worker staffing with a ratio of Caucasian social workers to Caucasian children of 1:5 (African-American social workers to children averaged about 1:8).

THE FUTURE OF GROUP CARE

Childcare Staffing

Agency administrators suggested that they currently face numerous difficulties in hiring qualified workers. Twenty-seven percent of the sample said that there were "very few" qualified childcare workers to fill positions in group care. Their outlook for 5 years from now was worse. Thirty-five percent of these respondents were concerned that there would be "very few" qualified workers in 1996.

When asked what factors would draw more qualified applicants to the field, the majority of agency administrators (64%) suggested that increased pay for childcare workers would accomplish a great deal toward this end. Another fair proportion of respondents (46%) said that increased training and education for potential workers would make a great difference, as would recognition of the work as a "profession" (21%). Some of their thoughts are captured below in the following comments:

- It's difficult to assess this industry. It does not attract highly qualified staff. Maybe more direct services and classes in colleges would help.
AFDC-FC rate setting requirements limit the available pool of candidates severely, so that qualified people cannot be hired. Schools do not teach the skills required for childcare work. The field of childcare work does not have prestige or publicity among the community college and college population.
It would help if we could pay better wages and provide more benefits.
A program in college that would lead to a certification. Then, it would become a more well-known and respected profession.

Social Worker Staffing

A similar outlook was shared with regard to the future labor force of social workers, although agency administrators were somewhat more optimistic in this regard. Only 12% of the sample felt that there were "very few" qualified social workers in the field today and their outlook for 5 years from now was essentially unchanged, as 13% of respondents felt that there would be "very few" qualified social workers available. Nevertheless, a significant number of respondents ($n = 19$) changed their response from "some qualified workers" now, to "few" or "very few" qualified workers" in five years ($\chi^2 = 269.5$, df = 9, $p < .01$). Again, the barriers administrators reported regarding locating qualified workers were pay and training.

Program Development

Over 61% of respondents suggested that they planned to develop new programs within their agencies in the near future. The majority of these respondents planned to develop further the bed capacity of their agency. A sizeable proportion of the sample (17%) also expected to open a nonpublic school, 14% hoped to develop a specialized foster care program, and 12% listed a subacute treatment facility for severely emotionally disturbed children.

Issues for the 1990s

As these agency administrators face the next decade, we asked them to share their thoughts on the "major issues" facing group care. Forty-two percent of respondents reported that funding would be the primary issue throughout the next decade. Twenty-seven percent were concerned about finding competent staff, and 21% were worried about the severity of the problems children would bring to out-of-home care, such as:

- The impact of drug use on infants and children
- HIV-positive children
- An ever-growing number of dysfunctional and ill-prepared kids who will not fit into the world
- Gang involvement spreading to younger ages

Similarly, when administrators were asked how group homes would differ in the year 2000, about 5% of respondents were pessimistic, noting a decline in the profession, and 22% were troubled about the increase in "needy" children. Yet, the vast majority of agency directors saw growth in the profession, noting more specialized care for children (25%), more skilled staff (18%), and an increase in the availability of supportive services (15%).

DISCUSSION

Findings from this study suggest several issues with regard to the current state of group care and prospects for the future.

Agency Size

Corresponding to Dore and associates' study (1984), the size of the average group home is shrinking. In California, that average now stands at about 17 beds, far fewer than the large child-serving institutions of the past.

Cost of Care

Although this study did not attempt to measure quality of care, we know that the care children receive in group care settings is expensive. The average cost of care in this study was almost $2,900 per month. Assuming that a child were to remain in group care over 1 year (not an unlikely scenario), the government will spend over $34,000 per child, per year. For the average resident of a group home facility, this is well beyond the cost of a college education in the most exclusive private universities (these costs do not include additional court and social service agency expenses). Of course, these figures pale in comparison to the costs associated with mental health hospitalization, the California Youth Authority, or County Juvenile Correction Camps, but these are the costs we bear as a result of serious emotional abuse and neglect of children.

Services Needed

By the time children are served in group care settings their needs for mental health and health services are great. This is not surprising. Weston, Klee, and Halfon (1989) report that "between 30 and 80 percent of foster children examined for psychological problems are moderately to severely impaired." They also suggest that children in out-of-home care are 10 times more likely to use Medi-Cal mental health services than other Medi-Cal eligible children. Similarly, as the majority of dependent children come from poor families, the incidence of poor health is also greater among children in out-of-home care (Halfon & Klee, 1991; Halfon et al., 1989). Children coming to the attention of group care administrators reportedly also have significant needs for health care services.

Staffing

We find that childcare workers bear certain similarities to childcare staff working in daycare centers and preschools. Staff are generally fairly young, poorly paid, and highly mobile. The National Child Care Staffing Study (Whitebook, Howes, & Phillips, 1989) showed that 41% of all childcare staff left the job within 1 year. This rate is comparable to the rate we found in the group home survey, as well. In fact, these data show that group home staff may be even more mobile than childcare staff, as a whole, with a 50% annual turnover rate. The reduced quality of care that results from high turnover in daycare has been well documented (Anderson, Nagle, Roberts, & Smith, 1981; Phillips, 1987); we can expect the consequences for emotionally disturbed, abused, and neglected children to be equally problematic.

Staff turnover among childcare workers was related to agency size and ratio of children to workers. This may indicate that the intensity of the work and proximity to large numbers of disturbed children may contribute to worker burnout. Unlike what happens with daycare, however, group care workers' wages were not the primary factor determining their length of stay in the field. Nevertheless, childcare workers are not paid a great deal. The average full-time group care worker in our study made an annual salary of $15,538. Certainly, length of stay was related to wages. However, it is unclear from the data whether or not higher wages were a result of a worker's length of stay, or whether higher paying agencies, in general, kept workers longer.

Ensuring quality care and safety are two of the most important features of group care for children. Yet in our multicultural communities it is also important for agency administrators to provide ethnically diverse childcare staff and social workers for children to develop appropriate cultural identities. Although agency administrators were quite successful in recruiting and hiring people of color in their childcare positions, they were more challenged in this regard in hiring ethnic social workers. In particular, administrators faced serious difficulties in recruiting and hiring social workers who are either Asian, Pacific Islander, or American Indian. Although these ethnic groups are not widely found among children in out-of-home care, their complete absence among social workers in our sample is a matter of some concern.

SUMMARY

As we move through the next decade, group care staff will be challenged to meet the needs of more difficult-to-serve children. Funding for group care is not likely to increase substantially, particularly as other types of child care (e.g., kinship care) continue to dominate the overall growth in out-of-home care. Therefore, administrators may face serious near-term challenges. Few resources are currently available in the community to train potential group care workers, so that agency administrators may need to take on this responsibility themselves or urge community colleges and continuing education programs to take an active role in childcare training. As the disparity between funding and needs increases, administrators may also need to redouble their efforts in locating qualified staff who will take on the responsibility of child care and who will be willing to make a stable commitment to the children in their care. In the 1990s, group care administrators will focus their work on accessing quality mental health and health care services, locating and training culturally competent workers, and appropriately serving increasingly challenging children.

Summary of Key Findings and Recommendations Regarding Group Care

Finding	Recommendations
1. Agency size is shrinking considerably. Children are being served in smaller facilities, rather than in large, institutional care.	1. In light of the value placed on the family in P.L. 96-272 and on the importance of placing children in the most familylike setting when removed from their homes, this trend toward the use of smaller group care facilities for children is welcome. For young children in particular, institutional care does not generally provide children with a homelike environment and, if possible, should be explored only when other alternative care settings have been exhausted.
2. The array of services that may be available to children placed in group care can be wide. However, the cost for these services is also high.	2. Not all children need the same types of services; an older child may need independent living skills and drug abuse counseling, whereas a younger child may need intensive play therapy and transportation services to and from the birth home. The number of services provided by the agency may not be the best indicator of the quality of the group care setting, but the availability of specific services that meet an individual child's needs is. Therefore, careful review of the setting and its services should be explored before a placement is made. At the time of placement, a written case plan that details the extent to which these services will be available to the child should be developed.
3. The need for health care, mental health care, and special educational services are great.	3. Development of health, mental health, and education "passports" may go a long way in bridging the gap between children's needs and the services they receive. Passports should be provided to every child cared for under the supervision of the state and should allow for easy access to needed services, in addition to detailed information about the child's past referrals and access to agencies.

4. Turnover is high among childcare workers.

4. These data suggest that factors associated with turnover among childcare workers may have to do with the size of the agency and the ratio of children to staff. Many factors may contribute to the challenges these staff face, and efforts in several areas may be important in staff retention. Increased training, a well-developed career ladder that leads to higher positions of authority and responsibility for qualified staff, better pay, and perhaps a greater ability to work with small groups of children, even in agencies that serve large numbers of youngsters, may be helpful.

5. Children coming in to group care are increasingly difficult to serve.

5. Intensive training should be provided to childcare staff and social workers to ready them for the challenges they will face in managing children's behavior. Training should also be provided to familiarize staff with the services available in the community for these children and their families. Salaries are somewhat low in this field and could certainly be improved.

11

Similarities and Differences in the Characteristics of Children in Out-of-Home Care

Although children have been served by the child welfare system for over a century, we know very little about who these children are. Only in the 1970s and 1980s have large-scale studies been conducted that begin to answer our questions about the characteristics of children in out-of-home care. The great majority of these children have always come from poor, minority homes (Mech, 1983; Shyne & Schroeder, 1978). African-American children, in particular, have consistently been in the foster care population in numbers disproportionate to their numbers in the general population (Olsen, 1982b; Pelton, 1989), and today's data show no decline in this trend (Walker, Zagrillo & Smith, 1991). Other studies indicate that children in foster care have higher-than-average rates of emotional disorders and physical disabilities (Klee and Halfon, 1987; Schor, 1982; Maza, 1983).

In addition to general information regarding the demographic characteristics of children in out-of-home care, little describes their behavioral characteristics. Anecdotal evidence suggests that the children coming into care are increasingly difficult to care for and challenge foster care providers' abilities to provide stable, loving homes (Rosewater, 1990; Small, Kennedy, & Bender, 1991). Yet, few studies describe the level of behavioral disturbance among foster children. Hulsey and White (1989) studied the behavior of maltreated children placed in group homes and a similar group of children who remained with their families. The maltreated children in group homes showed more problematic behaviors than the children at home. However, the instability of the children's home environment provided better prediction of behavioral disturbances than any other factor.

In California, Fitzharris (1985) conducted a study of nearly 10,000 children served in residential care and examined factors regarding children's family histories, their behavioral problems, and their placement histories. Dependent children exhibited many problems, such as impulsivity, aggression, truancy, sexual acting out, lying, and delayed social development. Wells and Whittington (1993) also found that, compared to the general population, children in residential treatment had more behavioral and academic problems and displayed fewer social competencies than their peers. They note that these children "have serious interpersonal and academic problems, have a primary diagnosis relating to either conduct disorder, adjustment disorder, or disorder of impulse control, and have used a prior mental health service" (1993, p. 196).

Other studies have examined the behaviors of children in foster family care and have found a relationship between children's problematic behaviors and their age, gender, ethnicity, and prior placement history. Younger children have fewer behavioral problems, boys exhibit more problematic behaviors than girls, and African-American children show fewer signs of behavioral problems (Fein, Maluccio, & Kluger, 1990). (A study conducted by Dubowitz and Sawyer (n.d.) suggests, however, that African-American boys in kinship care have more behavioral problems.) Fanshel, Finch, and Grundy (1989a) noted more severe behavioral problems among children who had seen numerous placements as opposed to their peers with more stable placements. A study by McIntyre and Keesler (1986) also noted serious behavioral and psychological problems evidenced by foster children. In their sample of foster children, almost one-half of the study children showed signs of psychological disorder as measured by the Child Behavior Checklist (Achenbach & Edebrock, 1981).

Dubowitz and Sawyer (n.d.) have found that children placed in kinship care exhibit high levels of behavioral disturbance. Comparing their sample of kin children to a normative population, children residing in kinship care had more than double the rate of "clinical" behavioral problems; these problems also increased with age, especially for boys.

Dubowitz et al. (1992) also suggest that kin children have a variety of health needs, many of which are not discerned or treated by the CWS. Their analysis indicates health problems that are similar in nature and frequency to those experienced by other children in foster care and poor children, generally. Halfon and Klee (1991) also found that foster children have numerous health problems, although their findings indicated that many of these problems were undetected by foster parents. Corroborating these studies, Simms (1989) noted a high incidence (35%) of chronic medical problems in a sample of very young (1 month–6 years) children in foster care.

In addition to these behavioral and medical problems, children in foster care also show delays in educational attainment. Almost one-third of Fanshel and associates' sample (1989a) were behind their age-appropriate grade level, and a significant minority of other children and adolescents in foster care attend special education classes to meet their challenging educational needs (Whittaker, Fine, & Grasso, 1989).

A COMPARATIVE LOOK AT CHILDREN IN OUT-OF-HOME CARE

To contribute to our developing understanding of these children, we compared the demographic, behavioral, health, and educational characteristics of children in group care, specialized foster care, foster family care, and kinship care in California.

The sample of children portrayed in this chapter was drawn from the cross-sectional mailed surveys described in the previous chapters. Several questions were asked of group home social workers, specialized foster parents, and other foster parents, including (1) the age and ethnicity of children served in their homes or agencies; (2) behavioral or medical problems children have exhibited; and (3) problems of acculturation or racism that children may display. Respondents were also asked to choose one child over the age of 2 who had resided in their home or agency as a foster child for at least 6 months. (In the case of group homes, administrators were asked to have a social worker answer this set of questions. Specialized foster parents, foster parents, and kinship foster parents were asked to respond to a similar group of questions.) If more than one child fit these criteria, respondents were asked to select the child whose first name started with a letter closest to the beginning of the alphabet. Respondents were asked to answer several questions about the educational and health needs of these children in addition to completing the Behavior Problems Index (BPI), a standard measure, on the selected child.

The BPI, developed by Zill and Peterson (1989) is designed to measure the frequency and range of several childhood behaviors. Many items included in the BPI were derived from the Achenbach Child Behavior Checklist (Achenbach & Edelbrock, 1981) and other child behavior scales (Graham & Rutter, 1968; Kellam, Banch, Agrawal, & Ensminger, 1975; Peterson & Zill, 1986; Rutter, Tizard, & Whitmore, 1970). The behavioral problems summary score is based on responses to a series of 28 questions dealing with specific problem behaviors that a child may or may not have exhibited in the previous 3 months. Scores range from zero to 28; higher scores represent a greater level of behavior problems. Three response categories ("often true, "sometimes true," and "not true:) are used in the questionnaire, but responses to the individual items are dichotomized and summed to produce an index score for each child. Six behavioral subscales can also be used: antisocial, anxious/depressed, headstrong, hyperactive, immature/dependent, and peer conflict/social withdrawal.

The instrument was used in the National Longitudinal Survey of Youth (NLSY) and was developed for English-speaking and Spanish-speaking mothers. In that survey, the instrument was normed on a sample of over 3,500 children, oversampling somewhat for poor and minority children. Norms are available for comparison with boys and girls ages 4 through 15 (for this reason our results will only reflect results for children ages 4 and older). The NLSY data show internal consistency reliability of the instrument as fairly high with an overall alpha coefficient of .90; test-retest reliability on this scale is somewhat lower at 0.63. The alpha coefficient for the BPI in our sample was .93.

Age and Ethnicity of Children

Figure 11.1 provides a breakdown of the percentage of children in various age ranges served in group care and in specialized foster care in this sample.[1] Percentages are listed as a proportion of the total number of children in each sample. As the figure indicates, group homes largely serve older children and adolescents, whereas specialized foster homes provide services to younger children. In our sample of group care providers we found, however, that 296 children between the ages of 1 week to 3 years old were being served in group homes. This represents approximately seven percent of the 4,492 children described in the survey. Furthermore, our sample included 125 children (3% of the sample) ages 4 and 5. (These findings are consistent with statewide data indicating that the proportion of infants to 5-year-olds in group homes across the state increased from 7% to 12% between 1987 and 1989.) The shift toward the use of group care for infants and very young children is cause for serious concern and is also discussed in other parts of this volume, especially Chapter 6.

Figures 11.2 and 11.3 also show the ethnicity of children in our sample of group care and specialized foster care. As the figures demonstrate, proportionately more Caucasian children are in specialized foster care than in group care. Mirroring the high overall numbers of African-American children in the foster care system (which is about 40%), African-American children are highly represented in group care and specialized foster care (African-American children are more likely to be placed in kinship care than in any other placement type; however, their overrepresentation in the more intensive settings, such as group care and specialized foster care, is also worthy of note). African-American children

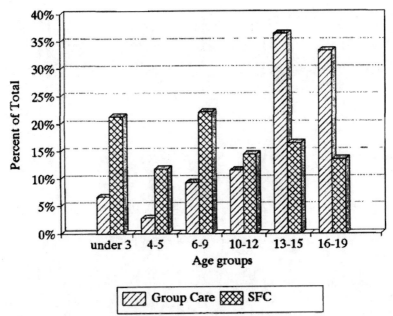

Figure 11.1.   Age of children in foster care.

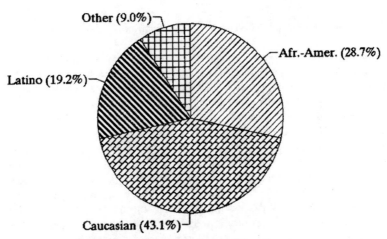

Figure 11.2.   Ethnicity of children in Group Care.

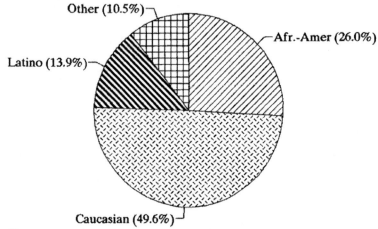

Figure 11.3. Ethnicity of children in specialized foster care.

represent almost 30% of the children in the group care sample, although their numbers in the general population are much lower (approximately 9% of the child population in the state). A similar situation is evident among African-American children in specialized foster care with about one-quarter of the sample including African-American children. Analyzing this sample in comparison to state wide data regarding children in group care and specialized foster care shows distinct similarities; this sample of children was highly representative of the overall population of children in group care and specialized foster care across the state.

Behavioral and Medical Problems of Foster Children

Agency administrators in group homes and specialized foster care agencies, as well as specialized foster parents were asked to identify the types of behaviors observed in the children they serve. Results from the survey indicate that children in both types of care exhibit a number of problematic behaviors that contribute to the difficulty in caring for their severe needs. A large majority of these children have a history of sexual abuse or physical abuse. Many show signs of acting out, aggression, sexual promiscuity, and substance abuse. Children served in specialized foster care are also seriously disturbed, although, taken as a group, they appear to be less difficult. Figure 11.4 displays the types of behaviors, problems, or past experiences that children "often" bring to foster care. In most areas, children's problems are noted as more severe by SFC agency administrators than by the actual foster parents caring for children. This

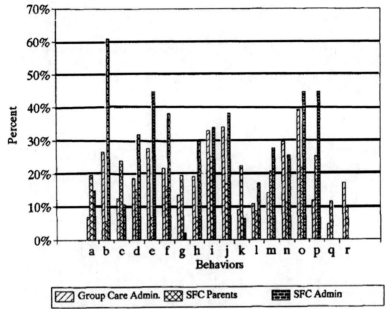

Figure 11.4. Behaviors "often" seen among children.
*Behaviors include the following: (a) aggressive to people; (b) gang affili-ated; (c) destroy property; (d) substance abuse behavior; (e) drug deal-ing; (f) misdemeanor crimes; (g) sexual acting out; (h) pregnancy; (i) self-induced injuries; (j) suicidal threats/attempts; (k) stealing; (l) tru-ancy; (m) runaway; (n) developmental disability; (o) eating disorder; (p) severely emotionally disturbed; (q) history of sexual abuse; (r) history of physical abuse.

may suggest that administrators are not as aware of the real concerns and needs of individual children in their care as are the direct service pro-viders. It may also indicate that administrators (at both the SFC agency level and the group care level) have a tendency to recall children with more problems.

The sample also included children who might be considered "medi-cally complex" or "medically needy." Figure 11.5 describes the types of medical issues administrators "often" see among children they serve. In this regard, children in specialized foster care show far more signs of medical problems than do children in group care. In particular, a signifi-cant number of children in SFC are prenatally drug or alcohol exposed. Although HIV-positive status or AIDS is a rarity in children in out-of-home care, affected children are more likely to be in group home care as opposed to specialized foster care. In fact, although only 2% of group care

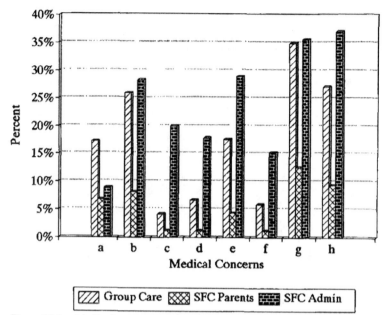

Figure 11.5. Medical concerns "often" seen.
*Medical concerns include the following: (a) infant drug addiction; (b) fetal alcohol syndrome; (c) external feeding tube; (d) oxygen dependency; (e) HIV/AIDS; (f) Down's Syndrome; (g) other special medical needs; (h) other special medical regimes.

administrators noted that they "often" served HIV-positive or AIDS children, another 3% indicated that they "sometimes" serve this population. As in earlier figures, we again see a far higher rate of medical need described by SFC administrators than by specialized foster parents.

Children coming into foster care also have special cultural issues. Given the expanding refugee and immigrant population in the western states, it is of little surprise that a significant percentage of the children in group care and specialized foster care evidence areas of special need such as refugee trauma, monolingualism, or as victims of racial violence. Respondents were asked the following question: "Please check any of the cultural characteristics on the list that are qualities of any of the children you have accepted into care." The wording of the question was designed to capture any difficulties administrators may have noted in their children over the years—not to capture the magnitude of the problem among current foster children. As Figure 11.6 demonstrates, group home children show far greater need in several areas of acculturation than specialized foster home children.

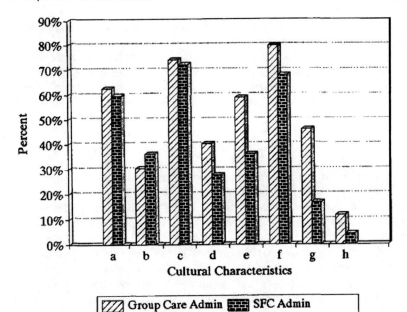

Figure 11.6. Acculturation issues.

*Acculturation issues include the following: (a) limited English proficient; (b) monlingual; (c) bilingual; (d) immigrant/refugee; (e) difficulty with acculturation; (f) internalized racial violence; (g) victim of racial violence; (h) other.

Portrait of a Typical Child in Out-of-Home Care

To gather more information about the children in out-of-home care, survey respondents were asked to provide some general information about one child in care. From this portion of the study a profile emerges of the typical child in care.

Group Care Children. Although children's ages ranged from 2 to 19, the average age of the child chosen for study was 13.4 ($n = 167$). The majority of the children were male (66%). Caucasian children were represented in the sample in about 47% of the cases, followed by African-Americans (26%), Hispanics (17%) and other ethnic groups (10%). Most children had been in group care for just over 1-year (15 months), although one child had been in his group home for approximately 6 years. The average cost of providing care to this sample of children was $2,991 per month (with a range from $1,365 to $8,577).

Specialized Foster Care Children. Of the 123 returned surveys, we received valid information on 87 (71%) children. Fifty-eight percent of our sample of children were girls (42% boys), about half (51%) were Caucasian, 21% were Hispanic, and 13% were African-American (15% were either listed as Asian/Pacific Islander, mixed, or other). Their ages ranged from 1 to 18, with a mean age of 12.1 years, somewhat below the average for group home children. The average monthly rate foster parents received for these children was $610 per month (ranging from $250 to $800/month). This group of children had been living with their foster parents for an average of 14 months, although some children also had been living in their present foster home for up to 6 years.

Specialized foster parents described these children's health as "excellent" in 54% of the cases, and "good" for 41% of the children. The average child was in sixth grade, and about 30% of the sample children had been held back or repeated a grade previously. Children generally received grades in the C+ range, and almost 40% of children were enrolled in some type of special education class. This included classes for learning disabilities (22%), speech and language (25%), severely emotionally disturbed (10%), classes for the mentally handicapped (2%), classes for the deaf or hearing-impaired (2%), or classes for the physically handicapped (6%). For the majority (over 80%) of the children in our sample, living with their present foster parents meant a change in their school. Nevertheless, in spite of these difficulties, almost one-half of the foster parents (47%) indicated that they were "very satisfied" or "satisfied" with the way their child was doing in school. (Questions regarding children's health status and educational status were not asked of group home children.)

Foster Family Care Children. Fifty-four percent of the children in foster family care were female (*n* = 189), 46% male (*n* = 160). The average age of selected children in foster homes was between 7 and 8 years (*M* = 7.66 years). Foster family children had been living with their caregivers for about 2.3 years, and the average monthly reimbursement rate for foster children was $480 per month (s.d. = $174).

In foster homes, 30% of selected children placed were Caucasians, 28% were African Americans, 22% Hispanics, and 14% other ethnicity. Same race placement was achieved with most Caucasian children in foster homes and was achieved with greater regularity among African-American children than with Hispanic children. Where 92% of selected Caucasian children in foster homes were placed with Caucasian families, two-thirds of African-American children were placed in African-American homes, and only 31% of Hispanic children with Hispanic caregivers (χ^2 = 211.5, df = 9, *p* < .001). When children were not placed with ethnically similar foster parents, they were almost always placed with Caucasians. Nearly one-half (48%) of Caucasian foster parents were caring for children of color.

Children were judged to be in good or excellent health by their providers, with only about 10.9% of children in fair health and 4.6% in poor health. Yet over two-fifths of these children were born prenatally exposed to drugs, according to their caregivers; about 10% were reported to have fetal alcohol syndrome (FAS). Twenty-five percent of children in foster care had other medical needs, such as asthma, and about 15% required other medical regimes, such as medications.

Children in foster family care were similar to kin children regarding behavior and school activities but appeared to be having more problems than children who are not in placement. About 61% of foster children were enrolled in school. Of these about one-third had either repeated a grade or were enrolled in special education classes. Somewhat fewer foster children required a change in schools than specialized foster children. When placed in foster care, about 59% of foster children were relocated to a different school.

Kinship Foster Care Children.   Similar to the children in foster family care, 52% ($n = 126$) of the selected children were female, 48% male ($n = 116$). In kinship homes, 63% of the selected children were grandchildren (including grandnieces and grandnephews), 33% were nieces or nephews, and 4% were otherwise related. On average, kinship foster children were also between 7 and 8 years old ($M = 7.91$ years). Selected children had been living in kinship homes for about 3.3 years, and the rate of reimbursement these providers received was about $367 per month (s.d. = $124).

African-American children were largely found in kinship foster homes. About 46% of selected children were African-American, compared with 32% Caucasian, 14% Hispanic, and 9% of other ethnicity.

Children were judged to be in excellent (47.8%) or good (41.2%) health by their relatives. Only about 9% were judged to be in fair health, and 2% were judged as in "poor or very poor" health. Similar to children in foster family care, many kin children were also exposed to drugs prenatally (about two-thirds), and about 10% were reported to have been born with FAS. Fifteen percent of these children had other medical needs (e.g., required surgery, had asthma), and about 15% of children required other medical regimes (e.g., medications). Over one-half (51%) of African-American children placed with kinship foster parents were born prenatally exposed to drugs.

Almost seven in 10 kin children described by the respondents were enrolled in school. Of these, about 23% of kin had repeated at least one grade, and about 26% were enrolled in special education classes. Of the children in special education classes, over one-half were in classes for learning disabilities, with over one-fourth enrolled in speech and language classes, and over one-fourth in classes for seriously emotionally disturbed children. Over two-fifths of their caregivers were satisfied or very satisfied with how their child was doing in school, and another 20% were somewhat satisfied. Unlike children placed in other settings, kin children were least likely to change schools when placed in foster care. About one-half of these children (49%) were required to change schools when placed with kin.

Behavior Problems.   Total scores for the group home sample of children were somewhat higher than total scores for children in specialized foster care. The total sample of group home children had a score of 21.75, whereas the specialized foster care population had a score of 17.14. Children in foster family care were reported to have somewhat more problems than children in kinship foster care but fewer problems than children in either group care or specialized foster care. Children in foster family care had a mean total score on the BPI of 15.6. At almost every age, children in foster family care had total scores that were more than 1 standard deviation above the mean compared to a national sample of children. Children in kinship care had fewer behavioral problems than other children in out-of-home care. Children's mean score on the BPI was 13.9. (Table 11.1 provides a breakdown of scores for the four groups.)

On the total BPI scale and on most of the subscales, group home children evidenced significantly greater behavioral problems than all other children in out-of-home care. Comparing our sample to the age-based norms established by the NLSY data, we find that the group home children in this sample were a highly disturbed group. That is, regardless of the age of the child, children were *at least* 2 standard deviations *above* the norm for a typical group of children the same age. Scores for three of the subscales (anti-social, anxious/depressed, and peer conflict) are very high compared to the national sample. The picture presented of group home children is rather sobering.

Specialized foster care children fare better than group home children. Nevertheless, scores for this group of children are also quite high and point to the extreme difficulties these children face in managing their behavior. Here, we see standard deviations far above the norm. However, the SFC children's average standard deviation above the norm hovers just below two (or less)—lower than the average for group home children. Although it is widely believed that specialized foster care acts as an alternative to group care, these data indicate that SFC children are largely a *less disturbed* group of children than those children in group care.

For specialized foster care, foster care, and kinship care children, we found no differences in children's BPI score based on the child's sex, age,

Table 11.1. BPI Scores

BPI Subscale	G.H. Mean Score	SFC Mean Score	Foster Mean Score	Kin Mean Score	F, df
Antisocial	5.06	3.74	3.08	2.92	33.26, 3/732***
Anxious/ Depressed	4.58	3.18	2.63	2.39	52.76, 3/737***
Headstrong	4.44	3.57	3.06	2.94	23.90, 3/744***
Hyperactive	3.76	3.24	2.89	2.71	11.41, 3/743***
Immature/ Dependent	2.55	2.22	2.13	1.85	7.36, 3/747***
Peer conflict	2.38	1.68	1.20	0.87	53.84, 3/748***
Total Score	**22.45**	**17.22**	**14.82**	**13.45**	42.18, 3/705***

* $p < .05$.
** $p < .01$.
*** $p < .001$.

months in care, medical needs, or ethnicity. (This is in contrast to Fein and associates' study [1990], which found that older children, boys, and Caucasians were more disturbed than other children in care.) In fact, few factors appear to be related to children's behavioral problems.

Surprisingly, the child's level of disturbance as indicated on the BPI and the number of hours seen by the child's social worker or the reimbursement rate the agency received were not related. As the data seem to indicate that there was little or no relationship between the behavioral disturbance of the child and the rate foster parents received for that child or between the child's disturbance and the number of social work services provided by the agency, it may be especially important to follow this issue closely. The BPI appears to be a robust test of behavioral problems (as indicated in the NLSY study), and responses to the BPI were also closely associated with foster parents' perceptions of the child's future prospects. Foster parents reported how well they expected their foster child to adjust to adulthood; these responses were compared to their responses to children's scores on the BPI. Three questions were asked to gauge their perception of the child's future adjustment: (1) I believe that this child will develop into an adult who ... forms close personal relationships easily; (2) Can care for self; (3) Can provide economically for self. We found that two out of three of these "future prospects" questions explained 60% of the variance in specialized foster children's BPI scores ($F = 13.77$, $p < .0001$).

Foster family parents appeared to have somewhat lower expectations for the children in their care than did kinship foster parents, and gave foster children a lower average rating than kin did for children in terms of their prospects for adult functioning. (There was no relationship between these "future prospects" questions and foster or kin children's BPI scores.)

Among the group home sample, children ages 6 to 11 had higher scores than the older children in the sample ($F = 5.58$, $p < .01$) on the BPI scale. This was again true for the antisocial subscale ($F = 4.87$, $p < .01$) although the differences were not significant for other subscales. Caucasian children tested higher (worse) on every scale and subscale. Analysis of variance tests showed Caucasian children to be significantly more behaviorally disturbed than African-American children on the total scale ($F = 2.77$, $p < .05$). Significant differences were again found between the high scores of Caucasian children and the relatively lower scores of African-American children on the anxious/depressed scale ($F = 3.33$, $p < .05$), the hyperactive scale ($F = 4.47$, $p < .01$), and on the peer conflict/social withdrawal scale ($F = 4.60$, $p < .01$). (Caucasians also had significantly higher scores on the peer conflict scale than children categorized as "other ethnicity.") Girls scored higher on the immature/dependent subscale than boys ($t = 4.38$, $p < .01$). However, there were no differences between gender on other scales.

The reimbursement rate each agency received per child was associated with the referral source from which the child had come; a few variables also appear to have an impact on the cost of group care. Analysis of variance tests showed a significant difference between the average rate paid by the Department of Mental Health ($3,614), the Department of Social Services ($3,003), and the Probation Department ($2,777) ($F = 4.33$, $p < .05$). A few variables (i.e., gender and number of services) taken together explained about 62% of the variance in rates ($F = 11.62$, $p < .001$). The number of services the agency provided predicted the rate the agency charged for services ($t = 2.30$, $p < .05$), and boys were more likely to be placed in facilities with higher rates of reimbursement than girls ($t = 2.14$, $p < .05$). Yet again, we found no relationship between the behavioral disturbance of the child and the rate of reimbursement the agency received to care for that child.

DISCUSSION

Our study points to the serious and acute nature of dependent children's problems. A significant number of children in foster care suffer from health problems, educational deficiencies, and are challenged with acculturation issues and racism. A large percentage of children were required to relocate to a different school when placed. Clearly, this type of change, at a time of great vulnerability, might have a good deal to do with children's abilities to cope well in the school environment. These findings also confirm other studies that point to the educational deficits children bring to foster care (Canning, 1974; Cohen, 1991a,b).

Children in foster care also are getting younger each year, and the increasing number of very young children in group care is especially distressing. Young children should not have ever-changing parents. In this sample, most children in group homes were expected to remain in care until emancipation; reunification outlooks for the whole sample were quite poor.

The vast majority of children in all placement settings exhibited behavioral problems that were reported to compromise their abilities to get along with others, to form close attachments, and to become responsible adult citizens. Certainly, there was a great difference between the level of behavioral disturbance among children in group care compared to children in kinship care. On average, children placed in kinship care show the fewest behavioral problems. Nonetheless, all children demonstrate elevated levels of behavioral problems, especially in comparison to national norms.

The findings concerning the relationships (or the lack thereof) between child behavior and placement characteristics should be judged with some caution. The survey measured child behavior while in placement for children who had been in these placements for varying lengths of time. There may be a differential "leveling" effect on child behavior resulting from the services provided at various reimbursement rates. For example, programs with higher reimbursement rates and more intensive services might be stabilizing childrens' behavior at levels close to those observed in less intensive settings, even though they admit into care children who are more disturbed than those admitted to programs with lower reimbursement rates. It may be that there is a threshold of problematic behavior (albeit a high one) under which all programs succeed in managing their residents. Group home programs at different reimbursement levels may be using services of varying intensity to maintain children at similar levels of behavioral disturbance. Research efforts linking behavioral measures *prior* to placement to level of reimbursement and type of program are necessary to address this issue adequately.

Nevertheless, the best possible match should be made between the needs of children and the ability of various care providers to meet their needs. This is fiscally and developmentally sound. We believe that our findings have implications for social workers in the way that they make placement decisions. These decisions can have serious consequences for children who are inappropriately placed in facilities that cannot meet their treatment needs and for children who should be in foster family care where they can develop long-term relationships. The findings also have implications for social workers' time with children. Indeed, we did not find a relationship between the number of hours social workers spend with children and children's behavioral problems. Yet, children with intense behavioral issues may need additional time and service from their social worker.

We had expected that higher-cost homes would serve either more behaviorally disturbed children or more medically needy children. In fact, we found no relationship between these factors and the cost of care. This also leads one to question the rate structure for care providers. Higher rates should be based on more resource-rich environments. These intensive service settings should be available and used for children with the greatest needs. This is not to argue for reducing the pay of foster care providers or group home operators, as their job is essential for the care of dependent children. Instead, procedures for more appropriate decision making regarding which children should be served, where, and the types of services they should receive once accepted into one or another setting must continue to be developed.

The need for further investigation is great. For example, if extremely disturbed children are being served in relatively low-cost settings, what explains the response of group home staff and specialized foster care staff that the appropriateness of their referrals were generally quite good? One might have expected that staff from relatively low-cost facilities and homes serving extremely difficult children would have been rather disgruntled with the process. Instead, a large majority of respondents were pleased with the appropriateness of the referrals to their agencies. The high level of satisfaction with the placement decision indicates the need for a closer look at this issue. Certainly, it would appear there is a group of children in foster care who present special difficulties and who might benefit from additional services if we hope to improve their prospects for adjustment later on in life. These children are not allowed, however, to benefit from additional social work support or more costly (i.e., presumably better trained) foster care placements.

Placement decisions are not well understood (Phillips, Haring, & Shyne, 1971; Wells, 1991); a great deal is left to the discretion of social workers who are acting on their limited knowledge regarding the child and the child's needs. Social workers' knowledge about the children they serve may also be related to the size of their caseload. Evidence suggests that social workers' working conditions and high caseload sizes are not conducive to knowledgeable decisions regarding children's placements (Hess, Folaron, & Jefferson, 1992). Other factors also play a role in placement decisions, such as the availability of bed space and financial considerations. Based on our data, it is fair to suggest that whatever steps that can be taken to improve decision making—be it in the form of training and education, reduced caseload size, or larger systems changes—would be helpful. Other measures may show promise, too. Efforts to design a mechanism to assess children's needs at the time of placement are important to make sense out of a complex and sometimes idiosyncratic decision-making process. Although the need for group care is not likely to diminish for some children, our study points to the possibility of shifting less disturbed children out of group care and into specialized foster care. For example, although our data do not tell us how the medical and behavioral problems of the young and very young children in specialized foster care and group home care compare, we believe that the great majority of younger children could be cared for in specialized foster care. The impetus for this shift would not be a cost-cutting measure (although this would be an additional outcome). Instead, it would reflect our commitment to serving a group of children in the most appropriate and familylike setting based on their individual needs.

Other efforts to explore placement decisions with regard to kinship care and foster family care are also important, although it would appear that there is a range of placement alternatives, from least intensive and restrictive to highly intensive, and children, on average, are placed in settings that may be suited to their individual needs.

Summary of Key Findings and Recommendations Regarding the Characteristics of Children in Care

Finding	Recommendations
1. Children coming into care have an array of medical, mental health, educational, and behavioral challenges.	1a. Children in all placement settings exhibit problems that most parents would be challenged to meet effectively. Training and re-training that prepares staff and foster parents for the difficulties they will face in their work is essential. 1b. Information for all providers about the availability of community resources for children and their families should be regularly available.
2. Many children placed in foster care are forced to change schools at the time of placement. If replacement is necessary, children may also be required to change schools a second or third time.	2. Efforts to provide a seamless system of educational services to children should be made whenever possible. Foster youth advocates whose specific job duties focus on the educational needs of these children might do a great deal in reducing the stress and confusion that often accompanies a change in school settings.
3. Children's behavioral problems appear to fall along a continuum, with the least behaviorally disturbed children found in kinship foster care and the most disturbed children found in group care. Yet, within a care setting, there is was little correspondence found between the behavioral disturbance of the child and the rate of reimbursement received for that child.	3a. Placement decisions are often based on an array of factors outside of the needs of the child. Careful training should be provided to social workers so that the services provided by a particular agency or family will match the needs of the child. 3b. When a child is removed from his or her birth home, a treatment plan should be developed that specifies the types of services needed in accordance with the child's individual needs. A range of placement alternatives should be considered, so that the best possible match can be made. 3c. Regular assessments of children's progress and satisfaction with their placement should be made whenever possible to ensure a solid match between the child's needs and the agency's or family's ability to serve those needs. 3d. Child welfare agencies should work with community providers to create a system for placement that allows social workers to make rational decisions based on the needs of the child.

NOTES

1. Some questions were not asked of all four types of providers (i.e., group care, specialized foster care, foster family care, and kinship foster care).

IV

Implications

12

Trends and Recommendations for the Next Decade

We now stand squarely amid the second decade of permanency planning looking toward and planning the third. In this concluding chapter we further discuss issues identified in earlier chapters and additional salient child welfare trends to plan for the next decade.

CHILD ABUSE REPORTS CONTINUE TO SPIRAL UPWARDS

Americans are taking action against child abuse by continuing to make reports—more than 1.7 million reports on 2.7 million children (albiet, not an unduplicated count) in 1992 (DHHS, 1992). The public is clearly committed to public and personal acts on behalf of vulnerable children. Each year the National Committee for Prevention of Child Abuse asks Americans if they have done anything personally to prevent child abuse; those numbers continue to grow. In an example, more than 112,000 calls were received by the National Child Abuse Hotline within 5 days following a recent TV special watched by 45 million people, entitled "Scared Silent: Exposing and Ending Child Abuse" (Rowe, 1993).

These high levels of reports continue to be a mixed blessing to our child welfare system. Although they clearly indicate substantial community awareness of and concern about child abuse, an adequate response to the needs identified by these reports continues to elude most agencies. Although we may develop better mechanisms for informing reporters about the actions taken on their reports, we cannot expect that a dramatically greater proportion of children reported as abused or neglected will receive ongoing services even if federal IV-B funds for child abuse investigations and in-home services will eventually increase from $250 million to half a billion dollars per year under the family preservation and support provisions of the 1994 budget.

A dramatic change might occur if additional states change the funding of their child welfare services from IV-B to the Emergency Assistance component of Title IV-A of the Social Security Act. This approach— already taken by several states, including Georgia, Pennsylvania, North Dakota, and Michigan—treats child abuse reports or the risk of out-of-home care as a family emergency. The states may then respond to the emergency with a package of services which are 50% reimbursable with federal funds. These services can include social work case-management services, cash costs for rent or home repair, and even the cost of emergency placement of the child where removal is determined necessary. These funds are limited to a maximum 6-month period every 12 months. The eligibility for these funds may be set above the AFDC level, in essence making services available to the great majority of families who need emergency economic and family services. There is general agreement that economic issues are a critical component of most child abuse reports and that families should not have to go through formal court proceedings and child welfare because of poverty alone (Besharov, 1992; Pelton, 1989). Our findings concur that neglect, most closely tied to poverty, is the reporting reason that most substantially increases the risk of out-of-home care. Refinancing of child abuse assessments and investigations (and reinvesting of existing resources into prevention programs) could dramatically expand our capability of responding.

Funds that are reinvested from IV-B or from the state or county contribution to serving high-risk families might be distributed to public and community agencies on the basis of risk factors like those identified in Chapter 2. Such efforts to fund at least in part on the basis of need, rather than on the basis of caseload alone, offer intuitive and practical advantages by allowing for more community-based work. Such work is beginning to occur with stronger collaborations between schools and child welfare agencies to develop family resource centers and on-site social services (Duerr, Berrick, & King, 1992; McCauley, 1993).

Population-based models that identify the likelihood that a child in a given community will be reported for child abuse or enter foster care provide a basis for evaluating such approaches. Wulczyn's (in press) groundbreaking work linking birth records and foster care records for children born in every zip code area in New York City offers a paradigm for evaluating the impact of community services to reduce child abuse and foster care stays. Such ecological approaches have been described elsewhere (Barth & Derezotes, 1990; Zuravin, 1989).

CHILD ABUSE ASSESSMENTS ARE THE MOST COMMON CHILD WELFARE SERVICE

Among child welfare services, ER contacts have become the child welfare service that most families receive; they contain the seeds of greatest harm and good. Child welfare workers make several million each year. Nationally, in 1982, 34% of the children whose child abuse or neglect report was confirmed entered substitute care—by 1988 the rate was 29% (Tatara, 1990). In 1976 in California, 40% of all child abuse reports were followed by ongoing in- or out-of-home services: Now only 8% result in additional services. Unfortunately, we have little data on the benefits that results from those ER contacts. Problems that arise from unhelpful or unnecessary investigations or removals generate more public interest, but recent research from Iowa (Fryer et al., 1990) indicates that clients' satisfaction with those contacts and the social workers who made them were strongly positive. Although they were less positive in cases that resulted in court dependency and supervision, they were still positive. On the whole, CPS social workers were judged as skilled, empathic, and helpful.

The 1980s has also witnessed substantial growth in the sophistication of child abuse risk assessment and investigations (the latter is a terrible term inherited from our history of having police authority remove children and should be replaced by *assessment and referral*). The challenge has been great. Imagine if child welfare agencies were informed in 1976 that they were to narrow their intake criterion, so that they were only providing ongoing services to one of five cases and that they had to do so without substantially increasing the risk of serious harm to children. Even without being able to forecast that this would occur in the midst of a sea of homelessness and crack cocaine, it would have seemed like an impossible task. To meet this challenge, child welfare agencies in many parts of the country have increased their training requirements and conducted additional training around risk assessment.

CHILD WELFARE SERVICES BECOME INCREASINGLY ARTICULATED AND ACCOUNTABLE

Every aspect of child welfare services is more clearly articulated today than it was in 1980. Programs and legal status have been clarified, so that social workers, at least, and most often families, know what is going on. This has been achieved with much compromise in the social worker flexibility. Clearer child abuse definitions, more time limits, and more administrative and judicial review affect every aspect of child welfare.

This trend may be ready to reverse itself. The interest in family continuity is partly a call for more social worker discretion in deciding which kind of family arrangement is best for individual children. The movement toward funding on the basis of economic need rather than child abuse disposition also has roots in the belief that more intervention should be done prior to entering the judicial labyrinth. Experts generally agree that more mediation and diversion from court is in the future. Great Britian has already begun the implementation of national child welfare reform that requires such an approach (Gaskins, 1993).

This does not mean that child welfare practice will become less accountable. The flowering of administrative data will almost certainly result in clearer analyses of individual and agency practice patterns. Outcome indicators like those used in this volume (e.g., reunification, adoption, and recidivism rates) will be routinely available (Courtney, 1993). The improved reporting and analysis of such data should, ironically, provide agencies with the justification to search for alternative methods to achieve their goals.

CHILD WELFARE SERVICES ARE FOCUSING ON INFANTS AND YOUNG CHILDREN

At least for now, the ages of children coming to the attention of child welfare services providers is dropping. The greatest growth in children's services has resulted from the massive influx of infants into foster care during the latter part of the 1980s—an influx that has only slightly abated since then. The roles of the child welfare social worker and the public health nurse are fusing around assessments of the adequacy of postnatal care, preventive home visiting, and assessment of harm.

The CWS is not ready for the influx of infants, as evinced by their relatively long stays in care. The existence of group home care for young children is evidence of the need to develop more alternatives for young and, especially, medically fragile children. When very young children cannot remain at home or cannot return home or to kin quickly, we strongly encourage placement for adoption. Adoption delayed is adoption denied. Although children of all ages can be adopted, children with the best chance of getting adopted and staying adopted are young children.

Another extension of the need to retool child welfare services to prevent the need for foster care for young children involves the lack of integration between family planning and child welfare services. In Chapter 2 we showed the importance of births as an explanation of the growth in child abuse dispositions. Other research suggests that unwanted births are particularly likely to result in child abuse reports (Zuravin, 1991). Furthermore, we have evidence that women who receive drug treatment services—a group at significant risk of involvement with the CWS—report that they rarely have discussions about sexuality or family planning with their counselors (Armstrong, Kenen, & Samost, 1991). Because CWS providers have a shared interest in reducing births among drug-involved families, they must collaborate with family planning services and drug treatment services to find strategies for reaching current and potential child welfare clientele.

KINSHIP FOSTER CARE SWELLS

There were an estimated 430,000 children in foster care in 1992 as contrasted with 274,000 in 1980 (Child Welfare League of America, 1983; Tatara, in press). The per capita foster care rate of 4.0 per 10,000 in 1980 grew to 5.8 per 10,000 in 1990. This reflects a 49% increase in the foster care rate despite only a 1% increase in the number of children 0–18. These figures are difficult to interpret because of the phenomenal growth of kinship foster care. We know from our data and from other published reports from New York and Illinois, that about 40% of the children in foster care are in kinship care (Wulczyn & Goerge, 1992). As these states contain nearly 40% of all children in foster care, the reduction of 70,000 kinship foster care children from the statistical tallies for these states would reduce the national foster care census by 16%. If other states are also showing at least two-thirds as much growth in kinship foster care, and our informal information suggests that this is a reasonable estimate, we would expect that another 70,000 children are in kinship care in these states. The overall tally of nonkinship children in foster care would be, quite approximately, 292,000 or 7% higher than it was in 1980. (Recognizing the roughness of these estimates and that some foster children were in kinship foster care in 1980, a somewhat greater change in the nonkinship foster care census may have occurred in the 1980s.) If we interpret family to include kin and recognize the vastly greater threats to family stability from poverty, drugs, HIV, and homelessness, we can argue that the 1980s shows considerable success in keeping children with their family. As social problems and poverty escalated at astounding rates, placement of children in nonkinship care increased slowly.

Using a family continuity standard for evaluating the CWS, the 1980s have indeed been a time of substantial advance. Measuring the 1980s by the permanency planning yardstick of child welfare's enabling legislation shows a somewhat different result. Although we expect that kinship foster care may result in a lifetime (i.e., permanent) commitment (despite the frequent lack of permanent legal ties), it is still not clear how this compares to kinship or nonkinship adoption.

The recent surge in kinship foster care is having unanticipated consequences on the CWS. Kinship care may be a welcome option for social workers and judges who have difficult decisions to make about leaving a child at home or placing the child into an unrelated (perhaps transracial) foster family home. Kinship care may be allowing more placements by mitigating some of the family disruption that might otherwise occur with placement. Our results have shown that kinship care enhances visitation with birth families and is more likely to result in the child remaining in a consistent school and neighborhood. A study on the residential arrangements of kinship foster care providers in Illinois found that many children remain within the same apartment complex (Goerge, Harden & Lee, 1993). Kinship care is also a blessed option for social workers concerned about the rapid reunification of children to risky homes. As research shows, children in kinship foster care are reunified at very slow rates. Indeed, less than 30% of children in kinship foster care are reunified by 18 months, whereas 30% of children in nonkinship care go home by 6 months. At the end of 3 years, fewer than one-half of the children in kinship care will go home. Indeed, our data indicates that when children go home from kinship foster care, they are 40% less likely to reenter care within the next three years. Kinship foster care is welcome news for those concerned about the diminished availability of conventional foster care providers and the growing cost of specialized foster care providers; and kinship foster care is good news for those who believe in lifetime families and the hope that these kinship arrangements are forever.

Kinship care is not an unmitigated good for those who worry about the rights of birth parents to get their children back expeditiously, for those who are concerned that government is taking over where extended family heretofore reigned, and for those eager for the day when foster care would become a therapeutic intervention rather than a setting in which preexisting problems may intensify. Although kinship care may provide many developmental opportunities for children, there are certainly compromises. One such compromise involves placements with kin whose advanced age or poor health may make the placement much shorter than "permanent." One influential judge became so concerned about the adoption of children by kin who were much older that he endeavored to have a regulation instituted that would limit adoption of a child by a person more than 60 years older. This proposal was defeated, and so was the subsequent proposal that would limit adoptions by persons 70 years older than the child. In California, the income of kinship foster parents who adopt is considerably below the poverty line and nearly one-half lack a high school education (Magruder, in press). Given the intergenerational consistency in educational attainment, and the strong link between education and health, and well-being the short-term advantages of family continuity in such cases must be weighed against the diminished futures predictable for many children in kinship care.

FOSTER CARE IS GETTING HARDER TO ENTER AND HARDER TO LEAVE

Foster care drift and limbo—the Scylla and Charybdis of the prepermanency planning era—are still pulling down their fair share of young futures. Still, we have a foster care system that is far harder to get into and somewhat easier to leave than it was in the 1980s. The reasons for leaving foster care have changed sharply during permanency planning. In California, returning home to the parent has continued to be the exit reason in about two-thirds of the cases. This figure peeked in 1986 at 72% of cases and is now at 66%. With nearly 20,000 case closings every year, that is a substantial difference. Some of the caseload growth is attributable to the growth in kinship foster care, but this does not dismiss the limited exits from foster care for nonkinship placements. Indeed, in California among children who entered nonkinship and nongroup home foster care since 1988, only 10% went home in 2 weeks, 20% by 2 months, 30% by 7 weeks, 40% by 1 year, and 50% went home by 2.5 years. (We do not have good pre-permanency planning data with which to compare these numbers.)

There is no definitive evidence that the administrative reviews instituted under permanency planning reduce drift and limbo. There does, however, seem to be some impact. When you plot the transition rate home from foster care, children go home quickly at first then the return levels off after about 6 months. Now, this return rate is rather smooth and downward sloping except it has substantial and upward bumps at the judicial review. At these permanency planning review points, the flow of children out of the foster care system is accelerated. The impact of those hearings on the lives of children and, specifically, on the reunification rate appear to be substantial. (It is also possible that some children would have gone home before then but remain in care until the review.) This finding seems consistent with Goerge's (in press) cited findings that case transfers expedite reunifications. Such transfers may add to the impetus to reconsider reunification—that is, "Can I send this child home rather than transfer her or him?" We need to learn more about the subsequent recidivism rate for children sent home under these circumstances.

Certainly, slow exits from care are a major issue. In the data we described, 25% of children go home by 6-months, but 2½ years later over one-half still have not gone home. Some policy analysts have used similar evidence of exit patterns—derived from event-history data on the reunification of foster children in Illinois—to argue that we need more court reviews (Goerge, 1990). In particular, they suggest that we need court reviews at 3 months in order to be sure that every possible child goes home at the time when children still have considerable likelihood of going home. Such early court reviews could also minimize lengthy stays of young children in institutional settings. Intensive family reunification services should span this review. We would also argue that these data call for continuing to study children who are reunificated up to 3 years later to understand why they were not returned home sooner.

SPECIAL-NEEDS ADOPTION GAINS AND LOSES PROMINENCE

There would be no permanency planning movement without the expansion in the 1970s of special-needs adoption. Special-needs and older child adoption convinced legislators and child welfare administrators that there was a way to exit the foster care system. This belief in the capacity of adoption to create permanent and loving families allowed for the institution of the permanency planning time frames institutionalized in P.L. 96-272.

Adoption began to provide a substantial outlet for children in foster care immediately following the passage of P.L. 96-272 all across the country. In California, adoption was a termination reason for less than 4% of children who left foster care, or one-in-nine exits from foster care other than family reunification at the outset of permanency planning. By 1990, adoption was the reason to exit foster care for about 10% of all children who left each year or, about one-in-four children who did not go home. Foster parent adoptions are an important innovation of the 1980s. In California, as in other states, well over 80% of all older child agency adoptions are by foster parents, and foster parent adoptions increased as the proportion of exits from 2.5% in 1986 to 4.5% by 1990. Indeed, just as many residential treatment programs developed an adoption component in the 1970s and 1980s, many adoption agencies are now developing a specialized foster care program in order to recruit and prepare families and to underwrite the unmet costs of the adoption. Both developments are supportive of family continuity for children.

Little did permanency planning's founding mothers and fathers expect that older child and special-needs adoption would fall from grace and that the likelihood of being adopted out of foster care would move forward for a few years and then stall. At this time, adoption does not provide a major exit from foster care for America's children. Our findings show this to be true for the vastly increasing proportion of children in kinship foster care, but it also appears true for children in conventional nonkinship foster care. Many children younger than 3 who do not live with kin have long-term foster care (or as they call it in New York State "independent living") as their permanent plan. Many, and perhaps most, of them are African-American and biracial.

The reasons deserve some mention. First, social workers and judges have never really believed in sufficient numbers that having a lifetime family was really important. They have lifetime families of origin, and most have children of their own and they love them until death do their part. Yet, they seem content to give other children under their supervision a family or group home until age 18. We find it hard to imagine succeeding in this age without any support after age 18. Yet, child welfare professionals find a hundred excuses for denying children adoptive homes—the biggest being that a child is unadoptable. Other frequently discussed reasons are that older child adoptions do not work out very well. This is not, however, supported by research (Barth, 1990; Rosenthal, 1993), even though there are some spectacular cases to the contrary. Finally, there is the excuse that there are no ethnically matched homes because adoption recruitment is poor.

Moreover, states do not save that much money when they place a child for adoption. The Federal government reimburses states for adoption subsidies and for foster boarding care at the same rate (Barth, 1993). Although administrative costs are lower for adoption cases than foster care cases, these savings are somewhat offset by home study and parental rights termination expenditures. In addition, federal reimbursement should be available for postplacement services, including spells in group home care, as needed. The absence of such federal support for adoption, as compared to foster care, is a further disincentive. (The great financial advantage of adoption accrues to the child through the continued support of their adoptive families; but children do not vote on public policy.) For adoption to have greater financial advantages to states, the federal sharing ratio for adoption subsidies and administrative costs should be increased (e.g. to 75%).

Another reason why children are not being adopted is that social workers and judges too often think of adoption as a mental health program and do not understand that it is a social services program. As such, they allow all kinds of psychological conjecture about the needs of children to override the basic needs of children to have a family that can see them through the thick and thin of housing and education and health care across the long term. Yes, adoption may aggravate some identity issues, but few youths would trade those transient identity issues for a lifetime of being completely on their own after age 18.

Relatedly, children are not adopted because there are not enough approved same race homes and because enough child welfare service providers believe that this shortage can be remedied by recruiting more same race homes or by family preservation to reduce future placements. No one can argue with the need for more adoptive parent recruitment or family preservation services on the grounds of fairness. Yet, given the virtual absence of evidence that better adoption recruitment can make a significant impact in adoption rates for children in care, and that family preservation can substantially reduce placement rates, these beliefs must only be viewed as naive. The effect of these ruses is to reduce the urgency to place today's foster child in adoption. Instead, we focus on recruiting families or preventing placement for tomorrow's foster child. To reduce unnecessary foster care we must refocus on placing today's young foster child before he or she becomes tomorrow's older group care child.

The proportion of children who cannot go home from foster care but can exit foster care by adoption needs to increase again. Many willing families are already available and interested in being adoptive parents, but agencies are ruling them out on the basis of reasons that may be more important to the social worker than the child. The Federal Office of Civil Rights has encouraged agencies to have a more flexible policy about racial matching, for example. Maybe shifts in sharing ratios between the federal government and the states or between state and local government will increase adoptions because of more striking adoption cost savings. Or perhaps intensive family preservation and reunification programs will more dramatically identify children who cannot go home and be used as a trigger for aggressive adoption. It may require all three of these changes for adoption to resume a prominent role in the next decade.

GUARDIANSHIP WILL EXPAND

As the demand for child welfare services has grown, the demand for a range of informal mechanisms for protecting children has also increased (Takas, 1992). Relative and nonrelative guardianships have become an increasingly significant outlet for children in foster care and for children cared for by kin who are not formally foster parents. Several states now have laws that allow paid guardianship status, and the American Bar Association is proposing still broader consideration of paid guardianship as an alternative to kinship foster care or kinship adoption. This is an area of child welfare practice that will grow sharply but that has virtually no research support. The legal and fiscal issues involving all forms of kin and fictive kin care are going to be a rich area of practice—for social workers and attorneys! At this point we see little reason to expand this classification. Children in foster care should get services. Adopted children get permanency. Children with guardians are assured of neither.

INTEGRATION OF FAMILY PRESERVATION, ASSESSMENT AND REFERAL

Family preservation services have lost some luster as a result of several evaluations with rather uninspiring results (e.g. Rzepnicki et al., in press; Yuan & Struckman-Johnson, 1992). The latest difficulties in showing placement prevention or cost-offset effects are partly attributable to the trends identified in Chapter 1 showing that the likelihood of getting into foster care had diminished a lot. Even family preservation control groups avoid foster care more than three-quarters of the time. The days of conceptualizing family preservation as a placement and cost-reduction strategy are numbered (Litter, Schuerman, Rzepnicki, Howard, & Budde, 1993).

As discussed, investigation has become the most used child welfare service. Each year in this country, nearly 800,000 families have contact with an ER social worker investigating a child abuse report (some of them even get more than one). Child protection services investigations have become the most recent child welfare services scapegoat. There is a steady hue and cry for the narrowing of child abuse definitions and for limits on mandatory reporting (Besharov, 1990). Most of these calls are caused by the potential infringements on civil liberties of "investigations" and because of the curious notion that if we had fewer investigations, we would have more resources to use to provide services.

At the same time, voluntary family maintenance has become all but extinct in California and is on the endangered list in other states. Formal in-home services were getting shorter each year, although they appear to have increased somewhat as a result of crack cocaine (Barth, in press). In the meantime, in parts of the country that have embraced brief intensive family preservation services, some in-home service programs have shrunk to a 28-day model. The result is that by the end of this decade, ER investigations and family preservation interventions may be indistinguishable.

This can work to the good. Reconceptualizing "investigations" as "assessment and referral" and allowing more time for social workers to provide direct linkage services might, at best, reduce entrances into foster care and trips to court and, at least, provide more assistance to families in trouble. Intensive family preservation services have shown that families receive some benefit from relatively brief (i.e., less than a month) interventions (Fraser et al, 1991). We need to harness this good for more clients. As many as one-third of child abuse reports might result in focused 2-day to 20-day family preservation services (in conjunction with powerful school-based social and health services, one hopes). Families that have the wherewithal to benefit from services at home will receive them very briefly. This could also be a very unfortunate trend if all services become abridged—the many families involved with substance abuse may need considerably longer services.

In the next decade we will see considerably more financial support for in-home services. The call to invest as much in families at home as we do in families in out-of-home is finally finding hearing ears in Washington. Increases in Title IV-B funding for in-home services have begun with the first Clinton budget. Perhaps more critical, several states are moving toward using the Emergency Assistance provisions of Title IV-A (an uncapped federal program) to provide up to 6 months (per year) of service that can include respite care, drug treatment services, housing assistance, and concrete benefits, such as a home or car repair. An entitlement to substantial in-home services (even if limited to 6-months) might finally achieve the long-postponed goals of the reasonable efforts provisions of permanency planning.

THE LENGTH OF FOSTER CARE IS RISING AGAIN

Nationally, the length of foster care appears to have been cut sharply since permanency planning. At the same time, the ages of children in foster care have come down in recent years. Infants have come into care in droves in recent years, and hey are not going home in any hurry. Data from California, New York, and Illinois indicated that only 25% of very young children entering foster care are back home by 1 year. With the enormous growth of foster care for African-American children and the severely constrained exits from foster care (because of kinship foster care or because of institutional racism that judges many of these children unadoptable), we have a lot of years of foster care ahead of us. Placement with relatives is no longer a common reason to exit foster care as it once was. In California placement with relatives has diminished from 12% of foster care exits in 1985 to 4%.

African-American children enter foster care at a rate higher than expected by population characteristics alone, but more of the reason that they are in foster care in such large proportions is that they stay longer. African-American children are clearly less likely to leave foster care, within the time frames of this study, they were one-half as likely to go home and one-fifth as likely to be adopted as Caucasian children. Our findings, like those of other child welfare researchers in the 1980s, indicate the "disproportionate" representation of "minority" children in foster care. Our findings add some clarity to questions about whether the causes of this disproportionality and how it operates. First, we learn that the minority ethnic or racial group of children represented in foster care at levels much higher than expected in the population are African-American; California's substantial Asian population is represented in foster care at a rate well below the expected rate on the basis of population, and Latino children are represented at the expected per capita rate.

The next decade may bring more careful conceptualization and measurement of "disproportionality." This could tell us whether the disproportionate representation of African-American children in foster care indicates that African-American children enter foster care at a rate that exceeds their need for protection or that other ethnic groups enter foster care at a rate that is less than or equivalent to what is needed. We do have some limited information from child abuse reports data in this volume that addresses this question. African-American children are disproportionately referred to child protective services for the conditions most likely to lead to foster care: severe neglect, multiple referrals, and caretaker absence or incapacity. Much of the disproportionality of foster care use by African-American children is attributable to economic conditions that result in higher rates of neglect and caretaker incapacity. This proposition is further evinced by the finding that the condition of poverty is associated with a slower transition home.

Children of color may be entering foster care according to their need for protection and care. If this is so, then we will not see much benefit for minority children from reforms in our child welfare system that reduce the "disproportionate" entrance of minority children into foster care. We will see greater benefit from reducing the need for protection and care—fundamentally through greater economic opportunity. We believe that the foster care census could be reduced with reforms that offer concrete services for family preservation and family reunification and may shorten stays in foster care. The advancement of treatment foster care as an alternative to group home care, especially for younger children, is also likely to accomplish some of the goals of speedier transitions home and greater likelihood of a subsequent adoption. Adoption programs that focus on home finding rather than matching could also lower the foster care census.

THE EXPANSION OF SHARED FAMILY CARE

Just as ER investigations and family preservation approaches will be merged in the 1990s, so will family maintenance and family reunification. The conflict between the protective capacities of placement and the family preservation capacities of in-home services will be reduced with a new model of service. "Shared Family Care" involves preserving families by placing them in care together. More precisely, shared family care describes the "planned provision of out-of-home care to parent(s) and children so that the parent and host caregivers simultaneously share the care of the child and work toward independent in-home care by the parent(s)" (Barth, 1993, p. 273).

Shared family care arrangements are increasingly abundant in home-less shelters for families, substance abuse treatment residences for pregnant and parenting women, and adolescent mothers in foster care. The concept is too good to be ignored, as it provides the child the protection of foster care and the family preservation of family maintenance services to be so limited in use. Shared family care arrangements will become a more central part of child welfare services in the near future.

Policymakers must find ways to accommodate shared family care. Revision of Title IV-E of the Social Security Act that would allow states to apply for waivers (as they can do under other titles, such as IV-A and XIX) would allow states to experiment with paying foster care costs even if the mother and child reside in the same household. Also, the Emergency Assistance provisions of IV-A can be used quite flexibly and are ideal for paying for short-term shared family care.

THE INFORMATION AND OUTCOME AGE ARE DAWNING

Child welfare service providers are attempting to round the corner and move from the *recordkeeping* age to the *information* age. In many ways we are now in an intermediate stage that we might call the *data* age. We are finding ways to condense the time and storage needed for recordkeeping and to improve our retrieval of information about children and families.

We are learning to code and manage data. The next great challenge is to turn this routinely collected data into information that we can use for policy, administration, and practice.

Children's services professionals are going to continue to hear about individual-level administrative data. At least two major federal initiatives so guarantee. In an effort to supply an adequate knowledge base for national child welfare policymaking, Congress in 1986 directed the U.S. Department of Health & Human Services to establish a new federal data-collection system for foster care and adoption. This legislation has resulted in the planning (though not yet implementation) of the Adoption and Foster Care Analysis and Reporting System (AFCARS). When the AFCARS is implemented, perhaps not for several more years, each state will be responsible for developing mechanisms that will produce AFCARS-compatible data from their own information systems. These data, forwarded to the federal government on a quarterly basis, will provide detailed information about all children who have lived in (or recently been adopted from) foster care placements during that period. When implemented, the AFCARS will be a national system of foster care and adoption data, providing a large amount of comparable indicators at the individual-case level. The system should provide the federal government with a national data resource of quality and integrity for monitoring and analyzing the foster care caseloads, both in the states and nationally. After the data have been collected for several years, an extensive time-series of foster care caseload data will be established. The data will lend themselves to analysis by a variety of statistical techniques that examine aggregate trend data, yielding an array of information about the foster care population and aggregate patterns of caseload change.

The creation of the AFCARS will represent substantial progress toward developing national data resources for child welfare policy support. Using the AFCARS, researchers will be able to profile the national foster care caseload and to analyze the characteristics of the population of children in care, the nature of their service environment, and many of the transition events that mark a child's foster care career. The AFCARS data will begin to provide the type of comprehensive reporting that policymakers have demanded for years. However, the usefulness of the AFCARS for analyzing trends will be restricted to a fairly small range of issues, mostly involving changes in aggregate caseloads and case flows. In technical terms, the AFCARS will be made up of a set of repeated cross sections of the national foster care population (and state subpopulations). Cross-sectional data have inherent limitations. They supply a clear snapshot of the foster care population at certain points, but even when analyzed across time, the cross-sectional data cannot accurately reflect certain continuities in the foster care system. Because they cannot fully capture the movements of individual children between placements and into and out of care, critical aspects of foster care and service patterns will be obscured (Goerge, 1992).

Chapin Hall at the University of Chicago is coordinating a multistate foster care data archive that would complement the AFCARS and make available a wealth of new information about foster care, foster children and their families, and related human services. After just one year in operation the data archive has generated a single data set of placement histories of foster children in care since 1988 in Illinois, New York, Texas, Michigan, and California. It is longitudinal, preserving for study the case histories of the population of children who have experienced substitute care. It will have a multistate focus and will contain data from at least 10 large states by the end of the initial 5-year period; this will comprise more than two-thirds of the nation's total foster care population. Finally, in addition to containing comprehensive data on children in foster care, the archive will incorporate data from other sources, especially from agencies providing human services and financial assistance to children and families and from those maintaining vital statistics. In instances where children have had contact with more than one agency, the various data records for each such child may be linked, so that the longitudinal records in the foster care database can be enriched by an array of data to add to the basic characteristics of foster children. Each of these systems contains the data required to make truly longitudinal databases—some states have already computerized foster care data going back almost twenty years. This reduces the need for expensive data collection, which is a prohibitive feature of most longitudinal research. The foster care will help them to understand the value and limits of child welfare information of all types.

This emerging information age will eventually (but not in the short term) lead to the *outcome* age. We already have stunning new capabilities to understand the changes in placement status that result for children. As we show in this volume, we are developing ways to explain the status changes as a result of the characteristics of children. The great challenge that we must address next is to determine the impact on case status of the services we provide given the characteristics of children and families (and previous services provided).

The information age will eventually force us to focus more clearly on our outcomes. We will more definitively than ever before need to determine the goals of child welfare services. In time, we will be able to trace the pathways of children born in each community as they experience foster care, criminal justice, general assistance and a university education. As the capacity or incapacity of child welfare services to prevent long-term problems for children become clearer, the strategic use of child welfare services is going to be hotly debated. Indeed, if the social fabric continues to fray at the rate we have witnessed in the 1980s, we may witness sharp differences in health, education, and career outcomes between similarly situated children who do and do not receive child welfare services and between children who receive foster care and adoption. The bright light of the information age will make the debate on those outcomes glow hot. We can expect that at some point, funding will be tied to achieving these outcomes. The complex moral, judicial, and statistical issues that must first be resolved and the current nascent nature of data may make that day closer to the end of the next decade than this one.

In order to realize the benefits of the information age, child welfare administrative data must be made useful to those who create them: child welfare workers. Many of the limitations of existing administrative data stem from the lack of interest and often disdain directed by social workers at the task of recording such information. Future management information systems will provide on-line access for social workers to information about the families and children under their care. Furthermore, they will be designed to expedite recordkeeping, rather than to complicate it further.

RATIONALIZING OUT-OF-HOME CARE

The information age will bring new opportunities for the CWS to rationalize placement decisions. As shown in our discussion of children entering group home care, we are currently able to trace the differential service careers of children of a given age and reason for entering the CWS through a variety of placements. The weakness common to our current foster care management information systems is that they provide too little information about children's behavior characteristics and service characteristics. This can be remedied by developing a reasonable-size set of indicators that help to describe the child's behavior at entrance and exit from placements (Courtney, Barth, & Allphin, 1993). The next piece is to add a description of the service elements available in each level of out-of-home care available to children. Finally, using large-sample statistical methods, we can estimate the transitions from placement type to placement type controlling for previous placement histories. In this way we can continue to test such time-honored but also untested assumptions, such as whether early placements in group care can prevent subsequent failures in foster care, whether g oup care stabilizes children so they can go home sooner, and whether the sense of belonging in kinship children results in fewer placement changes even for difficult children.

INDEPENDENT LIVING SKILLS PROGRAMS WILL EVOLVE

This book has had little to say about children who age out of foster care. The latest trends in foster care have turned policymakers' heads toward the very young children entering care. At this time, there is not a sufficient data trail that links these entering children with the exiting youths. We know from our work and others', however, that many children are leaving care at very slow rates. We also know that the adolescent population in the United States is swelling again. Adoption appears overmatched and, at best, seems to be losing its acceptance. This predicts the expansion of the need for services for youths who will walk a long path of foster care.

The 1980s has seen great advances in the development of independent living skills programs for youths about to leave foster care. These youths certainly deserved better preparation, and now they are getting it. This should not be mistaken, however, for a satisfactory solution to impermanency planning. Many adult children—between the ages of 18 and 28—who come from sound home environments and families and who are in, or finished with, college live with their mothers or fathers. Almost one-third of single men, and 20% of single women between the ages of 25 and 34 were living with their parents in 1990 ("Adult children come home," June 16, 1991). Independent living is not an acceptable goal for the great majority of children in foster care. Analogously, providing independent living skills program services at age 16 rather than adoption at age 6 is like providing *job club* rather than a college education. As O'Brien (1993) writes: "Abolish the goal of independent living.   The child should under no circumstances be allowed to sign a waiver stating he doesn't want to be adopted and that he wants his goal changed to "independent living." This is akin to asking a child to sign his own homelessness warrant or, in some cases, his own death warrant" (p. 6). Independent living skills programs must continue to expand their focus more on finding adoptive and birth parents and other kin who can provide lifetime family connections. They will also seek to encompass more hard services and provide an earlier start in preparing for life after foster care.

SPECIALIZED FOSTER CARE WILL EXPAND

Not only is the length of foster care growing. The quality is also improving. Treatment or specialized foster care is clearly an important advance of the 1980s across the United States and Europe. Children who would have been institutionalized or in congregate or shift care a few years back—children infected with HIV and children who are seriously emotionally disturbed—are now living with families. These specialized foster care arrangements are critical to the continuity and developmental appropriateness of such children's care (and the longevity of foster parent's career's). Unfortunately, the demonstration that specialized foster care is a powerful and personal intervention, especially for young children, has not yet resulted in the eradication of group home care for infants and toddlers. It is hard to believe, but our data show infants and young children continue to be placed in large shelter facilities and institutional residences as their first placement. We hope this is a unique California phenomenon but recognize with consternation that our years of research have found few things about California to be unduplicated elsewhere. The cost-to-benefit ratio of such an arrangement could hardly be lower—a lot of money is spent to do what almost every family could do much better for a lot less. We believe that the growth of group care for young children is partly a result of "defensive" social work practice, in which social workers make placement decisions on the basis of these concerns about the safety of the placement (rather than the well-being of the child). Greater availability of treatment foster care should reduce the need for this practice. The placement of young children in shift care where they have one parent in the morning and one in the afternoon and go to bed with still a third is, in all but the rarest of circumstances, an unnecessarily costly and developmentally hazardous practice.

CONCLUSIONS

Child welfare services are certainly a weather vane for the greater society. The fraying of the social, educational, and health services system that is resulting from our recent economic downturn will send more families to our doors. Over the last 30 years, children have been exposed to an increasing risk that they will lose one parent to divorce or death. In the future decades, they face an increasing probability that they will lose both parents to divorce, drugs, disease, and death. The cost of caring for children will continue to grow and the value of having children will diminish in the face of greater economic pressures. Child welfare services have done well to keep apace of the changes in America's families in the 1980s, but the evidence is clear that we have not changed fast enough to stem the growing tide of children in temporary out-of-home care; we will need to do still better in the 1990s if we are to show more than lip service to the still-unrivalled goal of a permanent, safe, lifetime family for every child.

Permanency and family continuity are concepts that serve as proxies for child welfare. In theory, child welfare can occur for children without either permanency or family continuity. Yet, child endangerment can occur despite a sense of permanency and family continuity. Children who grow up in violent communities, lead-infused housing, and ill-equiped schools are endangered. Our child welfare system will almost certainly fail if it allows itself to be satisfied with permanency and family continuity as its goals. Children are entitled to reach adulthood having experienced a safe, healthy, and nurturing environment and to experience the benefits of a family that advocates for them and offers them the opportunity to develop into responsible and self-sufficient adults. An adequate child welfare system must rest on the shoulders of a society with an economic and health and human services infrastructure that supports families. The challenge of the next decade is to make sure that the conceptualization of factors that contribute to child welfare and our commitment to family continuity are consistent with the provision of services that maximize the welfare of all children.

References

Achenbach, T. M., & Edelbrock, C. S. (1981). Behavioral problems and competencies reported by parents of normal and disturbed children aged four through sixteen. *Monographs of the Society of Research in Child Development*, 46(1), Serial No. 188.

Adoptalk. (Winter 1990). The addicted child: Summary of Judy Howard's presentation (pp. 4–5) Paper presented before the North American Council on Adoptable Children, Minneapolis, MN.

Adult children come home. (June 16, 1991) *The San Francisco Chronicle*, A1, A16.

Albert, V. (1988). *Welfare dependence and welfare policy: A statistical study*. Westport, CT: Greenwood Press.

Aldrich, J., & Nelson F. (1984). *Linear probability, logit, and probit models*. Newbury Park, CA: Sage Publications.

Allison, P. (1984). *Event history analysis*. Newbury Park, CA: Sage Publications.

American Humane Association. (1989). *Highlights of official aggregate child neglect and abuse reporting*. Denver, CO: Author.

Anderson, C., Nagle, R., Roberts, W., & Smith, J. (1981). Attachment to substitute caregivers as a function of center quality and caregiver involvement. *Child Development*, 52, 53–61.

Ards, S. (1989). Estimating local child abuse, *Evaluation Review*, 13(5), 484–515.

Armstrong, K., Kenen, R., & Samost, L. (1991). Barriers to family planning services among patients in drug treatment programs. *Family Planning Perspectives*, 23, 264–271.

Ashby,L. (1984). *Saving the waifs: Reformers and dependent children, 1890–1917*. Philadelphia, PA: Temple University Press.

Bailey, T., & Bailey W. (1986). *Operational definitions of child emotional maltreatment*. Denver, CO: American Humane Association.

Barth, R. P. (1990a). Disruption in older child adoption. *Public Welfare*, 46(1), 23–29.

Barth, R. P. (1990b). On their own: The experiences of youth after foster care. *Child and Adolescent Social Work Journal*, 419–440.

Barth, R. P. (1991). Adoption of drug-exposed children. *Children and Youth Services Review*, 13, 323–342.

Barth, R. P. (1993a). Fiscal issues in special needs adoption. *Public Welfare*, 51, 21–28.

Barth, R. P. (1993b) Shared family care: Child protection without parent-child separation. In R. P. Barth, J. Pietrzak, & M. Ramler (Eds.), *Families living with drugs and HIV*. New York: The Guilford Press.

Barth, R. P. (In press). Protecting the children of heavy drug users at home. In D. Besharov (Ed.), *Protecting the children of heavy drug users*. New York: The Guilford Press.

Barth, R. P., & Berry, M. (1988a). *Adoption and disruption: Risks, rates, and responses*. Hawthorne, NY: Aldine de Gruyter.

Barth, R. P., & Berry, M. (1988b). Child abuse and child welfare services. In M. Wald & M. Kirst (Eds.), *Conditions of children in California*. Berkeley, CA: PACE.

Barth, R. P., & Berry, M. (In press). Implications of research on the welfare of children under permanency planning. In R. Barth, J. D. Berrick, & N. Gilbert (Eds.), *Child welfare research review*. New York: Columbia University Press.

Barth, R. P., & Derezotes, D. S. (1990). *Preventing adolescent abuse*. Lexington, MA: Lexington Books.

Barth, R. P., & Sullivan, T. R. (1985). Collecting competent data on behalf of children. *Social Work, 30*, 130–137.

Barth, R. P., Berrick, J. D., & Courtney, M. (1990). *A snapshot of California's families and children (second snapshot)*. Berkeley, CA: Family Welfare Research Group.

Barth, R. P., Berrick, J. D., Courtney, M. E., & Pizzini, S. (1990). *A snapshot of California's families and children pursuant to the child welfare reforms of the 1980s*. Sacramento, CA: Child Welfare Strategic Planning Commission.

Barth, R. P., Albert, V., Lawrence, R., & Courtney, M. E. (1993). *Budget allocation methodology in child welfare services in California*. Berkeley, CA: Family Welfare Research Group.

Bartholet, E. (1993). *Family bonds*. New York: Scribners.

Bell Associates, J. (1992, March). *The National Foster Parent Survey*. Paper presented before the Child Welfare Training, Child Welfare Research and Demonstration and Adoption Grantees Conference, Washington, DC.

Benedict, M. I., & White, R. B. (1991). Factors associated with foster care length of stay. *Child Welfare, 70*(1), 45–58.

Benedict, M. I., White, R. B., & Stallings, R. (1987). Race and length of stay in foster care. *Social Work Research & Abstracts, 23*(4), 23–26.

Berrick, J. D., Courtney, M. E., & Barth, R. P. (1993). *Specialized foster care and group home care: Similarities and differences in the characteristics of children in care. Children and Youth Services Review, 15*, 453–475.

Berry, M. (1992). An evaluation of family preservation services: Fitting agency services to family needs. *Social Work, 37*(4), 314–321.

Besharov, D. J. (1990). Getting control over child abuse reports. *Public welfare, 48*(2), 34–40.

Besharov, D. J. (1992). Improving child protective services: How to expand and implement the consensus. *Children Today, 21*(2), 14–17.

Blumen, I., Kogan, M., & McCarthy, P. J. (1955). *The industrial mobility of labor as a probability process*. Cornell Studies in Industrial and Labor Relations No. 6. Ithaca: Cornell University Press.

Brace, C.L. (1876). *Placing out plan for homeless and vagrant children. Proceedings of* the National Conference of Charities and Corrections. In V. A Zelizer (Ed.), *Pricing the priceless child: The changing social value of children*. New York: Basic Books.

Bronfenbrenner, U. (1979). *The ecology of human development*. Cambridge, MA: Harvard University Press.

Bush, M. (1984). The public and private purposes of case records. *Children and Youth Services Review, 6*, 1–18.

California Child Welfare Strategic Planning Commission. (1991). *The vision for the children of California*. Sacramento, CA: State Department of Social Services.

Canning, R. (1974). School experiences of foster children. *Child Welfare, 53*, 582–587.

Carbino, R. (1980). *Foster parenting: An updated review*. Washington, DC: Child Welfare League of America.

Carson, N. H. D. (1981). *Informal adoption among black families in the rural south*. Ph.D. dissertation, Northwestern University.

Child Welfare League of America. (1992). Kinship care: A new look at an old idea. *Children's Voice, 6–7*, 22.

Center for the Study of Social Policy (1990). *Kids count data book: State profiles of child well-being*. Washington, DC: Author.

Chamberlain, P. (1990). Comparative evaluation of specialized foster care for seriously delinquent youths: A first step. *Community Alternatives: International Journal of Family Care, 2*,(2), 21–36.

Chamberlain, P., & Reid, J. B. (1991). Using a specialized foster care community treatment model for children and adolescents leaving the state mental hospital. *Journal of Community Psychology, 19*, 351–362.

Children Now (1991). *California: The state of our children in 1991: The county data supplement 1991*. Los Angeles, CA: Author.

Child Welfare League of America. (1983). *U.S. foster care population for 1980: Final estimate*. New York: Author.

Child Welfare League of America. (1992). Kinship care: A new look at an old idea. *Children's Voice, 6–7*, 22.

Chipungu, S. S. (1991). A value-based policy framework. In J. E. Everett, S. S. Chipungu, & B. R. Leashore (Eds). *Child welfare: An africentric perspective*. New Brunswick, NJ: Rutgers University Press.

Cohen, D. L. (June 5, 1991a). Foster care reforms often ignore problems children face in school. *Education Week, 1*, 15, 17.

Cohen, D. L. (June 12, 1991b). Foster youths said to get little help with educational deficits. *Education Week*, 8–10.

Cohen, J. (1990). Things I have learned (so far). *American Psychologist, 45*, 1304–1312.

Cohen, N. (1986). Quality of care for youths in group homes. *Child Welfare, 65*(5), 481–494.

Costin, L. B., Bell, C. J., & Downs, S. W. (1990). *Child welfare: Policies and practice*. (4th ed.). White Plains, NY: Longman.

Courtney, M. (1993). Standardized outcome evaluation of child welfare services out-of-home care. *Children and Youth Services Review, 15*, 349–369.

Courtney, M. E. (1992). Reunification of foster children with their families: The case of California's children. Unpublished Ph.D. dissertation. Berkeley, CA: University of California.

Courtney, M. E., Barth, R. P., & Allphin, S. (1993). LCA report. Unpublished manuscript available from the authors.

Cox, D. R. (1972). Regression models and life tables. *Journal of the Royal Statistical Society, Series B, 34*, 187–202.

CWDA (County Welfare Director's Association). (1990). *Ten Reasons to Invest in the Families of California: Reasons to Invest in Services Which Prevent Out-of-Home Placement and Preserve Families*. Sacramento, CA: Author.

Daley, S. (October 23, 1989). Treating kin like foster parents strains a New York child agency. *The New York Times,* B4.

Dore, M. M., Young, T. M., & Pappenfort, D. M. (1984). Comparison of basic data for the National Survey of Residential Group Care Facilities: 1966–1982. *Child Welfare, 63*(6), 485–495.

Dubowitz, H. (1990). *The physical and mental health and educational status of children placed with relatives: Final report*. Unpublished manuscript. Baltimore, MD: The University of Maryland Medical School.

Dubowitz, H., Feigelman, S., & Zuravin, S. (1993). A profile of kinship care. *Child Welfare, 72*(2), 153–169.

Dubowitz, H., Feigelman, S., Zuravin, S., Tepper, V., Davidson, N., & Lichenstein, R. (1992). The physical health of children in kinship care. *AJDC, 146*, 603–610.

Dubowitz, H., & Sawyer, R. (n.d.). School behavior of children in kinship care. Unpublished manuscript. Baltimore, MD: University of Maryland.

Duerr, M., Berrick, J. D., & King, D. (1992). Second year evaluation reports: LEARN. Chico, CA: Duerr Evaluation Resources.

Fanshel, D. (1982). *On the road to permanency: An expanded data base for service to children in foster care*. New York: Child Welfare League of America.

Fanshel, D., Finch, S., & Grundy, J. (1989a). Foster children in life-course perspective: The Casey Family Program experience. *Child Welfare, 68*(5), 467–478.

Fanshel, D., Finch, S., & Grundy, J. (1989b). Modes of exit from foster family care and adjustment at time of departure of children with unstable life histories. *Child Welfare, 68*(4), 391–402.

Fanshel, D., & Grundy, J. (November, 1975). Computerized data for children in foster care: First analysis from a Management Information Service in New York City. New York: Child Welfare Information System.

Fanshel, D., & Shinn, E. (1978). *Children in foster care*. New York: Columbia University Press.

Farber, M. A. (November 22, 1990). Mirroring New York's ills, kinship foster care grows. *New York Times,* B1, B4.

Feig, L (1990). Drug-exposed infants and children: Service needs and policy questions. Washington, DC: U.S. Department of Health and Human Services.

Fein, E. (1991). Issues in foster family care: Where do we stand? *American Journal of Orthopsychiatry, 61*, 578–583.

Fein, E., & Maluccio, A. N. (1992). Permanency planning: Another remedy in jeopardy. *Social Service Review, 66*(3), 335–348.

Fein, E., Maluccio, A. N., & Kluger, M. P. (1990). *No more partings: An examination of long-term foster family care.* Washington, DC: Child Welfare League of America.

Finch, S., Fanshel, D., & Grundy, J. (1986). Factors associated with the discharge of children from foster care. *Social Work Research and Abstracts, 22*(1), 10–18.

Finkelhor, D. (1990). Is child abuse overreported: The data rebut arguments for less intervention. *Public Welfare, 48*(4), 23–29.

Finkelhor, D., Gomez-Schwartz, B., & Horowitz, J. (1984). Professionals' Responses. In D. Finkelhor (Ed.), *Child sexual abuse: New theory and research.* New York: The Free Press.

Fitzharris, T. (1985). *The foster children of California: Profiles of 10,000 children in residential care.* Sacramento, CA: Children's Services Foundation.

Fraser, M., Pecora, P. J., & Haapala, D. (1991). *Families in crisis.* Hawthorne, NY: Aldine de Gruyter.

Friedman, R. M. (1988). *The role of therapeutic foster care in an overall system of care: Issues in service delivery and program evaluation.* Unpublished manuscript. Tampa, FL: Research & Training Center for Children's Mental Health, University of South Florida.

Fryer, G. E., Bross, D. C., Krugman, R. D., Denson, D. B., & Baird, D. (1990). Good news for CPS workers. *Public Welfare, 48*(1), 38–41.

GAO (U.S. General Accounting Office). (1989). *Foster parents: Recruiting and preservice training practices need evaluation.* GAO/HRD-89-86, Washington, DC: Author.

Garbarino, J. (1976). A preliminary study of some ecological correlates of child abuse: The impact of socioeconomic stress on mothers. *Child Development, 47,* 178–185.

Garbarino, J., Gutman, E., & Wilson, J. (1986). *The psychologically battered child.* San Francisco, CA: Jossey-Bass.

Germain, C. (Ed.) (1979). *Social work practice: People and environments, an ecological perspective.*

Gaskins, R. (1993). Comprehensive reform in child welfare: The British Children Act 1989. *Social Science Review, 67,* 1–15.

Gershenson, C., Rosewater, A., & Massinga, R. (1990). *The Crisis in foster care: New directions for the 1990s.* Washington, DC: Family Impact Seminar.

Giles, T., & Kroll, G. (1991). *Barriers to same race placement.* St. Paul, MN: North American Council on Adoptable Children.

Gill, M. H. (1975). Foster care-adoptive family: Adoption for children not legally free. *Child Welfare, 52,* 712–720.

Goerge, R. M. (1990). The reunification process in substitute care. *Social Service Review, 64*(3), 422–457.

Goerge, R. M. (1993). *Special education experiences of foster children: An empirical study.* Chicago: University of Chicago, Chapin Hall Center for the Study of Children.

Goerge, R. M. (In press). *Child Welfare Research Review.* New York: Columbia University Press.

Goerge, R. M., Harden, A., & Lee, B. J. (1993). *The physical movement of children placed with relatives.* Chicago, IL: Chapin Hall Center for Children.

Goerge, R. M., & Wulczyn, F. H. (1992). Foster care in New York and Illinois: The challenge of rapid change. *Social Service Review*, 66(2) 278–294.

Goodman, L. A. (1978). *Analyzing qualitative and categorical data: Log-linear models and latent structure analysis*. New York: ABT Books.

Graham, P. J., & Rutter, M. L. (1968). The reliability and validity of the psychiatric assessment of the child—II: Interview with the parent. *British Journal of Psychiatry*, 144, 581–592.

Gray, S. S., & Nybell, L. M. (1990). Issues in African-American family preservation. *Child Welfare*, 69(6), 513–523.

Grinnell, R., & Jung, S. (1981). Children placed with relatives. *Social Work Research & Abstracts*, 17(3), 31–32.

Gruber, A. R. (1978). *Children in foster care: Destitute, Neglected . . Betrayed*. New York: Human Sciences Press.

Halfon, N., & Klee, L. (1991). Health and development services for children with multiple needs: The child in foster care. *Yale Law and Policy Review*, 9(1), 71–95.

Halfon, N., Jameson, W., Brindis, C., Lee, P. R., Newacheck, P. W., Korenbrot, C., McCroskey, J., & Isman, R. (1989). Health. In M. Kirst and M. Wald (Eds.). *Conditions of Children in California*. Berkeley, CA: Policy Analysis for California Education.

Hasler, B. S., (1986). Dividing the pie: The allocation of resources to substate areas. *New England Journal of Human Services*, 6(4), 28–32.

Hawkins, R. P., & Breiling, J. (1989). *Therapeutic foster care: Critical issues*. Washington, DC: Child Welfare League of America.

Hawkins, R. P., Meadowcroft, P., Trout, B. A., & Luster, W. C. (1985). Foster family-based treatment. *Journal of Clinical Psychology*, 14(1), 220–228.

Hays, W. C., & Mindel, C. H. (1973). Extended kinship relations in black and white families. *Journal of Marriage and the Family*, 35(1), 51–57.

Heckman, J. J., & Singer, B. (1984). A method for minimizing the impact of distributional assumptions in economic models for duration data. *Econometrica*, 47, 247–283.

Hegarty, C. (1973). The Family Resources Program: One coin, two sides of adoption and foster family care. *Child Welfare*, 52, 91–99.

Hess, P. M., Folaron, G., & Jefferson, A. B. (1992). Effectiveness of family reunification services: An innovative evaluation model. *Social Work* 37(4), 304–313.

Holt, J. D. (1978). Competing risk analyses with special reference to matched pair experiments. *Biometrika*, 65, 159–65.

Hudson, J., & Galaway, B. (1989). *Specialist foster family care: A normalizing experience*. New York: Haworth Press.

Hugi, R. (1983). *Children and the state: Responsibilities and expenditures*. The Children's Policy Research Project. Chicago, IL: The University of Chicago Press.

Hulsey, T., & White, R. (1989). Family characteristics and measures of behavior in foster and nonfoster children. *American Journal of Orthopsychiatry*, 59(4), 502–509.

James, J., Womack, W., & Stauss, F. (1978). Physician reporting of sexual abuse of children. *Journal of the American Medical Association*, 240, 1145–1146.

Jenkins, S. (1967). Duration of foster care: Some relevant antecedent variables. *Child Welfare, 46*(8), 450–455.

Jenkins, S., Diamond, B. E., Flanzraich, M., Gibson, J. W., Hendricks, J., & Marshood, N. (1983). Ethnic differentials in foster care placements. *Social Work Research & Abstracts, 19*(4), 41–45.

Johnson, I. (1990, November). *Kinship care: Issues and challenges.* Paper presented before the American Bar Association. Arlington, VA: Fifth National Conference on Children and the Law.

Kadushin, A. (1978). Children in foster families and institutions. In H. S. Maas (Ed.), *Social service research: Reviews of studies,* (pp. 90–148). Washington, DC: National Association of Social Workers.

Kadushin, A. (1980). *Child welfare services.* New York: Macmillan.

Kahn, A. J., & Kamerman, S. B. (1990). Social services for children, youth and families in the U.S. *Children and Youth Services Review, 1 & 2,* 1–180.

Kalichman, S. C., Craig, M. E., & Follingstad. (1991). Professional psychologists' decisions to report suspected child abuse: Clinician and situation influences. *Professional Psychology: Research and Practice, 22*(1), 84–89.

Kamerman, S. B., & Kahn, A. J. (Winter, 1990). If CPS is driving child welfare— Where do we go from here? *Public Welfare, 48*(1), 9–13.

Kellam, S. K., Branch, J. D., Agrawal, K. C., & Ensminger, M. E. (1975). *Mental health and going to school: The Woodlawn program of assessment, early intervention, and evaluation.* Chicago, IL: University of Chicago Press.

Kelley, S. J. (1992). Parenting stress and child maltreatment in drug-exposed children. *Child Abuse and Neglect, 16,* 317–328.

Kennedy, J., & Keeney, V. (1987). Group psychotherapy with grandparents raising their emotionally disturbed grandchildren. *Group, 11,* 15–25.

Kirst, M., & Wald, M. (1989). Conditoins of children in California. Berkeley, CA: Policy Analysis for California Education.

Klee, L., & Halfon, N. (1987). Mental health care for foster children in California. *Child Abuse & Neglect, 11,* 63–74.

Knudsen, D. D. (1988). *Child Services: Discretion, Decisions, Dilemmas.* Illinois: Charles Thomas.

Korbin, J. E. (1991). Cross-cultural perspectives and research directions for the 21st century. *Child Abuse and Neglect, 15*(1), 67–78.

Kusserow, R. P. (1992). *State practices in using relatives for foster care.* Washington, DC: Department of Health and Human Services, Office of Inspector General.

Lawder, E. A., Poulin, J. E., & Andrews, R. G. (1986). A study of 185 foster children five years after placement. *Child Welfare, 65*(3), 241–251.

Lawless, J. E. (1982). *Statistical models and methods for lifetime data.* New York: John Wiley.

Lerman, P. (1982). *Deinstitutionalization and the welfare state.* New Brunswick, NJ: Rutgers University Press.

Lindholm, B. W., & Touliatos, J. (1978). Characteristics of foster families. *Social Thought, 1*(4), 45–56.

Lindsey, D. (1991). Factors affecting the foster care placement decision: An analysis of national survey data. *American Journal of Orthopsychiatry, 61*(2), 272–281.

Littel, J. H., Schuerman, J. R., Rzepnicki, T., Howard, J., & Budde, S. (1993). Objectives in family preservation programs. In E. S. Morton & R. K. Grigsby (Eds.), *Advancing family preservation practice*, (pp. 99–117). Newbury Park, CA: Sage.

Maas, H., & Engler, R. (1959). *Children in need of parents*. New York: Columbia University Press.

Magruder, J. (In press). Kinship adoption in California. *Children and Youth Services Review*.

Magura, S. (1979). Trend analysis in foster care. *Social Work Research & Abstracts, 18*, 29–36.

Maluccio, A. N. (1974). Residential treatment of disturbed children. *Child Welfare, 43*(4), 225–235.

Maluccio, A. N. (1991). The optimism of policy choices in child welfare. *American Journal of Orthopsychiatry, 61*, 606–609.

Martin, E. P., & Martin, J. M. (1978). *The black extended family*. Chicago, IL: University of Chicago Press.

Massachusetts Department of Social Services. (1992). *Who are the waiting children? An overview of the Adoption Services System of the Massachusetts Department of Social Services*. Boston, MA: Author.

Maza, P. (1983). Characteristics of children in foster care. *Child Welfare Research Notes, 1*, 1–6.

McCauley, K. (1993). Preventing child abuse through the schools. *Children Today, 21*, 8–10.

McIntyre, A., & Keesler, T. Y. (1986). Psychological disorders among foster children. *Journal of Clinical Child Pshchology, 15*(4), 297–303.

McMurtry, S. L., & Lie, G. W. (1992). Differential exit rates of minority children in foster care. *Social Work Research & Abstracts, 28*(1), 42–48.

Meadowcroft, P., & Trout, B. A. (1990). *Troubled youth in treatment homes: A handbook of therapeutic foster care*. Washington, DC: Child Welfare League of America.

Mech, E. V. (1983). Out-of-home placement rates. *Social Service Review, 57*(4), 659–667.

Meezan, W., & Shireman, J. F. (1985). *Care and commitment: Foster parent adoption decisions*. New York: State University of New York Press.

Meyer, B. S., & Link, M. K. (October, 1990). *Kinship foster care: The double edged dilemma*. Rochester, NY: Task Force on Permanency Planning for Foster Children.

Miller v. Youakim. (1979). Supreme Court 440 U.S. 125.

Minkler, M. (1993). *Grandmothers as caregivers: Raising children of the crack cocaine epidemic*. Newbury Park, CA: Sage.

Muehleman, T., & Kimmons, C. (1981). Psychologists' views on child abuse reporting, confidentiality, life and the law: An exploratory study. *Professional Psychology, 12*, 631–637.

National Association of Black Social Workers. (1991). *Preserving African American Families: Research and action beyond the rhetoric*. Detroit, MI: Author.

National Committee for Adoption. (1989). *Adoption factbook: United States data, issues, regulations and resources.* Washington, DC: Author.

National Commission on Child Welfare and Family Preservation. *A commitment to change.* Washington, DC: American Public Welfare Association.

Nightingale, N. N., & Walker, E. F. (1986). Identification and reporting of child maltreatment by Head Start Personnel: Attitudes and experiences. *Child Abuse and Neglect, 10*, 191–199.

Nutter, R. W., Hudson, J., & Galaway, B. (1990). *Survey of treatment foster care programs.* Unpublished manuscript. Edmonton, Canada: University of Calgary.

O'Brien, N., McClellan, T., & Alf, D. (1992). Data collection: Are social workers reliable? *Administration in Social Work, 16*(2), 89–99.

O'Brien, P. (Spring, 1993). Youth homelessness and the lack of adoption planning for older foster children: Are they related? *Adoptalk, 6.*

Olsen, L. J. (1982a). Predicting the permanency status of children in foster care. *Social Work Research & Abstracts 18*, 9–20.

Olsen, L. J. (1982b). Services for minority children in out-of-home care. *Social Service Review, 56*(4), 572–585.

Pappenfort, D., & Kilpatrick, D. M. (1969). Child caring institutions 1966: Selected findings from the first national survey of children's residential institutions. *Social Service Review, 43*(4), 448–459.

Pecora, P. J., Whittaker, J. K., Maluccio, A. N., Barth, R. P., & Plotnick, R. D. (1992). *The child welfare challenge: Policy, practice, and research.* New York: Aldine de Gruyter.

Pelton, L. (1989). *For reasons of poverty: A critical analysis of the American child welfare system.* Westport, CT: Praeger.

Peterson, A. V., Jr. (1976). Bounds for a joint distribution function with sub-distribution functions: Application to competing risks. *Proceedings of the National Academy of Science, 73*, 11–13.

Peterson, J. L., & Zill, N. (1986). Marital disruption, parent-child relationships, and behavioral problems in children. *Journal of Marriage and the Family, 48*(2).

Phillips, D. A. (Ed.) (1987). *Quality in child care: What does research tell us?* Research Monograph of the National Association for the Education of Young Children, Vol. 1. Washington, DC: National Association for the Education of Young Children.

Phillips, M., Haring, M., & Shyne, A. (1971). *Factors associated with placement decisions in child welfare.* New York: Child Welfare League of America.

Plotnick R., & Lidman R. (1987). Forecasting AFDC caseloads. *Public Welfare, 45*(1), 31–35.

Prentice, R. L., Kalbfleisch, J. D., Peterson, A. V., Jr., Flournoy, N., Farewell, V. T., & Breslow, N. E. (1978). The analysis of failure times in the presence of competing risks. *Biometrics, 34*, 541–554.

Proch, K. (1982). Differences between foster care and adoption: Perceptions of adopted foster children and adoptive foster parents. *Child Welfare, 61*, 259–268.

Rathburn, C. (1944). The adoptive foster parent. *The Child Welfare League of America Bulletin*, 23(9), 5–7, 12.

Rosenthal, J. A. (1993). Outcomes of adoption of children with special needs. *The Future of Children*, 3(1), 77–88.

Rosewater, A. (1990). *The crisis in foster care: New directions for the 1990s*. Washington, DC: Family Impact Seminar.

Rowe, J., Cain, H., Hundleby, M., & Keane, A. (1984). Long-term foster care. New York: St. Martin's Press.

Rowe, P. (1993). Child abuse telecast floods national hotline. *Children Today*, 21(2), 11.

Rutter, M., Tizard, J., & Whitmore, K. (1970). *Education, health and behavior*. London: Longman.

Rzepnicki, T., Schuerman, J. R., Littel, J. H., Chak, A., & Lopez, M. (In press). An experimental study of family preservation services: Early findings from a parent survey. In R. Barth, J. D. Berrick, & N. Gilbert (Eds.), *Child welfare research review*. New York: Columbia University Press.

Schor, E. L. (1982). The foster care system and health status of foster children. *Pediatrics*, 69(5), 521–528.

Seaberg, J. R., & Tolley, E. S. (1986). Predictors of the length of stay in foster care. *Social Work Abstracts*, 22, 11–17.

Selvin, S. (1991). *Statistical analysis of epidemiological data*. New York: Oxford University Press.

Senate Office of Research. (1990a). *California's drug-exposed babies: Undiscovered, unreported, underserved: A special report prepared for Senator Diane Watson*. Sacramento, CA: Author.

Senate Office of Research. (1990b). *Tackling California's demand for foster care*. Sacramento, CA: Senate Office of Research.

Shore, R. J., & Hayslip, B. (1992). *Redefining families: Implications for children's development*. New York: Plenum.

Shyne, A., & Schroeder, A. (1978). *National study of social services to children and their families*. Washington, DC: Department of Health, Education, and Welfare.

Simms, M. D. (June, 1989). The foster care clinic: A community program to identify treatment needs of children in foster care. *Developmental and Behavioral Pediatrics*, 10(3), 121–128.

Slaght, E. (1993). Reexamining risk factors in foster care. *Children and Youth Services Review*, 15, 143–154.

Small, R., Kennedy, K., & Bender, B. (1991). Critical issues for practice in residential treatment; The view from within. *American Journal of Orthopsychiatry*, 61(3), 327–338.

Stack, C. (1974). *All our kin: Strategies for survival in a black community*. New York: Harper & Row.

State of California Legislative Analyst office, (1985). *Child Welfare Services: A Review of the Effect of the 1982 Reforms on Abused and Neglected Children and Their Families*. Report No. 85–13. Sacramento, CA: Author.

State Department of Social Services (SDSS) of California. (1987). *Adoption regulations*. Sacramento, CA: Author.

Takas, M. (June, 1992). *Kinship care: Developing a safe and effective framework for protective placement of children with relatives.* Unpublished manuscript. Washington, DC: ABA Center on Children and the Law.

Tatara, T. (1990, October). *The relationship between CPS and Substitute care: An exploratory study based on national data on child abuse and neglect reports and substitute care populations.* Paper presented before the 12th Annual Research Conference of the Association for Public Policy Analysis and Management, San Francisco, CA.

Tatara, T. (In press). Some additional explanations for the recent rise in the U.S. child substitute care flow data and future research questions. In R. Barth, J. D. Berrick, & N. Gilbert (Eds.), *Child welfare research review.* New York: Columbia University Press.

Ten Broeck, E., & Barth, R. P. (1986). Learning the hard way: A pilot permanency planning project. *Child Welfare, 65,* 281–294.

Terpstra, J. (1990). Specialized family foster care. In N. J. Hochstadt & D. M. Yost (Eds.), *The medically complex child: The transition to home care.* London: Harwood Academic Publishers.

Testa, M. (1985). *Using proportional hazards models to measure progress toward achieving permanence after foster placement.* Prepared for the American Association of Public Welfare Information Systems Management Conference, Austin, TX.

Testa, M., & Wulczyn, F. (1980). *The state of the child.* The Children's Policy Research Project. Chicago, IL: The University of Chicago Press.

Thornton, J. L. (1987). *An investigation into the nature of the kinship foster home.* Ph.D. dissertation. Yeshiva University, New York.

Thornton, J. L. (1991). Permanency planning for children in kinship foster homes. *Child Welfare, 70,* 593–601.

Titmuss, R. M. (1971). *The gift relationship: From human blood to social policy.* New York: Pantheon.

Trussell, J., & Richards, T. (1985). Correcting unmeasured heterogeneity in hazard models using the Heckman-Singer procedure. In N. Tuma (Ed.), *Sociological Methodology 1985* (pp. 242–276). San Francisco: Jossey-Bass.

Tsiatis, A. (1975). A nonidentifiability aspect of the problem of competing risks. *Proceedings of the National Academy of Sciences, 72,* 20–22.

Tuma, N., & Hannan, M. (1984). *Social dynamics: Models and methods.* Orlando, FL: Academic Press.

U.S. Committee on Finance. (1990). *Foster care, adoption assistance, and child welfare services.* Washington, DC: U.S. Government Printing Office.

U.S. Department of Health and Human Services (DHHS). (1988). *Study findings: Study of national incidence and prevalence of child abuse and neglect, 1988.* Washington, DC: Author.

U.S. Government Accounting Office, Human Services Division. (1993). Foster care: Services to prevent out-of-home placements are limited by funding barriers. Washington, DC: U.S. Government Printing Office.

Voluntary Cooperative Information System. (1993). Research Notes: U.S. Child substitute care flow data. Washington, DC: American Public Welfare Association.

Wald, M. S. (1988). Family preservation: Are we moving too fast? *Public Welfare,* 46(3), 33–38.

Wald, M. S., & Kirst, M. (Eds.). (1988). *Conditions of children in California.* Berkeley, CA: PACE.

Walker, C. D., Zagrillo, P., & Smith, J. (1991). *Parental drug abuse and African American children in foster care.* Washington, DC: National Black Child Development Institute.

Washington Department of Social and Health Services. (1992). *Allocation Committee Interim Report.* Olympia, WA: Author.

Watahara, A., & Lobdell, T. (1990). *The children nobody knows: California's foster care dependency system.* San Francisco, CA: California Tomorrow Youth At Risk Project.

Webb, D. B. (1988). Specialized foster care as an alternative therapeutic out-of-home placement model. *Journal of Clinical Child Psychology. 17,*(1), 34–43.

Wells, K. (July, 1991). Placement of emotionally disturbed children in residential treatment: A review of placement criteria. *American Journal of Orthopsychiatry,* 61(3), 339–347.

Wells, K. (1993). Residential treatment as long-term treatment: An examination of some issues. *Children and Youth Services Review,* 15(3), 165–171.

Wells, K., & Whittington, D. (1993). Characteristics of youths referred to residential treatment: Implications for program design. *Children and Youth Services Review,* 15(3), 195–217.

Weston, D., Klee, L., & Halfon, N. (1989). Mental Health. In *Conditions of Children in California.* Berkeley, CA: Policy Analysis for California Education.

Whitebook, M., Howes, C., & Phillips, D. (1989). *Who cares? Child care teachers and the quality of care in america. National Child Care Staffing Study.* Oakland, CA: Child Care Employee Project.

Whittaker, J. K., Fine, D., & Grasso, A. (1989). Characteristics of adolescents and their families in residential treatment intake: An exploratory study. In E. A. Balcerzak (Ed.), *Group care of children: Transitions toward the year 2000.* Washington, DC: Child Welfare League of America.

Wolins, M., & Piliavin, I. (1969). Group care, friend or foe. *Social Work,* 14(1), 35–53.

Wulczyn, F. H. (1991). Case load dynamics and foster care reentry. *Social Service Review,* 65(1), 133–156.

Wulczyn, F. H. (In press). Status at birth and infant foster care placement in New York City. In R. Barth, J. D. Berrick, & N. Gilbert (Eds.), *Child welfare research review.* New York: Columbia University Press.

Wulczyn, F. H., & Goerge, R. M. (December, 1990a). *Public policy and the dynamics of foster care: A multi-state study of placement histories.* Washington, DC: U.S. Department of Health and Human Services, Office of Assistant Secretary for Planning and Evaluation.

Wulczyn, F. H., & Goerge, R. M. (1992). Foster care in New York and Illinois: The challenge of rapid change. *Social Service Review,* 66, (2), 278–94.

Wulczyn, F. H., Goerge, R. M., Hartnett, M. A., & Testa, M. (1986). Children in substitute care. In M. Testa and E. Lawlor (Eds.), *The state of the child: 1985.* Chicago: University of Chicago, Chapin Hall Center for Children.

Yamaguchi, K. (1991). *Event history analysis.* Applied Social Research Methods Series, vol. 28. Newbury Park, CA: Sage.

Young, B. (1980). The Hawaiians. In J. McDermott, W. S. Tseng, & T. Maretzki (Eds.), *People and cultures of Hawaii: A psychocultural profile.* Honolulu: University of Hawaii Press.

Yuan, Y. Y. T., & Struckman-Johnson, D. L. (1992). Placement outcomes for neglected children with prior placements in family preservation programs. In R. P. Barth, J. Pietrzak, & M. Ramler (Eds.), *Families living with drugs and HIV.* New York: The Guilford Press.

Zelizer, V. A. (1985). *Pricing the priceless child: The changing social value of children.* New York: Basic Books.

Zellman, G. L. (1990). Child abuse reporting and failure to report among mandated reporters: Prevalence, incidence, and reasons. *Journal of Interpersonal Violence, 5*(1), 3–22.

Zill, N., & Peterson, (1989). *National Longitudinal Survey of Youth Child Handbook.* Columbus, OH: Ohio Center for Human Resources Research.

Zuravin, S. J. (1989). The ecology of child abuse and neglect: Review of the literature and presentation of data. *Violence and Victims, 4*(2), 101–120.

Zuravin, S. J. (1991). Unplanned childbearing and family size: Their relationship to child neglect and abuse. *Family Planning Perspectives, 23*(4), 155–161.

Author Index

Subject Index